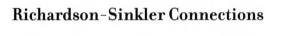

Richardson-Sinkler Connections

Richardson-Sinkler Connections

Planting, Politics, Horses, and Family Life, 1769–1853

Edited by Harriet Clare Sinkler Little

THE UNIVERSITY OF
SOUTH CAROLINA PRESS

© 2019 University of South Carolina

Published by the University of South Carolina Press
Columbia, South Carolina 29208

www.sc.edu/uscpress

Manufactured in the United States of America

28 27 26 25 24 23 22 21 20 19   10 9 8 7 6 5 4 3 2 1

Library of Congress Cataloging-in-Publication Data can be found at
http://catalog.loc.gov/.

ISBN: 978-1-61117-972-9 (hardback)
ISBN: 978-1-61117-973-6 (ebook)

For eight generations of Sinklers—past and present—who have assiduously preserved family documents and memorabilia for more than 250 years

Contents

Preface

In 2008 Harriet Clare Sinkler Little, William Henry Sinkler, and Norman Sinkler Walsh donated their collection of Sinkler family documents to the South Caroliniana Library. Included were numerous letters written to their third great-grandfather, William Sinkler, the majority of them from his first cousin and brother-in-law, James Burchell Richardson. Encouraged by Dr. Allen Stokes, Harriet Little continued her transcription of these letters, while extending her search for William Sinkler's letters to James Burchell Richardson (thus far not found). Additional letters and other documents were located, some in other South Caroliniana Library collections, some at the Rubenstein Library at Duke University, and several at the South Carolina Historical Society.

In addition to the aforementioned letters are many written by James Burchell Richardson's wife, Ann Cantey Sinkler Richardson, to her brother, husband, and son; those of Margaret Cantey Sinkler to her son and other family members; letters written by various family members to William Sinkler's son Seaman Deas, while he was attending medical school in Pennsylvania; many written by the Richardsons to their son William Henry Burchell Richardson, while he attended South Carolina College and later; and more from other Sinkler and Richardson relatives, friends, and business associates.

Most of the letters are from the Sinkler Family Papers, 1705–1984, in the South Caroliniana Library at the University of South Carolina, Columbia. Those that are from other archives are noted individually.

Editorial Method

Transcription has been verbatim et literatim of complete documents, although the placements and forms of datelines, salutations, postscripts, and so on have been standardized. Each document is given a heading identifying the writer and recipient, and the location of each has been noted, if known. Addresses are retained for the information they provide—for example, notes, mode of delivery, and other related facts. In cases where archaic spelling was obvious, words have usually been left as they were, without emendation. In some cases, clarification seemed necessary, and these have been set aside in brackets or explained in footnotes.

When deemed helpful, explanations of events and identification of names are provided in footnotes. Also included is a listing of "People of Interest" and "Places of Interest."

In an effort to avoid needless repetition, names are occasionally abbreviated—for example, JBR for James Burchell Richardson. This is always done in close proximity to the full name, so it is hoped that it is not confusing. A list of abbreviations has been included for further clarification.

Several genealogical charts have been included for clarification of family relationships. While the utmost care has been taken to provide accurate information, there are some cases where ambiguous or conflicting data has made this difficult. Nevertheless, it seems potentially helpful to provide these charts despite those conditions.

In some cases, siblings have been omitted in an effort to confine charts to a single page; this has not always been noted on the chart. The author's records include sources and detailed explanations, but it would have been cumbersome to have included them here. The reader should view them as aids to understanding family connections but not as research sources.

Acknowledgments

Allen Stokes, who accepted the Sinkler documents on behalf of the South Caroliniana Library in 2008, suggested this project in a way that I could not refuse. He meticulously proofread all my transcriptions, occasionally enlisting additional help with arcane terms and spelling, and was always available when I needed guidance and support. Without his help, this book would not exist.

Others who helped in ways large and small were Perry Richardson Bishop, Eliza Couturier, Joe Cross, Meg Gaillard, Nancy Gaillard, Keith Gourdin, Charles Howell, Richardson Hyman, Gerhard and Wally Karwinski, Terry Lipscomb, Paul Little, William Henry Sinkler, Harvey Teal, and Norman Sinkler Walsh.

Also: Mike Coker at the Berkeley County Museum, Katherine Richardson at the Camden Archives and Museum; Pat Kruger, Doreen Larimer, Cortney Price, Pattie Rivers, and other members of the Charleston Chapter of the South Carolina Genealogy Society; Marianne Cawley, Nic Butler, Lish Thompson, and Dot Glover at the Charleston County Public Library's South Carolina Room; Grahame Long, Jan Hiester, and Jennifer McCormick at the Charleston Museum; Nancy Cave at the Clarendon County Archives; Harlan Greene, head of Special Collections at the College of Charleston Libraries; the staff at the Dorchester County Library, Summerville; Steve Tuttle and Bryan Collars at the South Carolina Department of Archives and History; Beth Bilderback, Ron Bridwell, Henry Fulmer, and Elizabeth West at the South Caroliniana Library, and Sumter Genealogical Society.

Abbreviations

People

NOTE: Abbreviations are used sparingly, and usually quite close to the person's name to avoid redundancy, but this guide is provided in case the abbreviation is not immediately obvious.

ACSR   Ann Cantey Sinkler Richardson, daughter of James Sinkler and wife of James B. Richardson

CR   Charles Richardson, younger brother of James B. Richardson

CS   Charles Sinkler, older brother of William Sinkler, sometimes referred to as "Col. Sinkler"

EASM   Elizabeth Allen Sinkler Manning, William Sinkler's daughter, and wife of Richard I. Manning

HDS   Henry Deas Lesesne, nephew of William Sinkler's wife, Elizabeth Allen Broün

JBR   James Burchell Richardson, oldest son of General Richard Richardson and Dorothy Sinkler

JPR   John Peter Richardson, younger brother of James Burchell Richardson

JS   James Sinkler, father of William Sinkler and Ann Richardson

JSD   James Sutherland Deas, younger brother of William Sinkler's mother-in-law, Mary Deas

MCS   Margaret Cantey Sinkler, wife of James Sinkler and mother of William Sinkler

MDB   Mary Deas Broün, sister of William Sinkler's wife, Eliza Allen Broün

PG   Peter Gaillard, builder of the plantation known as the Rocks

RR   Richard Richardson, father of James B. Richardson

SD   Samuel Dubose, cousin of William Sinkler

SDS   Seaman Deas Sinkler, William Sinkler's son and a medical doctor in Charleston

TG   Thomas Gaillard, Charleston lawyer who moved to Alabama to be-
      come a cotton planter
WHBR William Henry Burchell Richardson, son of James B. Richardson
WHS   William Henry Sinkler, son of William Sinkler
WS   William Sinkler, son of James Sinkler of Old Santee, and builder of
      Eutaw Plantation

Sources

DU   Duke University, David M. Rubenstein Rare Book and Manuscript
      Library
SCDAH South Carolina Department of Archives and History
SCHS South Carolina Historical Society
SCL   South Caroliniana Library

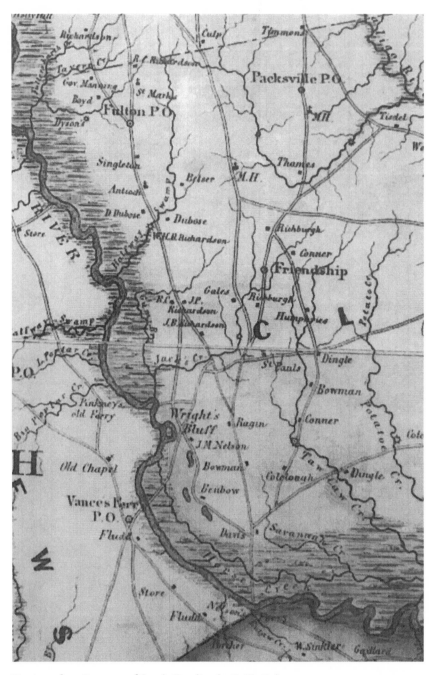

Portion of an 1854 map of South Carolina by J. H. Colton.
Courtesy South Carolina Department of Archives and History.

Chapter 1

Signs of the Times

Introducing the Families

With current technology providing multiple forms of instant communication, many of us find it difficult to conceptualize how people corresponded two hundred years ago. Yet, for numerous reasons this correspondence was even more critical during the early nineteenth century, especially for those not living in cities. Families and friends were often separated by many miles, and visiting was a major undertaking, occasionally requiring multiple means of transportation. Frequently, those able to travel carried with them letters from others to be delivered at their destinations to friends and family. Sometimes this was the only way of transmitting money. Letters refer to the enclosure of specific amounts of money—in some cases breaking the total payment into smaller sums sent in multiple letters.

In his study of the planter-class culture, Steven Stowe suggested that their language "shapes how individuals perceive events and relationships and how they feel about themselves and the world." He also noted that "letters often were the very substance of relationships otherwise strained by distance, gender differences, or emotion" and collectively "became a transcript of a family's life."[1] This is certainly exemplified in the correspondence of the Richardson and Sinkler families.

The Richardsons lived on the north side of the Santee River in what is now the Clarendon County–Sumter County border, while the Sinklers lived most of

1. Steven M. Stowe, *Intimacy and Power in the Old South* (Baltimore: Johns Hopkins University Press, 1987), 3–4.

the time on the south side of the river near Eutaw Springs, historically Berkeley but now Orangeburg County. Modern highways allow the trip to be made in less than an hour, but in the early nineteenth century, it was a circuitous trip through backwoods trails and swamps, which were often boggy and marginally passable. One account describes the roads as an "opening . . . cut through the woods, frequently following the route of a winding Indian trail, often barely wide enough for one vehicle to pass another, with trimmed pine saplings or other small trees laid across in boggy places."[2] From 1721, when the General Assembly established permanent road commissions, each parish was responsible for the maintenance of roads, causeways, and bridges. Funds for this purpose were raised by assessing inhabitants for that purpose.[3]

The trip also required the use of a ferry to cross the river—in this case Nelson's Ferry, originally called Beard's Ferry, which was near the confluence of Eutaw Creek and the Santee River. Very little specific information about this ferry exists, not even the width of the river at that point. However, a few miles downriver, at what was called White Oak Landing or Porcher's Bluff, just east of Greenland Swamp, the Santee was normally 270 feet wide and 18 to 20 feet deep.[4] It is

There appears to be no image of Nelson's Ferry available; this river ferry in Florida is probably similar in style. Courtesy of the Library of Congress.

2 Maxwell Clayton Orvin, *Historic Berkeley County South Carolina, 1671–1900* (Charleston, S.C.: Comprint, 1973), 65.

3 George D. Terry, "Champaign Country: A Social History of an Eighteenth Century Lowcountry Parish in South Carolina, St. Johns Berkeley County" (Ph.D. diss., University of South Carolina, 1981), 180–81.

4 Robert J. Kapsch, *Historic Canals and Waterways of South Carolina* (Columbia: University of South Carolina Press, 2010), 32.

obvious that this varied, as the rates could be increased by half "when it shall be between long and short ferry" and doubled "in times of high water" or "freshets." The rates set in 1799 varied from 12½ cents for a man on a horse to 75 cents for a four-wheeled carriage or a wagon with a team and driver. In 1807 rates were revised to correspond to that charged at nearby Vance's Ferry: they included more categories and ranged up to $1.00 for a wagon team or four-wheeled carriage. It is worth noting that there was no fee for ministers, soldiers, men on militia duty, or people attending church.[5]

The surviving Richardson-Sinkler correspondence indicates that the families did in fact visit frequently, sometimes for extended periods. It is easy to believe that the difficulty of the journey suggested lengthy visits to justify the effort. Many letters make reference to recent or proposed visits among various family members, and it is clear that the families were very close.

The letters span the period from 1769 to 1853, when the new country was growing and finding its way. This era included events such as the industrial revolution, the Lewis and Clark Expedition, and the move of the U.S. government from Philadelphia to Washington, D.C. The Napoleonic wars and related events in Europe engendered anxiety inasmuch as they directly affected trade, a constant concern for planters. The unease over the long buildup to the War of 1812 is evident in several letters. One of June 25, 1812, suggests ideas about the best way to serve the country, and others anticipate the effect on trade.

This was also a politically volatile period, which included the frequently shifting attitudes toward the importation of slaves, both from Africa and from other states. In 1803 James B. Richardson, as newly elected governor, "reversed his position and urged the legislature to consider reopening the trade," partially because he felt that it was virtually impossible to enforce, especially along the coast.[6] As he was a planter, it was clearly in his interests to have broad availability of labor, but several letters reflect the opinion that the Africans—those more recently imported—were more difficult to control. In any case, the slave trade continued legally until 1808, when it was ended by federal law.[7]

Although many contemporary historians use the term "slave" rather than the more general term "servants," that is not the case with these letter writers. The word "slave" is clearly used in wills and sometimes in reference to transactions, but individuals were most often referred to by name, or occasionally as "the boy," "your fellow," or—more rarely—"my Negroes." It was also common to refer to

5 David J. McCord, ed., *The Statutes at Large of South Carolina* (Columbia, S.C.: A. S. Johnston, 1844), 405, 428, 568.

6 Lacy K. Ford, *Deliver Us from Evil: The Slavery Question in the Old South* (New York: Oxford University Press, 2011), 97.

7 George C. Rogers, Jr., and C. James Taylor, *A South Carolina Chronology, 1497–1992*, 2nd ed. (Columbia: University of South Carolina Press, 1992), 63.

them by job function—for example, "miller," "cook," or, in the case of unskilled laborers, "hands."

This was likely a manifestation of the social system referred to as paternalism, whereby "the day-to-day governance of a slave population should be conducted similarly to how male household heads governed their white families, that is, with a combination of fairness and firmness, a balance of affection and discipline."[8] To some extent, this attitude was supported within the religious community: Baptist minister Richard Furman and Episcopal minister Frederick Dalcho both published pamphlets expressing their views that paternalism could function and make masters more kind and slaves more obedient.[9]

There is considerable evidence that the Richardsons and Sinklers practiced what Lacey Ford characterized as a looseness in the day-to-day operations, especially for artisans and mechanics.[10] Letters frequently mention the hiring of skilled craftsmen from each other, including brick masons or carpenters, and occasionally the involvement of slaves in decision making and handling of money. James B. Richardson wrote to his son at South Carolina College in 1825 mentioning his promise to send up a horse and slave for a few days. A subsequent letter notes that Jim, who had evidently been injured while in Columbia, had asked to be the one to make the trip. This same letter notes that Moses was being sent up to tend to Jim, and would be carrying money to pay the bills. A letter of the following year to William Sinkler notes that it was being carried by Hercules, WS's horse trainer, who had evidently made a delivery to Richardson and was carrying money to reimburse WS for the purchase.

Cotton had replaced indigo as a major export crop and would peak in price in the second decade and bottom out in the third.[11] In December 1801 the state of South Carolina "appropriated $50,000 to pay Phineas Miller and Eli Whitney for the right of South Carolina planters to use their machine called 'a saw gin, for cleaning the staple of cotton from the seed.'"[12] Closer to home, a September 1806 letter discusses the specifics of finding a builder of a gin; other letters discuss the production and price of the crop, and transporting cotton downriver to Charleston for export. As late as 1850, there is reference to a rice crop at one of the Sinkler plantations.

At first glance, it might seem that letters were focused primarily on weather and health, but one must consider the importance of both factors in the lives of early-nineteenth-century families. Weather certainly controlled travel, and temperature extremes dictated many social events. Weather was also a major dynamic

8 Ford, *Deliver Us from Evil*, 147.
9 Ibid., 263.
10 Ibid., 163
11 Rogers and Taylor, *South Carolina Chronology*, 74, 82.
12 Ibid., 69.

in crop production, the primary source of income. An April 28, 1803, letter complains of late frosts that had destroyed the crops, while a letter of March 15, 1807, notes that the weather was bad for planting.

The late eighteenth and early nineteenth centuries presented a constant struggle to deal with a plethora of diseases. Malaria, not yet associated with mosquitos, was avoided to some extent by relocating away from the waterways, but even that was not possible for everyone. Of equal concern were common occurrences of "yellow fever, smallpox, dysentery, respiratory disorders, numerous helminthic (worm) infestations, and tetanus . . . abetted occasionally by epidemics of measles, diphtheria, whooping cough, scarlet fever, and mumps."[13] In 1836 a major cholera epidemic ravaged Charleston.[14] One has only to look at a family descendant chart to observe the high mortality rate of that period, especially for young children. It is no wonder that people found it difficult to refrain from sharing their concerns about the health conditions of their families.

It's More Than a Name

If the repetition of names in these letters seems daunting at times, one must keep in mind that many families followed English naming patterns common from about 1700 to 1875. This meant that the first son was habitually named for the paternal grandfather, the second son after the maternal grandfather, the third son for the father, and the fourth son for the father's eldest brother. Likewise, the first daughter was named for her maternal grandmother, second for paternal grandmother, third for the mother, and fourth for the mother's eldest sister.[15] Clearly there were exceptions, usually for reasons that were obvious: for example, James (named for his father) and Margaret Sinkler's oldest son, Charles, was named for his maternal grandfather, Charles Cantey, who died about the time the younger Charles was born. The source of the name of their second son, William, is less clear, as there seems to be no known William on either side of the family. One possibility is that his father was aware of his own grandfather having been named William, although this does not appear in any Sinkler records. In any case, the third son was named James, which could have been for either his father or grandfather. Their daughter, Margaret Anna, was named for her mother, Margaret. There appears not to have been an Anna, but her maternal grandmother was Ann Drake, and her paternal great-grandmother was Ann Cantey (maiden name unknown).

---

13 Peter McCandless, *Slavery, Disease, and Suffering in the Southern Lowcountry* (Cambridge: Cambridge University Press, 2011), 6.

14 Rogers and Taylor, *South Carolina Chronology*, 85.

15 Angus Baxter, "In Search of Your British and Irish Roots," https://www.genealogy.com/articles/research/35_donna.html (accessed July 5, 2018).

Throughout both families, there is evidence of adherence to this pattern. Richard Richardson's first son with Mary Cantey was named Richard Jr., but it is less clear where the names of the other six children came from. The sources of the names of the four sons of his second marriage (to Dorothy Sinkler) are likewise not all clear. The first, James Burchell, is probably a combination of Dorothy's father's first name and Richard's mother's surname. It is unclear where second son John Peter's name came from, although his maternal great-grandfather was Peter Girard. Third son Charles was obviously named for his paternal grandfather, Charles Richardson.

James and Ann Richardson's oldest daughter, Dorothy, was clearly named for JBR's grandmother, and the second daughter, Margaret, for her maternal step-grandmother, Margaret Cantey Sinkler. The first James, who did not survive, could have been named either for his father or maternal grandfather. The next daughter, Sarah, was named for her biological maternal grandmother, but the next five daughters show no connection to family names beyond the two whose names included their mother's name as a middle name. Son William Henry Burchell may have been named in part for his uncle William Sinkler, and the youngest child, Richard Charles, was named for his grandfather, Richard Richardson, and great-grandfather, Charles Cantey, or—following the English system—his uncle Charles Richardson. The other son, named for his father, did not survive, but JBR's brother, John Peter, named a son James Burchell, which added to the confusion.

William and Eliza (named for her maternal grandmother) Sinkler named their firstborn James (paternal grandfather) and the second Archibald Broün[16] (maternal grandfather). That second son did not survive, nor did a subsequent son given the same name. Their son William died as an infant, so when they named a later son William, they added Henry, starting a line of five William Henrys. The third son, Seaman Deas, would have been named for Eliza's step-grandfather who was a family benefactor. They also had a Charles, who could have been named for his father's older brother, or his great-grandfather. Their only daughter, Elizabeth Allen, was named for her mother.

The Richardson Family

Richard Richardson (1704–1780) was a land surveyor who came from Virginia, probably in the early 1730s, although there is not consistent agreement on details. It is quite possible that he was attracted to the Sand Hills as a result of Governor Johnson's 1730 "Scheem . . . for Settling Townships" or plans for a 1739 "two-year reservation of the east bank of the Santee and Wateree, from Jacks Creek

16 Usually pronounced "Brow-oon," it was apparently also pronounced "Brown," as it was occasionally spelled that way.

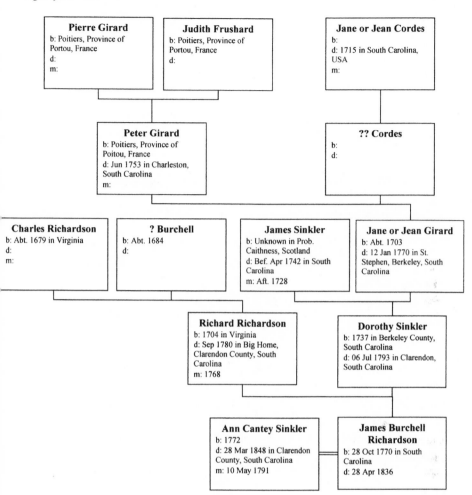

to Fredericksburg township (later Camden), for settlers from Scotland," which would have provided ample work for surveyors. This latter project, apparently based on the arrival of 350 Scots in North Carolina, never materialized. South Carolina historian Robert L. Meriwether said that Richardson did not petition for land for himself until 1744.[17] In any case, in 1736 he married Mary Cantey (1722–1767) in South Carolina, and they had seven children, the oldest being named Richard. Because the son also became a colonel of militia, there is occasionally some confusion over which Colonel Richardson is being referenced. After Mary's death, in 1768 Richard Richardson married Dorothea/Dorothy/Dolly

17 Robert L. Meriwether, *The Expansion of South Carolina 1729-1765* (Kingsport, TN: Southern Publishers, Inc., 1940), 19, 108.

Sinkler (1737–1793), with whom he had four sons, the oldest of whom was James Burchell Richardson (1770–1836).

From 1757, when he was commissioned a lieutenant in the Black River Head Company of the militia, until the end of his life, Richard Richardson was actively committed to military service.[18] He distinguished himself in the Cherokee War and the Tory insurrection known as the Snow Campaign and was appointed brigadier general on March 25, 1778.[19] Imprisoned in Charleston by the British, he was allowed to "linger out the last remaining hours of life at his family residence," where he died in September 1780. Shortly after he was buried, British lieutenant colonel Banastre Tarleton arrived and allegedly had the body exhumed before destroying property and burning the home. Ten-year-old James is said to have "jumped upon his father's military saddle and insisted that it should not be taken, whereupon the men were so amused at what they called the impudence of the little rebel that they gave it up to him."[20]

Richard Richardson's will of September 2, 1780, details numerous legacies to his wife and surviving nine children. Noteworthy is the amount of land in these bequests: specifically enumerated are more than 5,600 acres, with reference to other properties of indeterminate size.[21]

Little is recorded about Dorothy's raising four young boys after her husband's death, but she undoubtedly had ample support from friends and family. Her husband had been one of the moving forces behind establishing St. Mark's Episcopal Church, having also donated the land on which it was built, close to their home. Her stepson, Richard, lived nearby, and her brother, James Sinkler, and his family lived on the other side of the Santee. Although many miles separated them, it is clear that the families were in regular contact.

Throughout the 1801–03 correspondence with his young cousin, William Sinkler, it is obvious that James B. Richardson was cognizant of the need for male guidance. Letters also allude to his having felt the deprivation of his own formal education. There seems to be little evidence of schools in the area at that time. Ann Gregorie wrote that Wood Furman, a local surveyor and landowner, was teaching in the High Hills for a short time in 1770, but it would be the late 1780s before the Claremont Academy in Stateburg operated briefly and 1798 before there

---

18 George C. Rogers, *The History of Georgetown County, South Carolina* (Columbia: University of South Carolina Press, 1970), 69.

19 Benson J. Lossing, *The Pictorial Field-Book of the Revolution* (New York: Harper & Brothers, 1860), 444.

20 James Burgess, *Chronicles of St. Mark's Parish, Santee Circuit and Williamsburg Township* (Columbia, S.C.: Charles A. Calvo, Jr., Printer, 1888), 87–88.

21 General Richard Richardson, Last Will and Testament, dated September 2, 1780. Cathcart/Baskins Genealogy website.

was a movement to establish a public school.[22] When schools began to appear in the area during the 1800s, the Richardsons seem to have been very much involved.

By the terms of his father's will, James B. Richardson inherited at least 2,500 acres of land and Manor Plantation, although his mother was left the use of it for her lifetime.[23] It is not clear at what point he took over the management of the property, but over his lifetime he continued to amass considerable land. His will identifies extensive properties, but it is difficult to determine the accuracy of the acreage, as he frequently identified one tract as being part of another without clarifying the precise acreage. Also, bequests are sometimes followed by alternate heirs, and it is unclear whether the property was duplicated.[24] The acreage listed in his will totals over 18,000 acres, and his House of Representatives biography lists at least 10,990 acres.[25]

In the family tradition, he became involved with politics at least as early as 1792, representing Clarendon County in eight General Assemblies. It is worth noting that the 1790 constitution specified the following qualifications for holding office: members of the House of Representatives "had to own 500 acres of land and ten slaves or have real estate holdings worth £150 sterling ($11,000) free of debt; state senators had to have holdings of £300 sterling ($22,000) and governors £1,500 sterling ($110,000)."[26]

It is not clear what influenced James B. Richardson's interest in horse racing, but we know that his father had such a regard for horses that his last, Snowdrop,

Gravestone of Richard Richardson's horse, Snowdrop, in the Richardson family cemetery near Rimini. Courtesy of the Clarendon County Archives.

22 Anne King Gregorie, *History of Sumter County* (Sumter, S.C.: Library Board of Sumter County, 1954), 63, 174–75.

23 Richardson, Last Will and Testament.

24 James Burchell Richardson, Last Will and Testament, dated August 25, 1826. Sumter Genealogical Center.

25 N. Louise Bailey, *Biographical Directory of the South Carolina House of Representatives,* vol. 4, *1791–1815* (Columbia: University of South Carolina Press, 1984), 475.

26 Walter Edgar, *South Carolina: A History* (Columbia: University of South Carolina Press, 1998), 255.

is buried along with the family in the Richardson cemetery, near Rimini.[27] JBR's younger brothers John Peter and Charles followed similar paths, becoming planters, politicians, and racehorse owners, albeit perhaps less flamboyantly. Both predeceased JBR, and the youngest brother, Thomas, died as a teenager.

There were other Richardsons in the area that came to be known as the High Hills of Santee, but both families contend that that they were not related. Indeed, they further differentiated themselves by insisting that the Richard Richardson family at Big Home were "foot Richardsons," while the William Richardson family of Bloom Hill were "head Richardsons." The first referred to the very sociable, fun-loving nature of that family, which was actively involved in politics, partying, and horse racing and the latter to more intellectual pursuits and an interest in law.[28]

The Sinkler Family

The earliest Sinkler in the region was James (d. 1752),[29] believed to have come from Caithness, a county in the north of Scotland, probably around 1700, and settling at a place called Tuckers, in what was then Craven County.[30] Recent DNA tests have confirmed the northern Scotland origin. Sometime after 1728, he married Jean/Jane Girard Burchell (1703–1770), the daughter of Peter Girard (d. 1753), a Huguenot immigrant in Charleston. She had been first married to Peter Burchell (1698–1728), by whom she had two children. James and Jane had two more children, Dorothea/Dorothy (1737–1793), mentioned previously, and James (1740–1800).

This James settled on the south bank of the Santee River, southeast of St. Stephen, where he acquired extensive property and lived at a place he called "Old Santee." Together with his older half-brother, Peter (1725–1782), he cultivated indigo, a highly remunerative but very labor-intensive crop, the export market for which ended with the Revolutionary War. He next concentrated his efforts on cotton; Samuel Dubose credited him as being one of the first successful cotton planters, writing that in 1799 he "planted three hundred acres . . . and reaped

27 Richardson Cemetery survey, November 14, 2005, Clarendon Archive, Manning, S.C.

28 David Duncan Wallace, *The History of South Carolina* (New York: American Historical Society, 1934), 2:458.

29 Family and church records have historically used this date, but a petition for land submitted on April 7, 1742, by Jane Sinkler claims that her husband, James, was deceased. Brent H. Holcomb. *Petitions for Land From South Carolina Council Journals* (Columbia, S.C.: SCMAR, 1996) 1:145.

30 Anna L. Sinkler, "A History of the Sinkler Family," unpublished memoir, ca. 1945, SCL, Sinkler Family Papers, 1705–1984.

Pedigree Chart for

William Sinkler

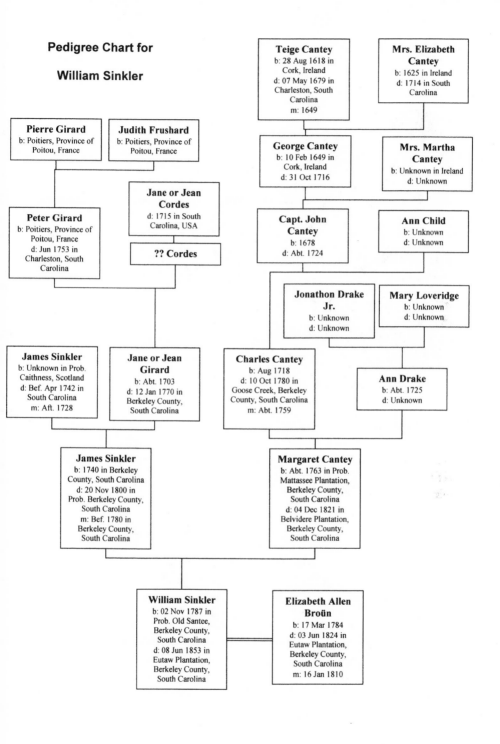

Teige Cantey
b: 28 Aug 1618 in Cork, Ireland
d: 07 May 1679 in Charleston, South Carolina
m: 1649

Mrs. Elizabeth Cantey
b: 1625 in Ireland
d: 1714 in South Carolina

Pierre Girard
b: Poitiers, Province of Poitou, France

Judith Frushard
b: Poitiers, Province of Poitou, France

George Cantey
b: 10 Feb 1649 in Cork, Ireland
d: 31 Oct 1716

Mrs. Martha Cantey
b: Unknown in Ireland
d: Unknown

Jane or Jean Cordes
d: 1715 in South Carolina, USA

Peter Girard
b: Poitiers, Province of Poitou, France
d: Jun 1753 in Charleston, South Carolina

?? Cordes

Capt. John Cantey
b: 1678
d: Abt. 1724

Ann Child
b: Unknown
d: Unknown

Jonathon Drake Jr.
b: Unknown
d: Unknown

Mary Loveridge
b: Unknown
d: Unknown

James Sinkler
b: Unknown in Prob. Caithness, Scotland
d: Bef. Apr 1742 in South Carolina
m: Aft. 1728

Jane or Jean Girard
b: Abt. 1703
d: 12 Jan 1770 in Berkeley County, South Carolina

Charles Cantey
b: Aug 1718
d: 10 Oct 1780 in Goose Creek, Berkeley County, South Carolina
m: Abt. 1759

Ann Drake
b: Abt. 1725
d: Unknown

James Sinkler
b: 1740 in Berkeley County, South Carolina
d: 20 Nov 1800 in Prob. Berkeley County, South Carolina
m: Bef. 1780 in Berkeley County, South Carolina

Margaret Cantey
b: Abt. 1763 in Prob. Mattassee Plantation, Berkeley County, South Carolina
d: 04 Dec 1821 in Belvidere Plantation, Berkeley County, South Carolina

William Sinkler
b: 02 Nov 1787 in Prob. Old Santee, Berkeley County, South Carolina
d: 08 Jun 1853 in Eutaw Plantation, Berkeley County, South Carolina

Elizabeth Allen Broūn
b: 17 Mar 1784
d: 03 Jun 1824 in Eutaw Plantation, Berkeley County, South Carolina
m: 16 Jan 1810

James Sinkler, reproduced from a miniature. Courtesy of the South Caroliniana Library, University of South Carolina, Columbia, SC.

from each acre two hundred and sixteen pounds, which he sold for from fifty to seventy-five cents per pound."[31]

The *Biographical Directory of the South Carolina House of Representatives* states that "although some records referred to him as 'Captain,'" his actual military service was not documented.[32] However, in a letter of June 9, 1779, he wrote to his nephew, Lieutenant Thomas Cooper, requesting that "you would come down That I might go home for a month" and described what Thomas needed to bring with him. Although he did not identify himself by rank, he clearly indicated that he was actively serving in Charles Town and had the authority to order a replacement.[33] It is difficult to determine how active he was in specific campaigns mentioned in the letter, or whether he was sharing information that had been passed on to him.

31 Samuel Dubose, "Reminiscences of St. Stephen's Parish, Craven County," in *History of the Huguenots of South Carolina* (New York: Knickerbocker Press, 1887), 68.

32 N. Louise Bailey and Elizabeth Ivey Cooper, *Biographical Directory of the South Carolina House of Representatives,* vol. 3, *1775–1790* (Columbia: University of South Carolina Press, 1981), 659.

33 James Sinkler to Thomas Cooper, June 9, 1779, SCL, Sinkler Family Papers, 1705–1984.

From the early 1760s until his death, James Sinkler served St. Stephen's Episcopal Church as commissioner, warden, and vestryman. As most planters did, he also served at various times as a justice of the peace, tax collector, and road commissioner. He represented St. Stephen in the First Provincial Congress, then several General Assemblies, being elected but then declining to serve in the late 1780s.[34]

After James's first wife, Ann Cahusac, died, he married Sarah Cantey (d. before 1780), with whom he had a daughter, Ann Cantey, in 1772. After Sarah's death, he married her half-sister, Margaret Cantey (1763–1821), with whom he had four children.

In June 1793, speculating that the higher pineland was healthier, he built a house there and temporarily moved his family, "blacks and whites included, of more than twenty persons," to stay until November.[35] This experiment was considered the precursor of the annual migration to what came to be known as summer villages, such as Pineville, Pinopolis, and Eutawville, which continued into the early twentieth century, when the use of DDT to control mosquitos obviated the necessity to move back and forth.

In 1769 he and his brother, Peter, purchased 800 acres just west of Eutaw Springs and bordering the Santee River on the north; this property would eventually become Belvidere and Eutaw plantations. It has been theorized that James moved to Upper St. John's Parish to avoid the periodic river flooding, referred to as "freshets." While it is clear that he farmed the Belvidere property, the house may not have been started before his death; the family did not move there during his lifetime.[36] His February 1798 will lists at least seven plantations and nearly 4,300 acres of land.

In 1786 James Sinkler was one of a group of twenty-one investors who incorporated a company to construct the canal to connect the Santee and Cooper Rivers. Construction did not start until 1793, but the Santee Canal was opened on May 1, 1800, allowing continuous travel between Columbia and Charleston.[37] Unfortunately, although he did not die until November 30 of that year, and despite his involvement, James Sinkler's name is not included on the plaque at the Old Santee Canal Park in Moncks Corner.

Sometime after JS's death, there was a lawsuit filed in the Court of Chancery by his nephew, John P. Richardson, on behalf of the executors versus the legatees of the estate, several of whom were both. Part of the confusion was over the fact

---

34 Bailey and Cooper, *Biographical Directory of the South Carolina House*, 3:659–70.

35 Dubose, "Reminiscences of St. Stephen's Parish," 53–54.

36 Anne S. Fishburne, *Belvidere* (Columbia: University of South Carolina Press, 1949), 8.

37 Kapsch, *Historic Canals and Waterways*, 47.

that JS had acquired extensive property after having made his will, but the stated purpose was to clarify four issues, which was done in court in May of 1802.[38]

1. There was no provision for son James, born after the will was made and shortly before his father's death. Although the will provided funds for educating the younger children, it specifically named William and Anna. The settlement provided for "a distributive share equally with the rest." Inasmuch as the younger James died in 1804, this issue became a moot point.

2. The property of Charles Cantey, who died intestate in 1780, was divided among his children, including Margaret Cantey Sinkler and Sarah Cantey Sinkler, deceased mother of Ann, who married James B. Richardson. James Sinkler would have been the guardian and, as such, would have had the use of the real estate and slaves that were left to both his wives and his daughter. Part of the issue was whether the marriage settlement to Ann Cantey Sinkler Richardson included property that would have been hers anyhow, and it is difficult to understand how much JBR gained from this.

3. Charles Sinkler, the oldest son, had been allowed by his father to manage property before he attained the age of twenty-one and received the profits for his own use. The lawsuit sought to clarify whether those profits should be considered an advancement on his share. It was decreed that his management was a temporary provision for his training, and should not be a part of his legacy.

4. When Ann Cantey Sinkler Richardson and James B. Richardson married in 1791, they were evidently given a very generous marriage settlement. James Sinkler's will refers to this, leaving to JBR "my northernmost tenement and half the lot of land in meeting [*sic*] street [Charleston] together with the thirteen hereafter named negroes . . . with thirty two negroes given my daughter as her marriage portion makes him fully equal to my other Children, and is given in lieu of any claim to any part of Estate Charles Cantey."[39] The court decreed that, despite this, JBR was entitled to a share of the estate.

Numerous letters contain references to "the disputed affair" or "the intestate" (legally a partial intestate, as it pertained for the most part to property acquired between the time of James Sinkler's will and his death). Although it was eventually settled in court in May of 1802, there were continued references to it as late as 1808.

---

38 Henry William Desaussure, *Reports of Cases Argued and Determined in the Court of Chancery of the State of South Carolina* (Columbia, S.C.: Daniel & J. J. Faust, 1817), 127–40.

39 James Sinkler, Last Will and Testament, February 1798, Charleston County Will Book 28 (1800–1807), 119.

Family Connections

When Richard Richardson married Dorothy Sinkler, he became the brother-in-law of her younger brother, James Sinkler. It is quite possible that the two men had known each other earlier, especially since JS owned at least two plantations in St. Mark's Parish. In any case, they both served in the 1st Provincial Congress in 1775, Richardson representing Camden District[40] and Sinkler representing St. Stephen.[41] Both served in other congresses and the General Assembly until late in life, so their political paths would have crossed frequently.

Peter Sinkler, the older half-brother of Dorothy Richardson and James Sinkler, is named as an executor of Richard Richardson's will, which refers to him as "my beloved friend." Unfortunately, Peter did not outlive RR by much, dying in January 1782 of typhus fever as a result of harsh treatment by the British, after having been betrayed by a brother-in-law and imprisoned.

James Sinkler's daughter, Ann Cantey Sinkler (1772–1848), would have grown up knowing her first cousin, Richard Richardson's son James Burchell Richardson (1770–1836), whom she married in 1791. One opinion is that marriage between cousins was quite deliberate, in that it "helped prevent the fragmentation of family estates while it bolstered the financial and political power," while deepening the "exclusive nature of lowcountry society."[42] However, another view is that "cousin marriage, frequent for planter offspring, had as much to do with the limited social contacts of a planter's daughter previous to betrothal as it did with financial consolidation. Some girls preferred to marry suitable cousins with whom they were familiar, rather than wed wealthy strangers picked out by their fathers."[43]

Together, James and Ann had twelve children, eight of whom survived to adulthood. Only two of those were male, which brings up another issue: there was no pretense made regarding the partiality for male offspring. While JBR's letters clearly show his pride in all his children, they likewise highlight his preference for males. On September 28, 1811, JBR refers to his "fine family of children (& two fine boys in particular)." Again, in a November 26, 1813, letter that Ann wrote to her brother, William, she is quite straightforward: "I acknowledge I did wish for a Son, more on account of my beloved Richardson than my own, we have but one poor little fellow [William Henry Burchell 1804–1879] who does not look healthy, and every Summer has a severe attack of the fever." This was obviously a reference to the recent birth of Julia Anna, her eleventh child; the last child was

40 Bailey, *Biographical Directory of the South Carolina House*, 4:475.

41 Bailey and Cooper, *Biographical Directory of the South Carolina House*, 3:659.

42 Lorri Glover, *All Our Relations: Blood Ties and Emotional Bonds among the Early South Carolina Gentry* (Baltimore: Johns Hopkins University Press, 2000), 49.

43 Catherine Clinton, *The Plantation Mistress: Woman's World in the Old South* (New York: Pantheon Books, 1982), 61.

a son, Charles, born two years later. Again, one rather strong view was that the "preference for male offspring went deeper than genealogy (name extinction) and inheritance; it was part of a larger ideological framework that proclaimed men superior and women inferior."[44]

James Sinkler's oldest son, Charles (1780–1817), was not quite twenty-one when his father died, and had apparently already left school (the Grammar School of the College of Charleston). He was left the use of several plantations, which he would inherit at his next birthday.[45] He represented St. Stephen in the General Assemblies and Senate contemporaneously with James B. Richardson and also participated in horse racing. In 1817 CS was elected president of the St. Stephen's Jockey Club.[46]

Margaret Cantey Sinkler (1763–1821), wife of James, seems to have enjoyed a special position in the life of her niece Ann Cantey Sinkler, whom she raised from the age of eight and who always referred to her as "Mother." Likewise, letters indicate that the Richardson nephews adored her. JBR's letters usually refer to her as "my good friend," and he seems to have encouraged her to spend time with them, which she apparently did. A November 23, 1805, letter from JBR to William Sinkler includes the information that he was "sorry the Boat is going down so suddenly, as it does not give your Mama an opportunity of getting her furniture up," suggesting that perhaps she was planning an extended visit and taking her bed, or was having some item brought from Charleston.

The following letter from JBR's next younger brother, John Peter (1772–1811), seems to exemplify the closeness they felt for Margaret, possibly enhanced since their own mother had died in July 1793. Certainly, some of the issues discussed in the letter are quite personal. JPR and his wife, Floride Bonneau Peyre (1772–1844), had had three daughters by then, one of whom had died; ultimately, they would have seven children.

∾

Sᵀ. Marks 15th July 1799

I now plainly see my Dear Aunt on what footing our correspondence must be continued. I have missed one opportunity and that too by the mere effect of Chance far from intentional, and I hold it has ceased; can that intercourse then, which has so many Charms for me, which brings such delightful sensations with it be entirely repugnant and insipid to the sentiments of my own Dear Aunt, of whom I deal on that subject I had form'd so high and favorable an opinion

44 Ibid., 46.
45 Sinkler, Last Will and Testament, February 1798.
46 Henry Ravenel, Jr., "Daybook for Henry Ravenel, Junior," September 4, 1817, SCHS 12–313–05.

of, If so! Am I not now intruding upon time and patience that might be more advantageously disposed of—than to employ it in reviving your amiable person and qualifications, in your every sphere, in the mind of an Absent tho warm Friend—I fear not feeling deeply interested in a correspondence which I acknowledge is sufficiently dull. You are not aware of that pleasure which on your part it affords to that friend I have just now been speaking of. Such however is the case—that I find you are unwilling to venture further than what is reciprocal on each side, or Letter for Letter—Be that as it may <u>I am unwilling</u> to debass [*sic*] myself of a pleasure, I feel not amongst the least that of conversing with my Dear Aunt whenever it is convenient, and when Fortune has placed a Barrier to our seeing each other. Were you not less neglectful however in writing than you have this time been, Nevertheless your goodness would still keep your Image, your affectionate worth, deeply engraven in my mind. I am ever under some new Obligation that will imprint it. The present my Aunt has now made me I feel and receive with pleasure, not so much for the intrinsic value, as for the disposition of Friendship it shews [*sic*] my Dear Aunt to be possess'd of for me. Safely therefore I shall deposit those Gifts, and use them preciously—And when I wear them, shall I not remember the Donor. That Gown especially—I have try'd them both on twenty times and till now I never thought I was proud. Charley hands you this and shall I tell you I almost begrudge him the pleasure he is about to receive in your company—because I cannot share the enjoyment—this is selfish—but yet it is like human nature—and sometimes I cannot restrain it—how wrong tho to wish for what it is not in our power to obtain for ought we not to feel content in any situation that brings health and [torn] as we now enjoy it—and when we have the Idea of its also being enjoyed at the blest Retreat of our dearest Friend. Where and with us long may it continue—I must now Conclude or I fear I shall begin to touch on the deranged situation of my Domestik [*sic*] affairs which I had much rather not call into recollection. You have ever my best wishes at heart and [torn] distant from I still retain them, wishing you all the happiness this world affords and as much as your goodness—Remember me to my young Cousins and Believe me to [be]

Yr. truly loving
And very affectionate Nephew
John P. Richardson

[Addressed to]
Mrs. Margaret Sinkler
Mr. Ch[arle]s Richardson
St. Stephens

There is no record of the relationship between James B. Richardson and William Sinkler prior to the death of James Sinkler, but it is apparent that immediately after James died in November 1800, JBR initiated a correspondence that continued until he died in 1836. It is interesting to observe how the relationship evolved from that of mentor/student to that of coequal planters and horse breeders.

It is not clear what type of education William had been pursuing during his father's lifetime, but within less than three months after his father's death, he was whisked away to a boarding school in Charleston, then six months later to Newport, Rhode Island. Despite the travel difficulties, it was not unusual for South Carolinians to pursue their studies in the north, frequently Philadelphia and Newport. Dr. Henry Ravenel (1790–1867), who received his medical education in Philadelphia, kept a "daybook" in which he described some of those trips. A November 1809 entry notes, "A dreadful storm of wind & rain at sea which lasted 2 days. Lost most of our sails." Of the four trips he includes, the two southbound required nine and eleven days, and the northbound were fourteen and twenty days.[47] Newport would have been an even longer trip.

James Sinkler's will provided income from investments to fund the education of his children, specifically William and Margaret Anna. Throughout this time, James B. Richardson's frequent letters were burgeoning with advice. It is probably not an exaggeration to infer that JBR was vicariously enjoying William's educational experience. In a January 7, 1802, letter, JBR acknowledged WS's apparent request for changing schools but reminded him of "your advantages in life, & comforts thereof, & in particular for the opportunity now afforded you," and continued with a dissertation on how and to whom he should be thankful.

In a letter of March 3, 1803, sent to Cambridge, Massachusetts, Richardson recommended that William pursue early completion of his studies, but subsequent letters sent to him throughout the summer indicate that he was in Cambridge the entire time. Perhaps this was a program that allowed students to be enrolled straight through the summer, which he apparently did. A lengthy July 12, 1803, letter is replete with detailed advice about attention to studies, social life and long-term goals; however, it includes a reminder that he (WS) should settle all his accounts, suggesting that JBR entrusted him to manage his educational expenses.

It was not until a November 23, 1810, letter that JBR acknowledged his having mentored WS, when "my mind guided and my hand pointed you to the way to goodness & greatness." It is logical to guess that this was great preparation for guiding his own son, William Henry Burchell (1804–1879), and JBR's letters to him, starting in 1822, are a continuation of strongly worded advice.

47 Ibid., 1–2.

Intrepid Ladies

The commonly held view of nineteenth-century, planter-class women is probably one of pampered ladies who were constantly waited on. While some may have given that appearance, the facts suggest otherwise. Edward McCrady observed that during and immediately following the Revolutionary War, many women, "like guardian angels, preserved their husbands from falling in the hour of temptation when interests and convenience had almost got the better of honor and patriotism." He further noted that some "parted with their . . . endearments of home, followed these husbands into prison ships and distant lands, where, though they had long been in the habit of giving, they were reduced to the necessity of receiving charity."[48] Many women needed to petition for compensation for property lost or destroyed during the war, and in doing so "they ventured into an alien and overwhelmingly masculine environment" that brought them up against severe traditional views.[49] Many women exhibited great strength in standing up for their rights, but most eschewed the opportunity to resist convention and work toward changing laws. While there were modest legal changes related to women's property rights, legislation "stopped short of eradicating inequalities."[50] Historian Drew Gilpin Faust noted that as late as 1861, when the women's movement and feminism were growing in the North, there was almost no impact in the South, where "understandings of womanhood had remained rigidly biological and therefore seemingly natural and immutable."[51] A woman had few rights: she was unable to vote or have any political views; once she married, everything she owned became her husband's—her land, her life savings, any slaves she owned, and her name.[52] There were obvious exceptions, especially within the Sinkler family: Jean/Jane Girard (1703–1770), wife of James Sinkler, left an extensive will that included slaves and real property; her grandmother, Jean/Jane Cordes (d. 1715) did, as well. Margaret Cantey (1763–1821), wife of the second James Sinkler, also owned property and left a lengthy will.

There was very little opportunity for education. Most girls were educated by their mothers or by a spinster aunt—if one lived nearby or in the household. Those who did attend schools or had tutors were probably taught some French,

48 Edward McCrady, *The History of South Carolina in the Revolution 1780–1783* (1902; repr., New York: Russell & Russell, 1969). 870–871.

49 Cynthia A. Kierner, *Southern Women in Revolution, 1776–1800* (Columbia: University of South Carolina Press, 1998), xxi.

50 Ibid., 191–92.

51 Drew Gilpin Faust, *Mothers of Invention: Women of the Slaveholding South in the American Civil War* (Chapel Hill: University of North Carolina Press, 1996), 5.

52 Kathleen Steeler and Jessica Brislen, "Women in 19th Century America," http://womeninhistory.tripod.com (accessed April 13, 2015).

music, drawing, needlework, and literature—and sometimes household management. An interesting comparison can be made to the British novelist Jane Austen (1775–1817), who would have been a near contemporary to Ann Sinkler Richardson. At the age of seven, Austen and her older sister were sent to two boarding schools, where they were taught "a little French as well as some drawing and needlework, and almost certainly dancing." When Austen returned home shortly before her eleventh birthday, that was the end of her formal education.[53]

All this suggests that girls were being groomed for managing their homes; indeed, there were few opportunities for employment, even for those who might have preferred not to marry. For those who did marry, they faced a life of running a household, frequently with an extended family. Unexpected guests were often offered a place at the dining table and a bed for the evening, and the proper hostess provided both with a smile. This necessitated organizing and managing a staff of household servants and planning and supervising meal preparation—often maintaining a kitchen garden. Managing a household included preserving food and making candles, soap, rugs, linens, pillows, and bedding; this latter included raising geese to provide the feathers and down. One historian claimed that "women administered food production, purchase and distribution not only in the planter's home, but for the whole plantation," including the dairy, the garden, and the smokehouse. She further described the mistress's domain as extending "from the mansion's locked pantry to the slave quarter hospital and the slaughtering pen for the hogs," adding that "most plantation problems were brought to her unless, being crop related, they fell within the sphere of the overseer."[54]

In time of illness, it was the mistress who provided nursing—frequently mixing home remedies—not only for the family but also for the entire plantation. She was also expected to make clothing for the family, which meant that most women became expert seamstresses.

Dorothy

Very little is known about Richard Richardson's second wife, Dorothy Sinkler (1737–1793), but the available facts paint a picture of a resilient woman. The product of Scottish and Huguenot heritage, she grew up on the south side of the Santee River near St. Stephen. She married RR in 1768 and bore him four sons; he was away during much of that time in command of militia and as a congressional delegate.

In 1780, before the oldest son was ten, she nursed her husband when he was brought home from a British prison to die at home. Some historians say that she was later forced to witness the exhumation of her husband's body and the burning

Dorothy Sinkler Richardson's grave in the Richardson Cemetery near Rimini. Courtesy of the Clarendon County Archives, Manning, SC

of her home, both at Tarleton's hand. That she was able to survive and raise her sons is testament to her strength. Although the youngest did not survive to adulthood, Dolly lived to see the older three become successful men. Their respect for her is probably best expressed in the epitaph on her tombstone:

DOROTHY SINKLER

SACRED

TO THE MEMORY OF

MRS. DOROTHY SINKLER RICHARDSON

RELICT OF GEN. RICHARD RICHARDSON

WHO DIED JULY 1793

AGED 56 YEARS

SHE WAS PIOUS & EXEMPLARY, DISTINGUISHED IN MIND & MANNERS

AND EMINENTLY DISCERNIBLE IN THE HIGHEST SOCIETIES IN WHICH SHE

ASSOCIATED.

THIS MARBLE WHICH DESIGNATES THE PLACE WHERE HER REMAINS

REST IS ERECTED TO HER MEMORY BY HER ELDEST SON

JAMES B. RICHARDSON

WHO EARLY BEREFT OF PATERNAL CARE FEELS THAT HE IS INDEBTED TO HER
MATERNAL CARE & ATTENTION, TO HER VIGOROUS & PRESERVING MIND OF
FIRMNESS & DETERMINATION SURPASSING DESCRIPTION AND TO HER
VIGILANT AND ENLIGHTENED INSTRUCTIONS FOR BEING ALL
THAT HE IS IN LIFE.

Margaret

Margaret Cantey grew up at Mattasee Plantation, in the same neighborhood as
Dolly, albeit about twenty-five years later. Born about 1763, she was probably
sixteen or seventeen when she married her neighbor James Sinkler of Old Santee
Plantation, the younger brother to Dolly. James had previously been married to
Margaret's older half-sister, Sarah, who had died when their daughter, Ann, was
seven or eight years old. Thus, Margaret started married life raising her niece, who
was only eight or nine years younger than she was.

When James Sinkler died in 1800, three of their four children were still at
home, and the family was in the process of leaving Old Santee to move to Belvi-

Margaret Cantey
Sinkler, reproduced
from a miniature painted
by Edward Malbone
in 1802. Courtesy of
the South Caroliniana
Library, University
of South Carolina,
Columbia, SC.

dere, where they were building—or planning to build—a home on Eutaw Creek. Family tradition is that Margaret built Belvidere; it is unclear from letters and other records exactly when she moved there permanently, but she was undoubtedly the mistress of the plantation.

Her nephew/son-in-law, James B. Richardson, who, along with Margaret, was an executor of James Sinkler's will, stepped in to mentor her thirteen-year-old son, William. However, she was actively involved in decisions and frequently accompanied her son to school, whether Charleston, Newport, or Cambridge. Margaret's letters indicate that she was the one to place her daughter, Margaret Anna, in school in Charleston and later in the North, frequently staying there herself—probably to assure that all was well. Her letters suggest that she did not like living in the North, even for brief periods of time. An 1803 letter states, "You well know how many miserable hours I spent there," further describing the time as "many painful weeks."

While letters do not clarify how actively involved she was in running the plantations, she was certainly aware of the essentials, such as her reference in a letter of February 10, 1802, that she would not have funds until the previous year's crops had been sold and paid for.

Margaret apparently had a long illness prior to her death on December 4, 1821, as noted in a letter written to William by his sister Ann. There was no mention of a specific illness, but yellow fever was prevalent during that time, and she was only fifty-eight.

Mary

Mary Deas (1762–1857) was born at Thorowgood Plantation[55] to Elizabeth Allen and John Deas, the latter having arrived in South Carolina from Scotland in the late 1740s, as a young boy. On August 17, 1780, Mary married Captain Archibald Broün (1752–1797), whose father was an earlier Scottish immigrant. Early in their marriage, both her father and her husband were stripped of their property, allegedly for having taken British protection. Although a young mother, Mary petitioned on her husband's behalf in 1783, a rather unusual step for a woman to take at that time. It is unclear how much influence this had, as Captain Broün himself later petitioned and in 1784 had his citizenship and estate restored.[56]

When her husband died—from long-term complications resulting from a bayonet wound at the Siege of Savannah—she was left to raise seven children, ranging

---

55 Located in what is now Goose Creek, the plantation name was sometimes spelled "Thorough-good" or "Thorogood." Elizabeth Allen had inherited the property from her father, then additional property from her stepfather, George Seaman, who made her his sole heir, which meant that she brought considerable wealth to the marriage. Robert J. Broün's research notes in Sinkler private papers, ca. 1971.

56 Kierner, *Southern Women in Revolution*, 122–23.

in age from two to sixteen. It is no wonder that one of her first concerns after the death of her oldest daughter, Elizabeth Allen Sinkler, in 1824, was helping her son-in-law, William Sinkler, raise his five young children. Letters throughout the period describe the support she and her other daughters provided in raising these children.

Some family memoirs suggest that she lived with one of her married daughters. However, numerous letters as well as Charleston city directories clearly show that the various addresses on Boundary, Archdale, and Tradd Streets were in her name, not that of a daughter. She was widely revered among family and friends, who frequently referred to her as "Greatie." When she died, she was nearly ninety-five.

Eliza

No letters written by William Sinkler's wife, Eliza (Elizabeth Allen Broün, 1784–1824), seem to have survived, but other letters refer to her "goodness and unremitted kindness and attention." William's sister, Ann, in a November 26, 1813, letter, noted that Eliza had sent her some ducks and hoped that she "will be lucky with them," which indicates that they were not for immediate consumption. Other letters mention produce sent to the Richardson family, and references to family visits. It is worth noting that William Sinkler had started construction of Eutaw Plantation in 1808, so when they married in early 1810, the home was quite new

Living room of Eutaw Plantation. Courtesy of the Library of Congress.

James B. Richardson-William Sinkler relationship chart. Chart does not include all siblings. Some sources indicate that the first James Sinkler died in 1752, but the 1742 date seems better documented.

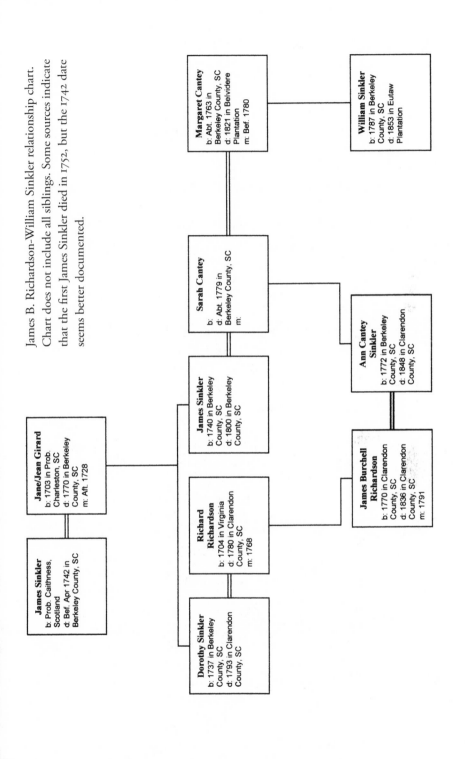

and likely not fully furnished. It is probable that she devoted much of her time to organizing their new home.

During the fourteen years of their marriage, Eliza had eight children, five of whom survived to be adults. The youngest infant died several months after her death in 1824 at age forty. Although there is no specific mention of yellow fever, it was still widespread during that time; and an August 26, 1824, letter from Ann Cantey Sinkler Richardson to WS mentions his "uneasiness about the yellow fever." WS never remarried.

William Sinkler wrote the following tribute to his wife, but appears not to have given it a title or possibly even to have finished it:

> Oh how shall I sustain
> This vast unutterable weight of woe?
> This worse than hunger, poverty, or pain;
> Or all the complicated ills below?
> She, in whose life, my hopes were treasured all
> Is gone—forever fled—
> My dearest "Eliza's" dead.
> These eyes, these tear swol'n eyes, beheld her fall
> Ah, no—she lives, on some far happier shore
> She lives—but (cruel thought) she lives for me no more.
>
> I, who the tedious absence of a day
> Removed, would languish, for my charmers sight;
> Would chide the lingering moments for delay
> And fondly blame the slow return of night;
> How, how shall I endure
> (O misery past a cure!)
> Hours, days, and years, successively to roll,
> Nor ever more behold the comfort of my soul?
> Was she not all my fondest wish could frame?
> Did ever mind so much of heaven partake?
> Did she not love me, with the purest flame?
> And give up friends and for my sake?
>
> Alas! I know too well
> How in her sweet expressive face
> Beam'd forth the beauties of her mind,
> Yes heightened by exterior grace
> Of manners, most engaging, most refin'd.
>
> No piteous object could she see
> But her soft bosom shar'd the woe

> While smiles of affability
> Endear'd whatever th' emotions of her heart
> Still shone conspicuous in her eyes,
> Stranger to every female art
> Alike to feign, or to disguise[57]

Ann

By contrast, Ann Cantey Sinkler Richardson (1772–1848) was a letter writer. Her husband, James Burchell Richardson, in an 1811 letter, refers to her as "no bad scribe," no doubt based on the fact that she undertook the burden of his immense correspondence during his illnesses. This was in addition to her own correspondence and other prodigious duties.

As mentioned previously, she was young when her mother died and her father, James Sinkler, remarried. Numerous letters reflect a very close and loving relationship between Ann and her aunt/stepmother Margaret, including extended visits both at their homes and elsewhere. A May 11, 1803, letter refers to her having spent seven weeks with Margaret in Charleston and leaving the two oldest daughters, about nine and twelve years old, with her to attend school. When Margaret died in 1821, it was Ann who nursed her at Belvidere during the long illness, possibly yellow fever. Her letter to her brother, William, in December reminds him "how kind and merciful is our heavenly Father, to give you so long a period to prepare for it."

Ann was eighteen or nineteen when she married her twenty-year-old first cousin, James B. Richardson, and bore him twelve children over a period of twenty-four years. During that time, they lost four of those children to the various illnesses then prevalent. The first son, James Sinkler Richardson (1796–1797), was buried at Old Santee Plantation, and the[n] later removal of his gravestone to St. Stephen's cemetery suggests that she may have been staying with her parents when he died. Letters frequently include parental concerns about the life expectancy of various children, especially Hermione and William Henry Burchell, both of whom struggled with various ailments but ultimately survived.

Raising this large family could have been considered a full-time job, but she had many other tasks. She was probably the one to supervise the moves back and forth between Momus Hall and their summer residence, most frequently referred to as Asylum. Although the homes were not far apart, the move involved relocating the entire household back and forth each year in late spring and late fall, as they attempted to minimize the exposure to disease associated with the swamp.

57 SCL, Sinkler Family Papers, 1705–1984.

And the sewing: while she undoubtedly could not have personally made all the clothing for such a large family, it was surely her job to plan and supervise the task. We know that this was not all relegated to slaves, as an April 4, 1819, letter to her brother states, "I could have done them better if I had of had more time to put the binding on." "Them" refers to what she called "horse clothes" she was making for him. At least two jockey suits of that era survive, but it is not known whether either one might have been the one referenced.

As all these accomplishments suggest, Ann Cantey Sinkler Richardson was a very busy woman. Yet she managed to correspond with the extended family and provide considerable insight into family life.

Back To Business

It is unclear just when William Sinkler returned from the north, but James B. Richardson wrote him a letter on October 5, 1805, to St. Stephen. Subsequent letters that year include topics such as harvesting cotton and instructions on brick-making, and a November 23 letter commends WS on "the care & management of your business." Over the years, letters make frequent reference to sharing labor, seed, and material. Along with the business advice, JBR also offered personal opinions, such as he did in an April 9, 1806, letter, which says that William was "too slow & tedious . . . & will in a little time loose the finest Girl," who would have made him a good wife.

JBR and WS were clearly sharing construction labor, as a December 22, 1808, letter attempts to explain why WS had "been kept out of the use of your Cotton Gin," evidently under construction. WS would probably have been building his plantation home, which would eventually come to be called Eutaw. In 1810 JBR referred to sending down his boat with "our corn and fodder" and suggested that WS set the freight rate. It is unclear whether "our" referred to these two men or to JBR and someone else.

There also seem to have been frequent property exchanges. A letter of September 20, 1806, refers to William Sinkler's use of "the Swamp land," and one of January 22, 1808, acknowledges WS's having sent Mr. Gourdin's letter with an offer of land, which Richardson was not interested in pursuing. In a November 23, 1810, letter, JBR seemed to be agreeable to selling unspecified property to WS for five hundred pounds, "and if you choose, take your filly at $250 in part." (The letter clearly states "pounds" and "$" in the same sentence.)

The earliest mention of James B. Richardson's name in Charleston horse racing came in 1793,[58] and from about 1808 until the end of his life, he was a force to be reckoned with. In addition to Charleston, there is mention of Augusta and

---

58 John B. Irving, *The South Carolina Jockey Club* (Charleston: Russell & Jones, 1857), 16.

Pineville, as well as a local course at Manchester, near present-day Pinewood. It is clear that WS was also involved; a letter of January 25, 1807, acknowledges that JBR had "heard of your trade," but it would be another twenty years before William Sinkler's name would gain prominence in the South Carolina turf.

There are references to sharing trainers and grooms. Letters are replete with breeding and trading details, such as a July 8, 1810, allusion to WS's offer of "the Filly Corinna" and another, which JBR declined because, he said, "it is against numbers in horses." One has to reread a letter of February 10, 1806, to realize that "Nancy" is in fact a racehorse and not a person, as she is mentioned in the same paragraph as family members, Were it not for the adjacent reference to WS's "little mare" being sent to Charleston, her identity might still remain a puzzle.

In 1833 James B. Richardson won all the main races at the Washington Race Course in Charleston, plus the Sweepstakes, a total of five races over a span of four days. He was only the third person to have done so, the earlier ones in 1800 and 1827.[59]

As previously noted, during the years from 1792 to 1817, Richardson was serving in the state legislature, two of those years, starting in 1802, as governor—the first who was not from the lowcountry. An example of some of the nonlocal issues he dealt with in that office is a letter dated February 25, 1803, over the signature of Thomas Jefferson. Because the handwriting in the letter is quite unlike the signature, this may have been an early version of form letters sent to all governors. (There were then sixteen to seventeen states, Ohio having been admitted in February 1803.)

[President] Thomas Jefferson to [Governor] James B. Richardson
Washington. Feb[ruary] 25, 1803
Sir
Having found it difficult to determine how the names of gentlemen proper for the office of Commissioners of bankruptcy, and who are willing to accept it and the non-acceptances and re-appointments at such a distance [serving] and time, while the service is a sufferance, I take the liberty of including your blank commissions which I ask the favor of you to fill up with the names of gentlemen, whom you think [proper] for this office, & who shall have previously signified to you that they will accept. When filled up, I have [still] to request you to give me information of the names that they may be entered in the anals [*sic*] of the Secretary of State's Office. The interest which I am sure you feel in whatever relates to the state over which you [preside] will apologize for the Liberty I take in asking you to perform for me a duty which you can perform so much more advantageously for your state. I pray

59 Ibid., 57–59.

you to accept assurance of my high consideration & respect.

Th. Jefferson

Governor Richardson[60]

Another letter that has survived is one JBR wrote to President Jefferson on April 4, 1803, responding to the request for the status of the state militia.

Charleston 4. April 1803.

Sir,

The requisitions made by you in pursuance of the request from the House of Representatives of the United States have been received, and shall be duly attended to; all vigorous exertions shall be used to put this State in the best possible situation of defence by having the Militia diciplin'd and well armed, the latter of which they are deficient in, tho' the attention of the Legislature has been engaged on that subject, and considerable appropriations made for the purchase of arms, the greater part of which, has been expended in contracts, that I am in hourly expectation will be fullfil'd, which will then enable the state of South Carolina to be more formidable in defence, and the assertion of her infringed rights, which I flatter myself she will be ever willing and ready to do, against any power that may invade or oppress. I have directed the Adjutant General of the State to furnish you immediately with the return of Militia, their arms and accoutrements &c, and the State of the Arsenals and Magazine, in compliance with the Act of Congress on that subject, and in conformity with a copy of a return some time since received from the Secretary of War of the United States, which no doubt will be expeditiously transmitted you by that officer. With respect to the geographical divisions of the State, I cannot better at this time delineate, than by observing that it is divided into twenty six districts under a late judiciary regulation, six of which are situate on the Sea Coast, and in case of a war, would be subject to many ravages, as they are penetrable by small vessels, from their contiguous situation to Rivers and inlets; they are also more extensive in Territory than the interior or upper districts, and less in population, as upon the latter principle the division appears to have been founded. It is indeed to be desired that the violation of rights essential to our wellfare, and the infraction of treaty, may be found the unauthorised act of a subordinate agent, and not the leading measures of a System, in which case the negotiation presents a prospect of a peaceable redress of the injury, and I hope, will

60 "From Thomas Jefferson to James B. Richardson, 25 February 1803." Jefferson Papers at https://founders.archives.gov/documents/Jefferson/01–39-02–0495. (accessed July 10, 2018).

effectually provide against its repetition; for the continuation of peace to our Country is an object worthy of our best endeavors to retain; it is at all times desirable, but more especially so, when we are but just recover'd from the excessive depredations, sustained in the struggle for independence: yet those objects however desirable, the advantages however great, and the enjoyment however pleasing, must be lost to remembrance when their preservation is hazardous to the dignity and reputation of the nation which I assure you, of my prompt cooperation in any measures for its support.

With high considerations of respect and esteem I am

Sir Your most obedient

James B. Richardson[61]

Richardson later served in the Senate and also held numerous other county offices, such as road commissioner and school trustee.[62] He also seems to have encouraged William Sinkler to participate in politics and the military, as a letter of June 25, 1812, states. It is worth noting that many men joined militias and took pride in using the titles, usually acquired through elections among themselves. The use of "Colonel Richardson," or "Colonel Sinkler" often made it difficult to identify specifically which person this was. Michael Stauffer quoted David A. Cole as saying that men "were neither equipped nor trained to wage war; they were paid only if they were called out by the governor."[63] In a letter of July 28, 1830, JBR expressed pleasure on having heard that WS had agreed to be a candidate for senator for St. John's, Berkeley. Although he was not successful, perhaps it fulfilled a wish of JBR's that he pursue that goal.

By February 2, 1826, James B. Richardson insisted that he was becoming "more & more a recluse every day, & becoming more & more attach'd to it." Increasingly, his wife, Ann, was doing the writing. On August 26, 1824, noting that her husband was doing "extremely poorly" and could not write, she mentioned looking for tincture of iron, which had provided relief in the past. Later letters would note his increasing blindness.

In a July 1830 letter James B. Richardson wrote to William Sinkler, he mentioned being "aversed [*sic*] to disunion or nullification" and expressed concern about a potential civil war. It is likely that his declining health confined his political activity to sharing his views with others.

61 "To Thomas Jefferson from James B. Richardson, 4 April 1803," *Founders Online*, National Archives, last modified June 29, 2016, http://founders.archives.gov/documents/Jefferson/01–40–02/0105. (accessed July 7, 2018).

62 Bailey, *Biographical Directory of the South Carolina House*, 4:476.

63 Michael E. Stauffer, *South Carolina's Antebellum Militia* (Columbia: South Carolina Department of Archives and History, 1991), 2.

A letter William Sinkler received a few years later from Thomas Gaillard, then living in Alabama, makes reference to "Nullifiers and Unionists" and mentions plans to "move my Negroes to this State." The most effusive political views expressed were those of James S. Deas, younger brother of WS's mother-in-law and a contemporary. In 1850 he claimed to view with "much anxiety and alarm the progress toward emancipation." Later in the same letter, he avowed that "the only issue that I think at this time that the South would be united in is the 'Right of Secession,'" which he regarded as the least objectionable.

The Letters Fly

Although there was a post office as early as 1792, most people appeared to continue sending letters by friends or servants.[64] Many letters indicated the name of the person who was to deliver the letter, and sometimes there was an admonition to place it only in the hands of the addressee.

On July 8, 1810, James B. Richardson wrote to William Sinkler that "the Post fly's [*sic*] to & from us twice a week." While the touch of sarcasm is obvious, it is also plain that this was considered a true marvel compared to years of sending mail by others. Letters to and from greater distances were yet another matter. On February 10, 1802, William received a letter in Newport, Rhode Island, in which his mother Margaret acknowledged having received "this moment" a letter of January 6. Likewise, on May 11, 1803, his sister Ann noted having received his letter one month after the date indorsed at Cambridge. Nevertheless, the letters moved—whether quickly or slowly—offering a window onto the events that shaped these families during this period.

---

64 Harvey S. Teal and Robert J. Stets, *South Carolina Postal History, 1760–1860* (Lake Oswego, Ore.: Raven Press, 1989), 11.

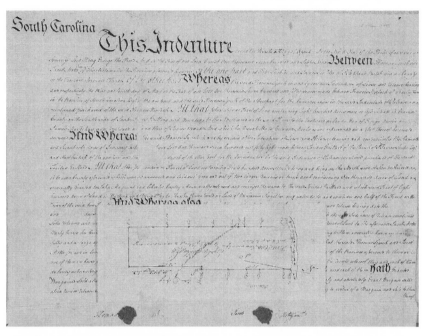

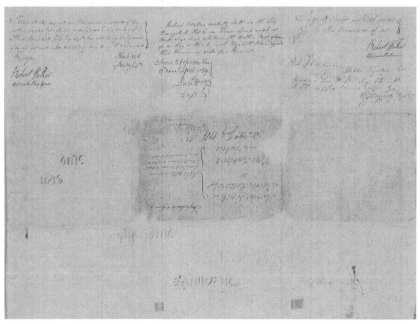

1769 Indenture (bill of sale) for 800 A. tract on Eutaw Springs purchased by Peter and James Sinkler from Thomas Lynch and Jacob Motte. Courtesy of South Caroliniana Library, University of South Carolina, Columbia, SC.

Chapter 2

Family Matters

Family relationships are often complicated, but few more so than that of James Burchell Richardson and his wife, Ann Cantey Sinkler Richardson. They were first cousins, he being the son of Dorothea/Dorothy/Dolly Sinkler Richardson and she being the daughter of James Sinkler, both of whom were children of Jean/Jane Girard Burchell Sinkler and the earlier James Sinkler. This also meant that Ann's mother, Sarah, and her stepmother, Margaret, who were half-sisters, were James Burchell Richardson's aunts.

When James and Ann married in 1791, James's first cousins, Charles and William Sinkler (and later James) became his brothers-in-law. Also, his aunt Margaret became his mother-in-law. Fortunately, they all appear to have been great friends, and letters show no evidence of friction among them. The fact that James Burchell Richardson was only seven years younger than Margaret made them close contemporaries, which could have been a factor.

Ann's father, James Sinkler, of Old Santee—a plantation southeast of St. Stephen—died on November 20, 1800, before completing the construction of Belvidere Plantation on Eutaw Creek, a tributary of the Santee River in Berkeley County, also referred to as Upper St. John's Parish. It is unclear whether construction had even begun before he died. A document shows that on April 19, 1769, Thomas Lynch and Jacob Motte, Jr., sold eight hundred acres on the south side of the Santee River to Peter and James Sinkler for £3,500.00 "SC money."[1] The plat attached to that document does not name the property, but a creek crossing

---

1 Indenture (bill of sale), April 19, 1769, SCL, Sinkler Family Papers, 1705–1984. Per SCDAH, in current money, the sale price would be about $105,000. Peter Sinkler was the older half-brother of James Sinkler.

diagonally north-northwest to the river names its origin as "Eutaw Springs." Ultimately, this creek, known as Eutaw Creek, would separate Belvidere Plantation on the northeast and Eutaw Plantation on the southwest.

James's 1798 will names his wife, Margaret, executrix; other executors were nephews James Burchell Richardson, John Peter Richardson, and Charles Richardson, and son Charles Sinkler "when he attains the age twenty one years."[2] This information is of interest in light of complaints in one of Margaret's letters about having to wait on executors and the court to get money.

Most bequests were real estate and slaves, with interest from "funded stock" to be applied to educating William and his younger sister, Margaret Anna. Although there was another son, James, born shortly before his father died, there was no new will. This was one of the factors that precipitated a lawsuit filed by John P. Richardson, executor, referred to in the previous chapter. Letters refer to concerns family members had over the matter, such as one on January 7, 1802, which mentions the hope that the intestate might be settled by April. Records indicate that the case was not heard until May.[3] Disagreement over property division seems to have persisted for several years.

When James Sinkler died, this left the barely thirteen-year-old William, his seven-year-old sister, Margaret Anna, and the infant, James, dependent solely on their mother, Margaret Cantey Sinkler. The older brother, Charles, had evidently left school by this time; it is likely that he helped run Old Santee Plantation, where they lived, plus others that his father had bequeathed to him when he became twenty-one. Letters suggest that he traveled frequently (to Charleston, Philadelphia, New York, and other places), and his mother's letter of April 28, 1803, refers to his "extravagances," as do other letters from JBR. Nevertheless, it is clear that at times he acted as a courier between his brother and James B. Richardson, at later times even being entrusted with the task of vetting a school being considered for William, perhaps even participating in the selection.

It is unclear who made the decision for William to attend boarding school, first in Charleston, then in Newport, Rhode Island. It may have been Margaret's choice, but more likely it was on the advice of JBR, who appears to have taken on the personal responsibility of mentor. At least four of JBR's letters insist that WS study science and literature, and in March 1803 he noted that he "can trace your improvement in writing: The goodness, Orthography, Grammar, and proper application of Capitals."

In a February 8, 1801, letter to William, he suggested that he had firsthand experience: "in a place like Charleston vices of every species are daily exhibited to the human eye" and he warned him that he might "at length fall a victim, and

2 Sinkler, Last Will and Testament, 119.
3 Desaussure, *Reports of Cases Argued,* 127.

become an admired [*sic*] of those vices." This same letter suggests that the letter be kept and reflected on "when the mind inclines to be led away." On February 20 of the same year, he commended WS on remembering "the counselling of an aged parent" who knew the "value of a good education." In the same letter, he insisted that William come to him—not his mother—for help and money.

Various letters mention the inclusion of money and the requests for receipts. Brother Charles noted money included in letters, and an April 28, 1803, letter from James B. Richardson mentions fifty dollars in his letter and the same in a letter being sent by his mother, stating that this was the "safest way to transmit."

It is quite clear that Margaret was in total agreement with this arrangement. In a long letter to her son, written on February 10, 1802, she insisted, "I hope my William will always attend to his counsel & convince him you possess gratitude for his great attention to you." Despite this recommendation, she included considerable advice of her own. In response to his apparently having sought her guidance regarding his interest in studying for the clergy, she enumerated the many factors involved and insisted that he should delay the decision until completing his studies. JBR's letters never mention the topic, so it is likely that he was not consulted on that subject.

It is not surprising that James B. Richardson empathized with his young cousin as he, too, had lost his father when he was even younger. Comments in various letters suggest that he had not experienced the educational benefits that he anticipates William receiving. At one point, in an August 6, 1802, letter, he even admitted to envying the experience and, in a letter of July 12, 1803, articulated his expectations that WS would fill "some exalted Station of honor in your Country placed there by the confidence of your fellow Citizens." It is not until November 23, 1810, that he acknowledged his role as mentor.

It is somewhat ironic that William was constantly criticized for not writing frequently enough, while at the same time being admonished to concentrate on his studies. Nonetheless, letters make clear that he received strong support and encouragement from JBR, his mother, Margaret, and his sister, Ann.

⁓

FROM JAMES B. RICHARDSON TO WILLIAM [SINKLER, PROBABLY IN CHARLESTON]
JAMES VILLE [S.C. 8 FEBRUARY 1801]

My Dear William,
Altho' I have left you but a few days more than a week, that period wears the appearance of a Month. The time too, was spent in the gayest society, and those my heart holds most dear which frequently occasions it to glide off with double rapidity, as it passes imperceptible from the agreeable manner in which it is spent. Possibly however, this tedious time was occasioned by my anxiety for

your recovery of the indisposition in which I left you, I trust indeed, that long 'ere this, my Dear William's health has been thoroughly restored, and his mind engaged in the noble pursuit of science and literature; to accumulate that invaluable treasure which will qualify him in due time for every avocation in Life, to which his Country may call him, or the exigency of his family may make indispensable, and which no vissicitude [*sic*] short of death can deprive you of. It may not be unnecessary for me here to repeat what I have so often exerted my abilities to impress indellibly upon your mind, "That those are your valueable moments of improvement, and that however hard the burthen may now appear, yet when well discharged, will be found that only means, which will qualify your mind, make it keenly susceptible of all those <u>rich enjoyments</u> which heaven has in store for all below who seek it"—To some in life, who have tasted more extravagantly of the bitter cup of misfortune (and there are none wholy exempt) the expression of "<u>rich enjoyments</u>" would appear so extravagant that no demonstration could justify. But believe me when I assure you that the improved, and unsullied mind, which aims at Christian perfection, knows indeed, a resemblance of the heavenly enjoyments, from those enjoyed in this Life. To acquire this in your present situation it will be necessary to be subordinate to all in authority over you, to obey with pleasure and alacrity, and with avidity comply with all requisitions or injunctions; believe completely in the integrity of those, with whom your friends have thought proper to place you, for true it is that the well disposed youth, whose mind and manners are indicative of a virtuous heart, whose feelings share the ill of others in misfortunes, and inwardly participates in their joy—will never know the want of a Friend at all times. Upon the subject of your situation in a gay City, I shall not now say much, I will use U as a <u>subject </u>to engage my next leisure <u>halfhour</u>, which you must not expect will be very frequent, for my engagements are too numerous in life to spend more time with you my young friend, than I find is absolutely necessary for your good; however, in a place like Charleston vices of every species are daily exhibited to the human Eye, and however horrible they may appear at the first view, the pure & unsullied mind from frequently witnessing the same, will not view them with less horror only, but if not supported with the purest principles, & firmest determination, will at length fall a victim, and become an admired [*sic*] of those vices—which at first sight, his spotless mind contemplated as a <u>devouring monster</u>. I will now leave this, as I think I have given you sufficient testimony that I am no stranger to those variegated scenes in Life, altho' I have conducted myself, as thus far to pass my day, untinctured with their Banefull influences. You must treasure to yourself my counseling, for tho' not such as may come from the Pen of many; no one can give stronger assurance, of the goodness of its intention. Preserve this letter until I have the pleasure of seeing you, and when the mind inclines to be led away with vain pursuits, give it your perusal, and one moments reflection, when you will find reason & good sense, reassurance, dignified situation. I arrived at your Mama's early on the day after I left you, and had the happiness to find her well, entirely freed from the recent effect of her indisposition. She tenderly inquired after the health of her William, but was as much reconciled as could possibly be, to your separation—I spent but a little time there, before I prosecuted my journey to my home, where I found my family all in health, which happiness <u>we</u> all continue [torn] of—I have given you a Prolix detail of a <u>friendly</u> [torn] tho' not <u>prolific</u>, and have run out my time allotted for you—therefore I must bid you adieu—first telling you that Mrs. Richardson & the Girls all desire their Love to you—

I am with sincere affection
Dear William
Your friend very truly
James B. Richardson
8 February 1801

[Addressed to]
Master William Sinkler

~

FROM JAMES B. RICHARDSON TO WILLIAM [SINKLER IN CHARLESTON] JAMES VILLE [S.C., 20 FEBRUARY 1801]

My Dear William,

Your very acceptable Letter, I did not receive untill a few days past, how this delay was occasioned I cannot account for, from the great regularity in the Post. I must confess your long silence gave me great surprise, and no concern could be more acute from one friend for another, than I experienced in not learning early from you, as I had left you indisposed. I am now happily relieved, and am indeed glad to hear of your restoration from the attack of Fever, so as to continue your engagements in the Pursuits of Literature; I trust you may long continue in the enjoym[en]t of the invaluable blessing and experience no further interruption in your Studies. It gave me pleasure to observe you had treasured in remembrance, the counselling of an aged and experienced Parent, you can scarcely err, while you retrace that good and upright conduct, which activated and guided him through Life; Experiense taught him to know, from its want, the value of a good education, and therefore he placed upon the acquirements its true estimation. I am very sensible that your being in the Country, in the Bosom of your friends, and the desireable society of your fond and worthy Mama; are bribing allurements to a mind like yours, which has so recently tasted the sweet effects. But when my William recollects with what exertions I urge the impression upon his Mind, of a ready remuneration of those fascinating <u>Baubles</u>, for the pure, but arduous search for wisdom; Reflection will serve to discover the comparison just, of one being tinsele while the other is the purest metal. I rec'd a Letter from your Mama, which intimates her intention of going to see you. I flatter myself my D[ea]r Boy, that it was occasioned by nothing that had been mention'd in your Letters to her; your resolution will serve you of my especial request, of all oppressions of whatever should concern your <u>Peace of Mind</u>, should be made known to me alone, for you must remember, the susseptible mind she possesses is at all times early affected, much more so then, when it has been long afflicted with a tedious indisposition; it would surely add To the oppresion, & thereby retard her recovery. Your Sister thanks you for your remembrance of her; but my little Daughters are greatly at a loss to account for the cause of your entire neglect of them. They are closely engaged at school, and make considerable proficiency—we are all in good health, except myself, who has some days past been greatly indisposed—we unite in Love & good wishes to you,

    I am with sincere regard
    Dear William
    Your friend very [page torn]
    James B. Richardson
    20 February 1801

[Addressed to]
Jamesville Feb[ruar]y 22nd
Master William Sinkler
Charleston
For the James Ville)
Post Office)

From James B. Richardson to William [Sinkler in Charleston]
James Ville [, S. C. 15 March 1801]

My Dear William,

    I confess my remissness in this long period of silence, but when I have to urge in expiation of what you may deem neglect towards you, I trust your generous mind will not only admit the same, but feel with your friend, for the unfortunate cause which has interposed and prevented his good intentions A variety of causes too numerous to detail, has baffled purposes which I had in view, and deprived me <u>pleasures</u> dear indeed, but alas! Whose provident care and precaution, can ward off the oppressive calamity of sickness, which from time to time has affected some part or other of my family; while I write you, my <u>little Hermione</u> lies in the arms of her fond Mother, when scarcely the most sanguine hope founded in

---

4 Hermione lived until 1840.

Christian fortitude, can make me ever expect to see her again restored.[4] Oh my William! if there are not justifyable causes to incapacitate the mind of an affectionate Father for the avocations & engagements in life; I know not what may be termed so.

But let me not too effectually disarm my young friend of his manly sensations, by representations of the afflictions of those who are, and ought be dear to him, nor touch too sensibly the sympathy of his friendly Bosom; which always heaves in tenderest wishes, for the good of mankind generally, and his friends especially—I trust my Dear William that 'ere many Days I may have it in my power to give you a more favorable statement of our situation; But God himself only knows what will be this termination. I duly received your favor of the 12. inst[an]t; it gives me great pleasure to hear of your good health, I wish you a series of time in its continuation, in this enjoyment of that most invalueable blessing, Man feels himself qualifyed for the most arduous undertakings, and I hope you will find no unsupportable difficulty in your commendable pursuit in [*sic*] literature—persevere in the good intentions you have professed, and God I hope will prosper them. I readily admit your attention towards me in your regular correspondence, and feel indebted for your strict performance in those injunctions I imposed upon you. I flatter myself you have been assiduously vigilant in writing your Mama, the <u>best of mothers</u> my William, one, who it appears to me, would forego all the enjoyments in life, for the gratification, the advantage, and happiness <u>of those she loves</u>; when I state this to you, I do not expect the relation to a mind afore a stranger to the fact. No, but because I derive pleasure of recounting the goodness of such meritorious worth. It has been my intentions for some time past to go and see your Mama, and to bring her with me to my habitation; but the same reasons which I stated previously to you in this, prevented me that desireable pleasure; I am afraid from the delay, that she may have thought hard of me, but I am sure when acquainted with true preventive, it will obliterate all censure. I have communicated your tender of affection to your Sister, who thanks you kindly, & bid me assure you she would answer your letter, when released from the troubles that oppress her—My little Daughters receives your love, and remembers your short opertimes [*sic*] spent with them with pleasures—Benjamin who is here, thanks you for the good wishes, & offers you as many in return—says he will be able to Build you a House, by the time you procure a Companion to inhabit it.[5]

Adieu my William, believe me with unfeigned regards, Your sincere and affectionate friend

James B. Richardson

5 "Benjamin" is undoubtedly Benjamin King, a Charleston builder and friend of JBR, who ultimately built Eutaw house for WS, starting in 1808.

15 March 1801

NB. Write your Mama by the first opportunity & mention this circumstance, or inclose this letter_____

[Addressed to]

3

Jamesville March 16 10

Master William Sinkler

Charleston

Fr. the James Ville

Post office—

﹏

FROM JAMES B. RICHARDSON TO WILLIAM [SINKLER]
JAMES VILLE [S. C. 8. APRIL 1801]

My Dear William,

The reception of your much esteemed favor of the 1st instant gave me great pleasure, as it assured me of your good health, and the unremitting attention you pay to your Education suffer me to assure you that it is exceedingly satisfactory to receive such information; I have used my best exertions to impress upon your mind, the high importance you should view the attainment of science and literature, and believe me my William, as you progress to proficiency, & as you will proportionably increase in my esteem and admiration; for altho' I bear you considerable affection in consideration of your Parents, and your merits too, still I do believe that affection would perish, if I could ascertain that Nature had endowed you with sufficient capacity, and you would not exercise it, to acquire that treasure, which no event, short of Death, could divest you of.

Thus you discover my thirst after erudition, without which I think no Man however good, can be great, and taking into consideration the mass of mankind destitute of it, I view them as drones in society, and Burdens to the age they live in; therefore as you will my estimation, so you must exercise your exertions to acquire a good Education, which will render you beloved by all men.

It gives me great satisfaction to inform you of the good health of my little family, and also that of your Mama's & her family Anna & James,[6] who are all with us, and I trust from the change of Society and Air she will derive some good effects, as the traces of disagreeable Pain in her side, yet remains sometimes to be felt. I am not at all surprised you should be desirous of your Mama's accompanying you to the Northward, but I am somewhat so, when I reflect upon your

6 James Sinkler was apparently born shortly before the death of his father but was not christened until May 3, 1801, at St. Philips Episcopal Church in Charleston. He died in 1804, but it is not known where he was buried.

having the vanity to expect she will abandon the society of friends very dear to her, to gratify your <u>Boylike</u> wishes. Besides It may not happen that the place you are situate at school, would be the one where your Mama should incline to spend her Summer, and that being the case, <u>we</u> should be deprived of her valuable Society, without your being the better for it. No my young friend! However desirous I may be to see you gratified in every rational wish, I assure you I cannot relinquish my promised portion, for your enjoyment of this.

I shall be in Charleston the 18 or 20 inst[ant]. And I hope for the pleasure of your Mama's company down, as she promises it, if no unforeseen occurrence should interpose to prevent __ in the interim I must beg you, (after offering <u>our</u> united Love to you) to believe me with sincere affection,

Dear William
Your friend very truly
James B. Richardson
8 April 1801
Master William Sinkler___

[no address]

[SCL: Sinkler, Coxe, Fishburne, Roosevelt & Wharton family papers]
From James B. Richardson to William [Sinkler in Newport, R.I.]
James Ville [S.C. 29 August 1801]

I received your esteemed letter my Dear William but a few days since, occasioned by my absence from home or business at Santee & the irregular attendance at the post office during that time. It was a circumstance affording great pleasure to all your friends to hear of your safe arrival at your destined Port in good health, this information is truly pleasing far more than compensates for this sympathetic feeling we experienced for all the inconvenience disagreeable situation you underwent during your passage. But my William, your long silence after your arrival has given me great opportunities of justly reproaching you with neglect when each moment of delay was more important than ten times that period at any other season. The fears and anxieties of your friends were all awakened for your safety, & would have remain'd suspend'd between the conflicting powers of Fear & hope. Some weeks longer had it not been for the attentive goodness of M[iste]r Rutledge (to whom I shall feel myself lastingly indebted) that favored me with a letter immediately as he knew of your arrival.

I received with pleasure the letter from M[ister]r Rogers,[7] who mentions the

7 Robert Rogers was the longtime owner of the Newport Academy, a private school in Newport, Rhode Island. Mr. Rutledge was evidently on staff. George Champlin Mason, *Annals of Trinity Church, Newport, Rhode Island* (Newport, R.I., 1890), 1:308.

entire approbation of your conduct the short time you have been with [torn] not be improper here to remind my William (of what I have so repeatedly told him) how important and necessary it is, at all times to preserve the good opinion, the esteem & affection of all mankind, much more so of those who have the guidance and care of our Person & Education, to have an implicit reliance on the friendship of your Tutor and obey all his commands with alacrity, pleasure, & steadfast adherence to every injunction however oppressive or counter to your warmest intimation, trusting that time and future events will bend them to your advantage, and afford you just cause to bless that humiliating, disposition to all in authority over you. The period wherein you must acquire science and Literature, now presents itself. Suffer my Dear William those golden moments, not to glide off without due regard, due improvement, that when time has run her course, till maturity has crowned your years. You may look back with pleasure at your time well spent, and the industry, care, and attention your friends well rewarded, in your highly improved mind.

I trust that your stay Northwardly will all benefit you in a good constitution, you must only be more guarded in the winter to prevent the penetrating cold which is more liable in that climate than ours to terminate in Consumption or more [torn] affect the lungs, but the healthy situation the summer throughout, & have to enable you well to endure the asperity of the winter. Since you left us, your Brother Charles has been very ill, which detained me so long there (where I had gone upon business which shall be part of the subject of my next Letter to you) that I got very sick, so did your mama & Mr. J[oh]n Richardson, we are all recovered, and the rest of the friends you have in the Asylum[8] have participated exuberantly of good health. I hope our good God will countenance us all in the enjoyment of that invaluable blessing of series of years in continuation. M[iste]r Rogers mentions your deposit of the Two h[undred] Dollars, which I intended as Pocket money, and to furn[ish you] with cloathes. These he mentions he will supply & I have not the least doubt but to your satisfaction, & when you are in want of money to expend, you must apply to him—his order on me that be duly attended to and if my William should wish more than he at present requires, & writes me to that affect, I will always allow him what is handsome reasonable. Please Present my best respects to M[iste]r Rogers & M[iste]r Rutledge, a letter accompanies this for each of them. All your friends, particularly your sister & little nieces, adjoin me in sincere love to you. I am with unfeigned regard

D[ear] William

8 Asylum was the name given to JBR's summer home, to which the family moved late each spring until fall to avoid what was then call "swamp miasma," believed to be the cause of malaria.

(torn) [Your sincere] friend & aff[ectiona]te Brot[he]r
[James] B. Richardson
Master W[illia]m Sinkler

[Addressed to]
James Ville Sept[emb]er 5th[arrived in Newport?]
Master William Sinkler
From the JamesVille [*sic*] Post Office
Newport Rhode Island

From James B. Richardson to Master William Sinkler
[in Newport, R.I.]
James Ville S. Carolina [7 January. 1802]

It has been some time indeed my Dear William since I have written you. This
however has never been for the want or inclination but has been owing to the
multiplicity of engagements both public & private, which had called me from
my home & family, & occupied my every attention. You may to be sure, enquire
with propriety, if no interval has taken place, whence I had been enabled to
have said a few words to you I answer with candor, there has such times ensued,
but they have not been sufficient for me to write you upon the various topics I
inclined, which tended to prevent my writing hitherto. I must acknowledge the
goodness of my William by mentioning the receipt of his favor two of which I
have renewed since my silence. The first afford'd me incomparable pleasure & satisfaction, it informed me of your good health, which is of the first consideration,
& of your pleasant & comfortable situation, & enumerated your determination
& the prospects which opened to your view of the acquirement of science &
literature. This was indeed gratefull to my mind, and gave me another cause to
tender my thanks to the great <u>giver of all good</u>, for prospering my exertions to
obtain a good education for you my William. The contents of your last letter did
not accord with those of the first, it illy comports with my feelings, my ardent
solicitation for your good in deeds, it was painfull to peruse, and equally astonishing how the character therein mentioned, should have gained that reputation
& respectibility abroad, which he is not entitled to, nor does not receive at home.
I cannot for one moment suffer myself to believe, that any personal prejudice
could tempt my William to a recital of this kind, more especially when the avow-
als contained in his letter are to the contrary, and the temper & goodness of his
heart are so well known to me. Every inquiry shall be duly made to discover some
proper place for your future residence, & some suitable person to engage in your
removal, but during this operation, in the interim of that period, I must rely
upon you my William, to exercise your best exertions to advance your education,

suffer no pecuniary inducements to lead you astray from that invaluable acquirement, and believe implicitly that more or less as you obtain its possession, as you enhance yourself in the esteem and respectibility of the world, and become thereby endeared to your friends, and all those whom you most highly prize and as you mention no corruption of Morals, (which would induce me to an immediate removal of you) but to his seminary being too throng'd, I must tell my William that he must advance himself as fast as he possibly can, & be content untill I can do better for him, in a more proper & suitable place, and you will thereby deserve, much more credit for your proficiency. I flatter myself it is unnecessary for me to remind you that for your advantages in life, & the comforts thereof, & in particular for the opportunity now afforded you, of treasuring to yourself (without interuption of sickness) that invaluable acquirements, which nothing short of Death can bereave you of, that you are not unmindfull of the source from whence they flow, nor unthankfull, by tribute, and adoration to the benign [torn] of them. Who support us all by his goodness, a father to the fatherless, who now deprives us of one valuable friend, for his good causes & best known reasons, but he erects the standard of another with equal fidelity. Who raises from obscurity the son that confides in him, & makes him a luminary, whereby man may behold his manifold kindness & adore him. Surely my William a <u>Being</u> thus good & great, deserves more than that <u>small tribute</u> which is required of us, & may I not hope that you perform them unremittingly, in a due & proper manner. It is with pleasure I mention the good health of myself & family, & that of your Mama & her's, I think her health much advanc'd, of which her appearance is indicative—we all join in tendering our best wishes for the preservation of yours, & in reminding you to be carefull of it, also, that each expects your communication, whenever your avocation will admit, if only a few lines, it will be satisfactory.

In my last to you I made some mention expecting your Pockett money, upon this subject you did not say a word in your last; I shall wait therefore in perfect readiness to transmitt you, whenever I receive your requisition, & you need not fear I shall allways have the candor to mention you, whenever I judge you are beyond the bounds of frugality; but as yet you have been <u>almost parsimonious</u>. In my last I hinted at giving you an account of the Division of the Lands of your fathers [*sic*] Estate.[9] I here inclose you the description of that portion you drew, which is between that of your Mama's & mine. The business of the Intestate[10] is

9 William's father, James Sinkler, died on November 20, 1800, and left an extensive and detailed will.

10 A lawsuit, referred to as a "partial intestate," was brought against the estate because of property JS had acquired after his will was made and also because of another child having been born. See earlier notes.

not yet settled, but I expect will be in April next. Adieu my Dear William, I am adjoined by all, in the offer of my Love & best wishes for your health & advancement, in whatever may be necessary for your happiness, here and hereafter.

I am with sincere regard
Your affectionate & faithful friend
James B. Richardson
7 Jan[uar]y 1802

[Addressed to]
JamesVille Jan[uar]y. 634
Master William Sinkler
New Port
Rhode Island
From the James
Ville Post Office

Margaret Sinkler to Master William Sinkler [in Newport]
Charleston 10 day February [prob. 1802]

I have this Moment My Dear William received your affectionate Letter of 6 of January & acknowledge you have Some cause of Complaint of the inattention of your friends—I wrote you two letters, and you have never acknowledged but the receipt of one—I might have wrote oftener My Dear & can only Plead ill health as the cause of my omission—for I never can Neglect a Child So justly Dear to me, as my William—but my Son, I intreat that you will write oftener, your Letters is the only Satisfaction, I receive in your absence so to know you are well is great comfort to me. You must be Sensible, of the many anxieties that fills a Mother's Bosom for the Welfare, of an absent Child—She is under apprehensions for his Safety—for his Conduct in Life—Many youths are led astray by bad Company which God forbid My Darling Child, should be among the Number. Support forever my William an unsullied reputation—with your honour untarnished. Great are the hopes I have [for] you, deceive me not—return to your Native land & your fond Mother's Bosom, Virtuous & happy for miserable should I be to receive my Son otherwise. I hope you pay great attention to your studies and will not return as many do—no better than when they went—I have not Seen young Gaillard, but am told his father is not at all Pleased with his being so little improved, & I have heard both the Mr. Richardsons, who Seen him at Columbia, say, they were astonished to see him return no better improved. Surely you will not let this be Said of you—you are old enough to know what is for your advantage—& tho you have no friend there to urge you on, you ought to be more attentive, depend upon the goodness of your Maker to Strengthen your good resolutions—He will never depart those, who implore his aid—which I hope my fatherless Son, will never forget to implore, you are of an age, now, that you most need a father's Care, but you are so unfortunate as to have none, depend upon your God & your own vigilance to make you a good & wise man. I think often of my William, but on Xmas Day more than usual, all of our family were together (at your Sister's) but yourself, depend upon it I regretted your absence extremely. I am pleased to find you spent the day so worthy of yourself as to attend to the duties of devotion, which I hope you will always continue to do—As to your Choosing the profession of a Clergyman—I know not what to say, my William—I think you ought to weigh maturely a thing of Such importance to your future good—I should have no objection provided, you thought you could live up to the Dignity of the Character you adopt—much are expected of the Clergy—these are not only to give us Lessons of Inspiration, but are to live up Strictly to their Calling, and setting their Congregation a good example—but you justly observe, you will be a better judge when you have finished your Studies—Your best friend would rather you would quallify yourself for a Statesman. Doubtless you will know who I mean by your best friend—no other deserves the epithet but Mr. James B. R.[11] I hope my William will always attend to his Counsel & convince him you possess gratitude, for his great attention to you. Mr. Dubose[12] is really married, & very unexpectedly by the friends of both sides. I wish I could tell you your Brother was like to be married—but I fear he is too much in love with Single State to alter his condi[t]ion. He is got much better than he has been tho still very thin—Mr. Bowen's friends are making great interest here, for him to be an assistant to Mr. Frost in the old Church—his being a pupil of the Deceased Bishop Smith—he has a Number of friends—it is generally thought he will get it—he and Mr. Parker are the only candidates—I wish Mr. Bowen could get it.

I Should certainly my William have no objection to sending you the whole of your fifty dollars but I have sat for my picture to Mr. Malbone[13] of Newport; I thought as he is reckoned to take extraordinary likenesses you would have no objection to Spend your fifty dollars for my min[i]ature—<u>You may</u> say—<u>Why not give it to me Mama</u>? I tell you why! Since your father's Death I never have

11 It seems clear that Margaret and JBR supported each other in advising WS. Margaret may have been somewhat coy in mentioning that JBR expected WS to be a politician.

12 Samuel Dubose (1758–1811) was first married to Elizabeth Sinkler, the daughter of James's half-brother, Peter Sinkler. After her death, he married Martha Walter in 1801 or 1802.

13 Edward Greene Malbone (1777–1807) was an eminent miniaturist from Newport, Rhode Island, who periodically traveled to other cities to work. He spent five months in Charleston, beginning on December 10, 1801, during which time he produced fifty-eight miniatures.

Called Sixpence of Money out of the hands of the executors—The money which is now there is <u>intestate</u> & I hope may be given my little James,[14] nor has any one a right to touch it until the Court decides whose it shall be—that cannot take place afore this last years crop—which I have a third of—there is not a bail of Cotton nor barrel of rice yet Sold, so you See my Son, it is the want of the ability & not Inclination—that I do not send it to you. Mr. Malbone Speaks of going to Newport I will give the Mini[a]ture to him [to] deliver you—I will get Mr. Richardson to supply you with Pocket Money—he is now in town, I will request him to forward it as soon as possible. There [*sic*] all on the <u>race Course</u>, while I, like a Solitary Individual Set alone—and writing my sweet William—this is truly a place of Confusion & bustle, ere this I suppose their hearts are at ease & they know the winning horse—I have Come to this Place, to put my little Anna to school. I have placed her with a Mrs. Jones & Shall let her Stay until June & then fetch her home, or if I can get a friend to accompany me, I will pay you visit & bring her & James with me—my health is yet extremely bad—I enjoy very little Satisfaction in life—your friends are all well in St. Marks, when I left it about a fortnight—except one valued friend, John Richardson who has had

A chair, sometimes called a chaise, shay, or one-horse shay, was a two-wheeled cart pulled by a single horse. Sketch by Virginia Wood. Courtesy of the artist.

14 James was Margaret's fourth child, born shortly before the death of her husband, James, whose will referred to only three children. His existence contributed to the "intestate" reference.

his knee dislocated from a fall out of his Chair Coming from Columbia—I am afraid he will never walk again, <u>without Crutches</u>. You know not how I pity him. My D[ea]r William He is very melancholy about it indeed—well my Son here is a long letter to make up for my Neglect—God bless you my Son, prays your affectionate Mother M Sinkler

Anna begs her love to you & sais [*sic*] write her—She hopes soon it will be in her power to answer you—tell the Dubose both of them howdey.

[Addressed to]
6
Master William Sinkler
Newport

∽

From James B. Richardson to William [Sinkler in Newport,
    Rhode Island]
[6 August 1802]

My Dear William,

It has been long since I have had the pleasure of writing you, or receiving one of your favor, for the first deprivation I cannot attribute any just cause which I think worthy [of] communication, yet it is requisite to say, it proceed'd not from inclination, & true affection for you, or the desire of enducing you to a constant correspondence; & for the latter, I feel myself at a loss to assign a reason, as I know you delight in the exercise of your pen, & I cannot be otherwise than assured your esteem & regard, has undergone no change. I therefore shall urge no more, in the hope that your excuse will be found equally good with my own, for this seeming neglect. You will not I expect be surprised, at the reception of the enclosed Letters, as ere this I trust the dear, <u>the dear</u> personages[15] is [*sic*] safely with you, deliver the same with y[ou]r own hands, & enjoy the comfort, the invaluable treasure I am deprived of. Oh! My William, must I confess I <u>envy</u> you that happiness, the enjoyment of such desireable society? Must I for once acknowledge I feel that despicable passion, inhabit my Manly, tho' feeling Bosom? Yes, & in my belief for such a friend, who would not <u>envy</u> another the enjoyment. But once you are the happy, thus blessed let me not omit to apprize you of the importance of your treasure, conjure you to be more attentive than ever, & to exercise your best exertions, to supply a tender affectionate mother, for the deprivation of a faithful friend, I would to heaven, that me & mine were

15 Probably William's mother, Margaret Sinkler, and possibly his younger brother and sister as well.

with you, which would be a completion of all our happiness. But it is denied by Providence, for mortals ever to be completely happy here on Earth, or if they are so, their frail nature is not capable of a true knowledge, only till we are bereft of those blessings, are we susceptible of estimating their just value. I request you will write me often, & particularly at the rec[eip]t of my every letter, & if your Mama should not be with you, to forward my letter to her through the most safe & direct channels, & mention to me, whither you have conveyed them.

I hope you all enjoy good health, (as I calculate ere this reaches you, they are with you) and that you make more satisfactory proficiency in your Education, & that before long you will be prepared for colledge. I gave your Brother Charles some direction with respect to your situation, which amounted nearly to saying that if you thought (& in his opinion) you was [*sic*] not advantageously situate for the requirement of your Education to remove you to such place as was high in repute & the prospect promised well; but that if you were progressing (admiting it was some slower) you had best continue, as a removal would tend at first to retard your process, & you might not be as satisfactorily situated. This however, was a proviso that you was [*sic*] not at this time fit'd for Colledge, in which case he would immediately summon you to the most suitable. I flatter myself my Dear William, those arra[n]gements will be acceptable to you, when I assure you that every measure I pursue, wherein you are interested, has deeply your good at heart; & that nothing on my part shall ever be wanting, to make you an accomplished man of Science and Literature; for such would be my anxious desire for my own Son, if It was please God I had one. You will please tender my best compliments to M^r. Rogers, & inform him that I have paid M^r. Barker by his desire, one hundred Dollars, on y[ou]r acc[oun]t, which I make no doubt, he may have acc[oun]t of 'ere this. Remember me affectionately to all with you, & in particular your good Mama <u>my justly valued friend</u> & tell your brother Charles that his prospect of a crop continues pleasing, tho' there has been excessive Rains, which yet continue, & will do partial injury in such lowlands as retain the water; his Domestics conduct themselves with propriety, & I trust will continue so till his return. It is with pleasure that I mention the health of my Dear family & myself, who are all seated under the protection of the <u>towering Pine</u>, they all desire their affectionate Love to you all, and the two little chattering girls in particular to their d[ea]rgrand Mama, who they often speak of in raptures of love. I must enjoin upon you my William, that you will not [word missing] endeavors, to [torn] your Mama to a longer stay from her friends, than the [torn] health shall require & herself indulged with the pleasure of her seeing you. Adieu my Dear William, believe my allways [torn] unfeigned regard. Your sincere & affectionate friend,

James B. Richardson

6 Aug[us]t 1802

Master William Sinkler

[SCHS 73-VI-19]
FROM JAMES B. RICHARDSON TO MAST[E]R WILLIAM SINKLER
    [IN NEWPORT, RHODE ISLAND]
JAMES VILLE S. CAROLINA [19 AUGUST 1802]

I have not received one letter from you my Dear William for some length of
time, why, or wherefore this neglect? My own feelings justify me in saying that I
deserve it not, & to be approp[riate]d with what I do not incur, is more than my
keen sensations will admit I should endure; the Cleolea [*sic*], & indignation of
supporting injustice, would fain lend me to resentment, yet calm consideration
urges lenity, & had me hope you have some cause, founded on the most plausible
pretext, for your seeming neglect. My last letter to you of the 6 August, made
some investigation, & contained a gentle admonition on this occasion, but the
offence (I may so harshly term it) has been abundantly aggravated since, by the
reception of several letters from you to different persons. Your Sister also complains of your inattention, yet confesses she has but little right, when you neglect
the communication of those from whom you might possibly derive some information (if not improvement). I hope however, that no indisposition has been
the preventive & to know this authentic from you would be highly sat[isfacto]ry,
yet for the want of that knowledge, I support the suspence [*sic*], under the kind
influence of hope, which carries & supports us through every vicissitude, attendant on this variegated life. You have no doubt 'ere this, the happiness of your
fond Mother's society, your situation therefore becomes amiable, I trust however,
you will never loose the remembrance of those deserving attributes, of your best
thanks to the great giver [of] all good, for that, and all other blessings you receive
from time to time; & that by your tender care & assiduous attention to a valuable
parent, & the discovery of your mental improvements, you will evince, that all
the sacrifices she has made through life on your account, promise fair an [*sic*] ample repayments, and afford her maternal bosom exquisite pleasure & happiness,
that she hath beheld you worthy of her sincere affection, & a Son deserving [of]
praise & commendation. This would be heartfelt pleasure to me, who feels a tender (& much greater) interest in your proficiency of science & literature, & your
general welfare, than from the Tenour of your conduct, I am led to believe you
immagine; But him who knows the hearts of all, cannot be a stranger to mine,
& to such sincerity as flow therefrom. Give my love to my fr[ien]d Charles, &
all the children—& to your good Mama in the most tender manner, & present
her with the inclosed.

    I am with real regard
    Your very sincere friend—

James B. Richardson
19 Aug[us]t 1802
Mast[e]r W[illia]m Sinkler

[Addressed to]
[James V]ille Aug[us]t. 2050
M[a]st[e]r William Sinkler
From James Ville Post Office
NewPort Rhode Island.

[SCHS-73-VI-19]
FROM JAMES B. RICHARDSON TO MASTER WILLIAM [SINKLER IN
    CAMBRIDGE, MASSACHUSETTS]
SENT NEAR JAMES VILLE 3 MARCH 1803

Dear William,

I received your affectionate letter of the 28 January last, this moment, and that of the 19. same month a few days since. It gives me infinite pleasure to hear of your good health, which I confidently presume, as you have made no mention to the contrary and silent upon the subject. I am happy that I can say, my family at this time enjoys that invaluable blessing health, but how long that pleasant situation may be theirs my God only knows, as the measles are in the Neighborhood, and prevalent in every family, my fears are awaken'd lastly it should communicate to mine; my trust however, is great and extensive in that Almighty goodness, which guards and supports us this life; my own health has not been reinstated since the severe illness in the summer, it is much amended, and I am enabled to exercise the discharge of the duties incumbent upon me, tho' not without experiencing frequent indispositions, which were unusual with me. It is pleasing to me my D[ea]r William to hear you speak from your letter, with such satisfaction in the acquirement of your Education, and know you tread the paths of pursuit with energy & hope; I flatter myself those manly exertions, by divine blessing, will be bless'd with success, and that the time may arrive (not far distant) when you will be reunited to your family, and serviceable to your Country, in any [situation] unbiased voice of <u>freed</u> <u>men</u> may place you; to affect this [blurred] object, my wishes, my exertions, have never been wanting [blurred] short of that invaluable acquirement, would have tempt[ed] you from the cares and caresses of a tender Mother. But the purpose of qualifying [blurred] deserve them better, & to be sensible to appreciate [blurred] is surely worthy of some <u>early</u> sacrafice [*sic*]. I have just returned from Charleston in company with my valued friend (your Mother) so far as Santee, I left her in better health, by much than I met her on her arrival in Carolina. I flatter myself that altho' less plethoric she will enjoy better health than for some time past she has done. The nature of my avocations in life, require some of my time in Charleston[16] whither I shall go in a few days, where I shall be adjoined by your Mama, who will make a happy addition in my family. I wrote you early in December last from Columbia, and am surprised you have not yet received it in that I mentioned some particulars respecting your Education, urging your strict application to your early completion of your studies; I cannot avoid here repeating my wishes for your particular attention, now especially as it is my wish if you enter College early this spring or summer, that you may pay me a visit about the holy days in December next; as it will not be in my power, situate as I am, to visit you. This to be accomplished will require your intense assiduity, in order you should make a figure during your stay among y[ou]r friends. Then I can communicate my intentions for your future pursuit. The approbation of my friendly conduct towards you, expressed in your letter of the latter date, with the state of estimation you hold me in; are gratefull and flattering & I hope such as my conduct will allways merit of you. Your Brother Charles arrived in Charleston, during a dissipated week, and when I was throug'd [*sic*] with business, so that I had not an opportunity of conversing with him concerning you; I therefore desire you will send me an estimate of your expences for Education, cloathing, and person, each district, and what will be the suitable period, and manner to transmit money for the same. I will make the enquiry of Charles Sinkler, but yours will serve me as a memorandum. I have no kind of objection to your learning fencing, or any other accomplishment your fancy leads you; but I beg you will not suffer them to divert your attention from the primary object of consideration, by the accomplishment of the mind, that well stored treasure, which temporal vissicitudes [*sic*] are not liable to divest you of; But fencing is a manly exercise, and through the walks of life may be found serviceable, therefore it accords with approbation. I enclose you Fifty Dollars, and should have sent to town and sent you more, but thought this would be more serviceable, than double the sum later. You will favor me with rec[eip]t for the same immediately [as it] comes to hand, which I reques'd you will not neglect.

I have written you a long letter my Dear William, but even that [blurred] not prevent me from observing the pleasure I derive on the rec[eip]t of your favors, more particularly when I can trace your improvement in writing: The goodness, Orthography, Grammer, and proper application of Capitals. Adieu my Dear William, our united love is tendered you. And believe me with sentiments of sincere affection. Your friend very truly,

James B. Richardson

Master William Sinkler

---

16 The 1803 Charleston races were held February 9–12, but JBR's presence could still have been related to horse racing matters.

[Addressed to]
Jamesville Ma[r]ch 8<u>th</u>
Master William Sinkler
Cambridge
From James Ville Post Office
Massachusetts

[Attached note: one side] Letter to William Sinkler from Gov. J. B. Richardson March, 1803[17]

[Other side] Ella Brock Sinkler, daughter in law of Charles Sinkler[18] told me that my grandfather had recounted to her a duel that he had fought or nearly fought, when he was a young man. [She] was much ashamed of it—Someone had spoken slightingly of the ladies of St. John's Parrish—
Francis W. Sinkler
Nov 4th 1939

FROM JAMES B. RICHARDSON TO MASTER WILLIAM SINKLER
[IN CAMBRIDGE, MASSACHUSETTS]
CHARLESTON 28. APRIL 1803

My Dear William,

I have but a few minutes to dedicate to you, Therefore I must employ them in what interests me most materially. Your health is an object of high importance, to me and all your friends, therefore I must [make] the inquiry after it; hoping you have enjoyed it, since I had last the pleasure of hearing from you; It is pleasing I can give you an assurance that we all participate of that invaluable blessing, and I trust may continue long in the possession of it. I have been not a little surprised at receiving any answer from you to my letter of the 3 March last covering Fifty Dollars, which I requested you would acknowledge the rect. of, as soon as it came to hand. Since that period I have received no letter from you which occasions me much concern; & I desire my William you will write by every opportunity, and mention very particularly all the letters you receive from me.

I here inclose you Fifty Dollars, and tomorrow or this evening, in a letter of your Mama's I will send you Fifty Dollars more, and so will continue to send you, in expectation of its being the safest way of transmit[t]ing, as in a case of miscarriage, the loss will not be so material, nor this object a temptation—you will observe my William to make immediate return of receipt in order that the same

17 JBR was governor of South Carolina from 1802 to 1804.
18 This was not WS's older brother but his (WS's) son (1818–1894).

may be entered in my Book. Your Sister, Mama, and the little girls, with James and my fine Son, all tender you their love. I am my Dear William

> With unfeigned affection
> Your sincere friend in haste,
> James B. Richardson
> Mast[er] William Sinkler

[Addressed to]
Postmarked Boston MS May 16 50
Forwarded
Master William Sinkler
Cambridge
Mail Massachusetts

From Margaret Sinkler to William Sinkler
 [in Cambridge]
Charleston April the 28 1803

Dear William,

Your letter of the 27 of March I have received my D[ea]r William wherein you complain heavily of my long silence—it has not been occasioned from my Neglect I will assure. I have written you repeatedly & cannot conjecture the reason of this detention as I have heard of no mail being lost.

I am sensible my Son it must occasion you great uneasiness for well do I know what suspence [*sic*] is—I have painfully felt its effects & would not inflict so heavy a punishment on any being that I loved—to one of your affectionate disposition the silence of your friends must be still more distressing and I hope you will make the necessary allowances—I believe it is impossible for your Mother who tenderly loves you to forget you.

You wish for a return of those pleasant moments you spent a travelling with me—I should be truly glad to see you here, my D[ea]r William but I have no desire to return to the Northward. You well know how many miserable hours I spent there—Nothing but your uncommon attention I believe supported me under the many painful weeks I passed through & after you left me I cannot tell what I endured—

We have had some late frosts here, which has destroyed the crops. I fear your Brother will be a sufferer heaven knows he dearly wants a good crop to supply his extravagence—I heard from him a few days ago he was well. tho' I have not see [*sic*] him sometime. I fear Charles writes you very seldom—you know he dislikes his pen very much. I fear William you are now fond of guns—as I observe you are very careless. Adieu my much loved William—

James, is positively so cross that I scarce know what I am about. He is vaccinated and has a very bad arm which keeps him fretting constantly he tells you howdey & often speaks of you. I am better in health than I have been for sometime Past—may heaven Preserve you is the Wish of

Your ever-fond & affectionate Mother

M. Sinkler

Enclosed you will find 50 dollars, sent you by the Governor—which he mentioned in his letter [he] wrote you this morning—he requests you will send him a receipt immediately as you get our letters—for both bills—MS

[Addressed to]

50

Master William Sinkler

Cambridge

Massachusetts

[Postmarked "CHARL. SC May 2" and "BOSTON. Ms May 16"]

FROM ANN C. RICHARDSON TO M[ISTE]R WILLIAM SINKLER
  [IN CAMBRIDGE, MASSACHUSETTS]
ST. MARKS MAY 11, 1803

My Dear William,

I received your much esteemed favor of the 3d of March a few days since which gave me great pleasure to hear you enjoy'd your health, which blessing I am happy to inform you is our situation at this time I include my Dear Mama my Brother and James. I had the pleasure of spending 7 weeks in Town with Mama and James I assure you she is quite well and hearty and looks exceeding well, we left her in Charleston about ten days ago and left Dorothy and Margaret[19] with her to go to School, you accuse me my Dear Brother of neglecting you, I acknowledge I deserve it in some degree but not as much as you think for I have written you twice lately neither letter you make mention of in particular one which I inclosed a letter to Anna and bid you to forward to her for me. I am certain they have miscarried, you must not my William give yourself any uneasiness in supposing you're neglected by your friends believe me it is no such things. I know of several letters my Mama wrote you while I was with her, and heard her express her surprise that you mentioned you had not received none also my Richardson as soon as he received your letter mentioning your wish to learn fencing, he immediately wrote you and remitted you the money for that purpose he has since written you and sent you money. I am much surprised you have not

19 James B. and Ann Richardson's daughters, born in 1791 and 1794.

received neither of those letters there must certainly be some thing amiss in the Post, and no [neglect] of your friends I assure you, believe me my Brother every thing in my power to give you satisfaction and make you happy. I will with the greatest pleasure do for you, I have, with truth given you a true state of our Dear Mama['s] health which I am certain is the cause of your being unhappy but my William I entreat you not to let your mind be too much affected let hope sweet hope support you and look forward to that happy period that will bring you again to Carolina and to your friends who wishes much to see you and none more than your Sister, yes my William! I say none most seriously do I long to see my darling Brother, it gives me inexpressible pleasure to hear your Brother say he intends you shall come and see us in November, Oh anxiously shall I look for that period; keep up your spirits my Brother trust in that great and good God he is all sufficient: you say you're unhappy, nothing can make you so but by being from your friends and not hearing often form [*sic*] them which I grant is a good cause, but my William remember for what reason you are separated from us, to lay up that treasure for yourself that no one can divest you of, that which will make you an ornament to your Country and a comfort to your friends; consider those advantages and the hope of shortly seeing us in your native land and I am sure you will make yourself happy and I assure you I will write oftener to you than I have done yet, and always let you know particularly of Mama's health. I have sent you a lock of my hair in return send me one of yours[.] Your Nieces and Nephews beg their love to you I am my Dear William till Death

Your truly fond and very affection[a]t[e]

Sister

Ann C. Richardson

Your letter was dated 3d of March and [blurred] the 4. of April one month after date indorsed at Cambridge.

[Addressed to]
James Ville May 14
M[iste]r William Sinkler.
Cambridge Massachusetts
Mail.

From James B. Richardson to Master William Sinkler
  [in Cambridge, Massachusetts]
Sent near James Ville 12 July 1803

My Dear William,

Your two letters of the 13 and 20 of June are now before me & which I received yesterday evening; the contents gave me considerable uneasiness in consequence of the information of your having been sick; I trust and hope ere this that inestimable treasure health is thoroughly restored you. It constitutes me much pleasure that I can inform you of myself & family participating of the like blessing; except my dear little Son who has had several attacks of warm Fevers; & tho some better this day, is extremely poorly and much reduced; you know not Dear William how many painful moments of inquietude afflict this paternal bosom of mine for the safety of my Dear boy, who has concentrated in his little frame my many pleasing hopes. It will be another source of gratefull pleasure to you, & indeed the most important to hear that your Dear Mama is in good health, and at present with me. This blessing I hope my good God will long, very long bestow upon each individual of us.

Need I repeat to my William my extensive confidence in the care and attention I expect him to bestow on his Studies, and daily avocations; his due & humble recollection of his God & anxious for a continuance of his goodness and mercy; no, I trust it is unnecessary; those impressions I hope have long been indelibly made, which from constant practice, have become interwoven with whatever is natural. You cannot be devoid of the pleasing expectation, known to be possessed by your affectionate Mother & myself of your acquirement, use then every exertion not to disappoint those affectations, which realized will be productive of so much happiness. You are now of an age to appreciate the true value of a good Education, and your observation will point out the objects that enjoy with peculiar pleasure its just reward. Ah! my D[ea]r William how pleasing the sight, for me to behold you, the person of my description, filling some exalted Station of honor in your Country placed there by the confidence of your fellow Citizens between whose suffrages are guided by merit and Talents, where nothing is inherited or attached to Birth; and to know your capability to discharge the trust reposed in you. In effect this desired object, lets your attention be engaged in that which will guarantee it, and suffer no delusive persuasions to divert you from your lau[d]able pursuits. I am well aware that your situation is not destitute of great incentives to divert you from the line of rectitude and propriety which it is necessary you should pursue; nor that your situation is not remote from those female allurements which too often draw youth into their vortex, which prove destructive when too closely pursued, to not only their morals, but their constitution. You will doubtless make it an object of your strict attention to avoid every thing that will prove subversive to those valuable principles I wish preserved. You mention in your letters the want of some money; the sum named shall be transmitted to you. This letter will cover one hundred Dollars, & succeeding ones immediately after will cover the remainder. Ere this, you have seen your Brother Charles who has in charge for you a hundred Dollars, which will compose a part of the sum wanted. No inducement can tempt me to question your improper use of money. I have too high an opinion of your good sense to suppose for a moment that you would expend your money in any other manner than you could in your moments of reflection, review with pleasure, or gratify a friend in the examinations, if he should ask it. You must be very well assured, that I have pleasure in supporting you as genteelly as any youth among your companions, of not a more considerable capital than yourself, but I should regret indeed, to see you involved in difficulties, by the indulgence of extravagance, or <u>youthful unwarrantable passions</u>: which I had myself sanguine in hoping will never be the case [words obscured].

It is my wish that you should return here this [torn] company with your Sister, to leave New York about the [torn] of October next, or the first of November; your Brother who spoke of coming in by land, mentioned his intention of get[t]ing you to accompany him, but I cannot support the idea of her coming without some male protector. Therefore it would be best you should come with her. Previous to your departure I shall desire you to pay all expences there incurred, & will provide you accordingly. Our united Love & best wishes attend you both for your success, health & happiness. I am with unfeigned regard Dear William,

Your friend very sincerely

James B. Richardson

NB. return me rec[eipt]ts immediately as this comes to hand for the money sent.

Mast[er] William Sinkler

From Charles Sinkler to Mister William Sinkler
New York–July 25–1803

[Blurred]

Your letter written for Philadelphia I duly receiv'd. I left that place on Thursday and arriv'd on Saturday. This morning I receiv'd the letter of 3rd Inst[ant] requesting to see me immediately or requesting an inclosure of 300 dollars,[20] which you will receive herein. The letter you mention having written the Governor—he had not received when I left Carolina. He gave me one hundred Dollars for you not expecting you would need more. In about a fortnight I expect to see you. Untill when Adieu. Write me immediately on the receipt of this.

I am D[ea]r William yours

Cha[rle]s Sinkler

[Addressed to]

M[iste]r William Sinkler

---

20 William's older brother, Charles, was apparently a frequent emissary of JBR's, although it is not clear why he was in New York. JBR's letter of August 7, 1803, suggests that WS may not have acknowledged receipt of the money.

From James B. Richardson to Master William Sinkler [in Cambridge, Massachusetts]
Sent near James Ville 7th August 1803

My Dear William,

In my last to you I promised to write you very soon, so indeed was it my intention, but a variety of circumstances have arisen in succession and from time to time, thus far has interposed & prevented my design. I hope since your last you have enjoyed good health. Your silence however has been a cause of inquietude, fearing lest your health being impaired, has been the occasion of it. I live in the flattering hope that 'ere long the reception of a letter from you will dissipate my fear & apprehension & announce your recovery to the pristine state of health[.] I derive pleasure while I give you information that my Dear family with my valued friend your Mother are in tolerable good health. The latter very good, & my little Son recovered (tho' quite thin) of the indisposition mentioned you in my last. I ardently solicit of my good god the lasting enjoyment of this invaluable blessing and that at least we may have the pleasure of meeting under its kind influence. Inclosed is a Bill of one hundred Dollars which I hope you may receive safe, and transmit the receipt for that, and the former remittances as they are absolutely necessary vouchers to substanciate my entries.[21] In your last my William, requiring a remittance of money you will suffer me to assure, there was no cause as a justification for doing so, to enumerate what you had received, as no information could result, that I was not acquainted with, for I must inevitably know what I have remitted, or I ought to know, in order to support my own transactions, it only then could tend to evidence your economy, or my disposition to restrict you, which latter case my William, I aver never was my desire or intention, and my own feelings justify me in the assertion; and so can your Brother Charles, who on his return to Carolina in February last presented me a Bill of money advanced for you, of One Thousand & Eighty odd Dollars, which he will say I met with cheerfulness. So my William in future, preamble your requisition with no recapitulation, I will suffice at all times to intimate your loans and whenever in my power they shall be redressed, for my confidence in you is great and implicite. When your brother Charles left Carolina he promised me that he would visit you, no doubt he will perform what will constitute him pleasure, & is desirable to me, when you see him, tender my Affection & best wishes, and mention the situation of our health, and that I shall expect to meet him very early in October next on my Circuit of review, which he will see by the Gazette commences in September. The declaration of War between France and England has produced a

21 Records for administering funds for William's and Anna's education.

considerable stagnation in the commercial transaction of our country.[22] This, as is reasonable to expect, affects the agricultural interest. Produce remains at a stand. The prices are quoted as before the declaration, but there is no business done, the wisest in prediction differ prodigiously in their opinions upon the operation of our Markets henceforth. I cannot avoid thinking sometime, it would be advisable to seize the favorab[le] crisis of changing to advantage <u>our species of property</u>, so fluctuating in its productive interest. My D[ea]r Mrs. Richardson and family adjoin in love to you. I tender the same with the assurance of being your Sincere friend and very affectionate,

James B. Richardson

[Addressed to]
  Postmarks: [CH]ARL, SC [BOS]TON 10
  AUG SEP How 40
19   2   50
  Master William Sinkler
  Cambridge
  Massachusetts
  Mail

22 The effect of the Napoleonic wars on international trade was a major concern for planters.

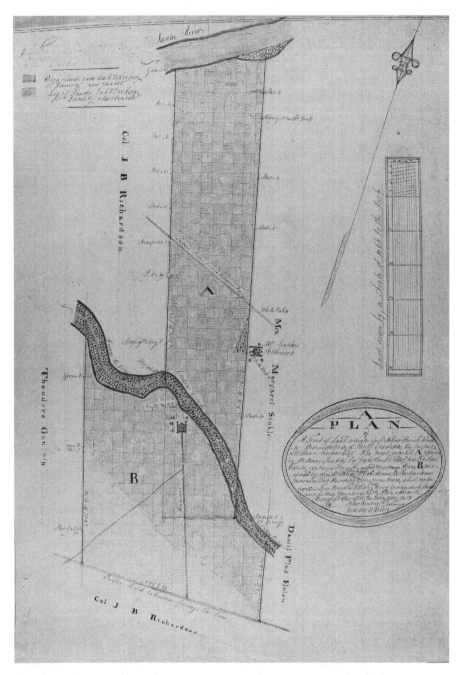

1818 plat by Peter Sanders and Sumter McKelvey, showing Eutaw and Belvidere plantations. Courtesy of South Caroliniana Library, University of South Carolina, Columbia, SC.

Chapter 3

Politics, Horses, Planting, and Other Business

It is not known when William Sinkler returned from Cambridge, but the first letter confirming his being back in South Carolina is in the fall of 1805. Judging from the address on the letter from James B. Richardson, William appears to have been at Old Santee, the Sinkler home near St. Stephen, rather than at Belvidere. JBR's letter expresses a real urgency in preventing the sale of that home to someone outside the family. While Old Santee is not explicitly named as the "ancient residence," it is unlikely he would have meant Belvidere, which was not old.

By the terms of James Sinkler's 1798 will, William was to inherit Belvidere and his older brother, Charles, would inherit Old Santee after their mother Margaret's death or remarriage. Margaret Cantey Sinkler outlived her son Charles by four years, so, although he lived there and managed it, he never inherited Old Santee. An 1807 plat shows the Eutaw Springs property having been partitioned to deed 275 acres to William, which seems strange, inasmuch as he had actually inherited it by the terms of his father's will. Possibly it was just a matter of clarification. It would appear that at some point James B. Richardson purchased the northeastern tract that included Belvidere house, as his daughter Dorothy seems to have been living there after the death of her husband in 1814. Letters from JBR to WS comment on her presence there and the fact that Dorothy and William visited frequently. At some point WS must have bought it back—possibly in 1818, as there was another plat drawn indicating that WS was purchasing 214 acres from JBR. Interestingly, Margaret's 1820 will leaves Belvidere to WS's oldest son, James, although it would seem that she did not actually own it and he appears not to have ever lived there. Further confusing the issue is JBR's 1826 will, which specifically names Belvidere and about 200 acres being left to daughter Dorothy, stating that he had previously given her a "Deed of Gift." However, records indicate that William Sinkler's son, Charles, owned Belvidere from the mid-1840s.

Subsequent letters are replete with instructions related to managing and planting the family plantations, making it clear that JBR continued his role as mentor. Gradually, there was a shift toward shared interests, such as the relay of instructions to overseers, arrangements for the sale of crops, the acquisition of property and supplies, and eventually horse racing matters. In a letter of September 20, 1806, JBR updated WS on arrangements for the construction of a gin, an informal agreement for WS's "using the Swamp land," and a request by another friend for the use of one of WS's carpenters.

It is difficult to determine exactly where WS was living, as letters were directed to him at "St. Stephen's, Santee," "St. John's, Santee," and "Springfield." From content in letters, Springfield appears to have been in the vicinity of Eutaw Springs but clearly does not refer to another later plantation of that name. It seems quite likely that it was an early name used for the property that was partitioned from Belvidere and would eventually be called Eutaw.

James Sinkler's will left extensive property to his son William on attaining the age of twenty-one (1808), but he had the use of it immediately following his father's death in 1800. WS had expressed a desire to build his own home as early as 1801 and appears to have started working toward that goal even before signing a construction contract with Benjamin King in March 1808 (see appendix B). JBR's letter of July 28, 1808, and others refer to the acquisition of material for the new house. While the east and west wings of the house were not added until 1820 and 1838 respectively,[1] the main house was completed soon enough for WS to bring his new bride there in 1810 and start a family.

Meanwhile, James B. Richardson continued his political activities, serving in either the state senate or the house until 1813, then again in the 1816–17 term; letters of November 23, 1810, and September 18, 1813, make mention of his returning to Columbia. In December 1812 he was elected a director of the new Bank of the State of South Carolina. Although it was a disqualifying position, he continued to serve in the senate until December 8, 1813, when it "was determined by that body (after protest and involved investigation) that he earlier had taken the oath as bank director."[2] Historian David Duncan Wallace characterized the bank as having been well managed and politically powerful,[3] so it must have been difficult for JBR to have made a choice.

---

1 F. M. Kirk, "Eutaw Plantation," *Charleston News & Courier,* October 7, 1935. There are no official records of this construction, so it is likely that Kirk got his information from the owner at the time, William Henry Sinkler III.

2 Bailey, *Biographical Directory of the South Carolina House,* 4:476.

3 Wallace, *History of South Carolina,* 2: 396–97.

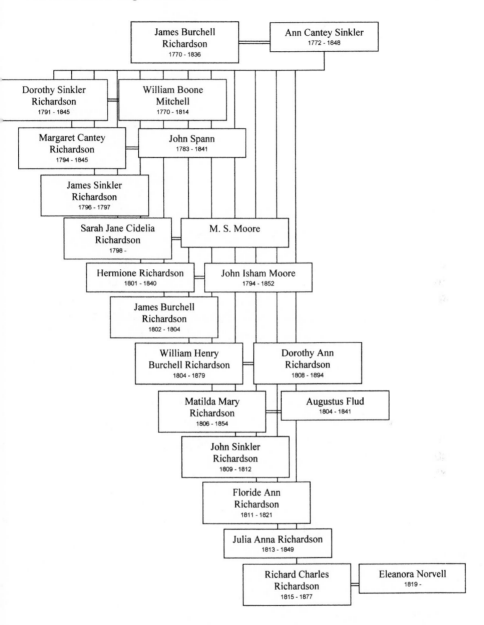

James and Ann Richardson continued increasing their family, with the twelfth child being born at the end of 1815. It is worth noting that by then their oldest daughter, Dorothy Sinkler Richardson, had married and had a child. This meant that by the time their last child was born, they were also grandparents.

A letter of September 28, 1811, makes reference to JBR's assuming the role of "second parent" after the death of his next-younger brother, John Peter. The Richardson brothers were very close, so it is no surprise that JBR would have assumed this responsibility. It is unlikely that he would have been required to provide financial support but probably undertook an advisory role.

Another example of fraternal loyalty, not mentioned in these letters, was when the youngest brother, Charles (1774–1829), ran successfully for Congress against John Kershaw and William Mayrant in 1812. JBR campaigned vigorously for his brother on the platform that John Kershaw had received an appointment from John Adams, and hence was a Federalist, while William Mayrant was crazy, so the only man fit for election was Charles Richardson. Mayrant filed suit against JBR for slander but lost his case when the court declared that every man had a right to judge and give an opinion of a candidate's fitness.[4]

It was during this time that Margaret Cantey Sinkler was carrying on a regular correspondence with John Peter Richardson's oldest child, Elizabeth (Betsey, 1794–1873). Many of the letters focus on sewing and weaving, including Margaret's acquisition of looms for weaving fabric. These looms would necessarily have been fairly large, as among the items being woven were bed sheets. It might be inferred that Margaret was encouraging her grandnieces[5] in pursuing these skills; a letter of August 25, 1813, requests some of "the silk yarn she [Betsey's sister, Flora] spins to form the cord of her Counterpanes." It is also quite likely that MCS was promoting the habit of writing letters.

In an undated letter, obviously written during this period, Margaret mentioned that she was sending Betsey's mother (Floride Bonneau Peyre Richardson) a small lump of indigo, noting that she had made "but very Little." Although indigo ceased to be an export crop after the Revolution, many people continued to make small quantities for their own use. It was not until the late nineteenth century that synthetic indigo came into general use, and it did not displace natural indigo until well into the twentieth century.[6]

In 1814 Betsey married Richard Irving Manning, and in 1845 their son married the daughter of William Sinkler, further entangling the family tree. Betsey had the distinction of having been related to six South Carolina governors. Already the niece of James B. Richardson, she was the wife, mother, and grandmother of the three Manning governors, as well as the sister and aunt of the two John Peter Richardsons who became governors.

4 Gregorie, *History of Sumter County,* 411.

5 Aside from being JPR's aunt, Margaret was the half-sister of Betsey's maternal grandmother, Elizabeth Cantey Peyre.

6 Kate Long, "The Chemical Era," 1–2. https://sites.google.com/site/kateannelong/the chemicalera. (accessed July 10, 2018)

Another activity of this period, not mentioned in letters, involved music. Probably around 1815, JBR encouraged Robin, "a full-blooded Negro, aged thirteen," to pursue his obvious musical talent. As a young child, Robin had made not only corn-stalk fiddles and reed flutes, as many children did, but also a violin fashioned from cypress shingles and horsehair strings. JBR was persuaded to send him to Charleston for lessons, and in four months Robin learned to play the violin and read a little music. He in turn instructed four other young boys to play instruments, and although they were evidently far less talented, the group eventually became widely known as the "Liliputian" band.[7] In addition to playing for dances at Momus Hall and Big Home, they were taken by JBR on a tour of the southern states, and the following year they performed a week of local concerts.

From about 1806, letters contain numerous references to horses—no big surprise, inasmuch as James B. Richardson had been an active participant in Charleston racing for more than ten years. He was not the first in his neighborhood: Richard Singleton and General Wade Hampton were well-known breeders, the latter also being a major owner of Washington Race Course in Charleston.[8]

An annual February event, race week had appeal not only for the participants but for all classes of the community, black and white. Charles Fraser described the week as being "devoted to pleasure and the interchanges of conviviality," noting that schools were dismissed, judges adjourned the courts, clergy often attended, and if a physician could not be found elsewhere, he was probably also at the races.[9] Another historian described the event as a "social equalizer," as it eased the tensions of upward mobility between the newly wealthy and established men. She further observed that the races could be "a prized form of recreation for slaves" and that trainers and jockeys often came in for a share of the purse.[10]

After the 1805 races, Colonel William Alston (1756–1839) decided to quit. He sold Nancy Air to John Peter Richardson prior to the general sale, in which many of his horses went to "Mr. Richardson" and Singleton.[11] This undoubtedly helped establish the stables of the Richardsons. At times, it is difficult to determine which Richardson—especially JBR and JPR—owned which horses. The winner was sometimes listed as "Col. Richardson," which could have been either, as both were lieutenant colonels in the South Carolina Militia.[12] This was due in part to Jockey Club rule 8: "Any member or members of this Club may start a horse, although the same be not his or their property; and he or they are solely to receive

7 Gregorie, *History of Sumter County,* 220–21, 432.

8 Irving, *South Carolina Jockey Club,* 14.

9 Charles Fraser, *Reminiscences of Charleston* (Charleston, S.C.: John Russell, 1854), 62.

10 Katherine C. Mooney, *Race Horse Men: How Slavery and Freedom Were Made at the Racetrack* (Cambridge, Mass.: Harvard University Press, 2014), 31–45.

11 Irving, *South Carolina Jockey Club,* 24–5.

12 Bailey, *Biographical Directory of the South Carolina House,* 4:476–77.

Washington Race Course viewing stand, erected in 1836. Courtesy of the Library of Congress.

the benefit of the purse, should they win: Provided, That two horses shall never be run from one stable for the same purse. A declaration to this effect to be made openly in the Club, upon honor, before starting."[13] This same problem occurred with Sinklers, as William's older brother, Charles—sometimes referred to as "Col. Sinkler"—and also WS's sons, James and William Henry, eventually raced horses. Even after Charles Sinkler's death in 1817, there are winner listings of "Col. Sinkler," and there is no evidence of WS having had a militia commission. His son James was too young at that time.

In addition to racing in Charleston, James B. Richardson and William Sinkler raced in other locales, the latter primarily in Pineville. A letter of February 10, 1806, includes horse racing details from Augusta and refers to WS's sending down his "little mare" to Charleston. Letters in 1807, 1808, and 1811 describe horse breeding and trading details.

Not all letters were about business and family matters. In a very long one of August 11, 1810, JBR attempted to define both friendship and happiness, claiming that friendship "too often leads us to believe with the utmost sincerity that they [our friends] really are what our fondest wishes would make them." He assures WS that he is happy "as much as falls to the lot of mortals, or as much as my nature & disposition will admit."

13 Irving, *South Carolina Jockey Club,* 193.

JAMES B. RICHARDSON TO WILLIAM SINKLER, ESQUIRE [IN
ST. STEPHEN'S, SANTEE]
ASYLUM 5. OCTOBER 1805

Dear William,

I am in much such health as when you left me yet in my bed, and my spirits
continue extremely low, my God only knows when I shall ever enjoy life again
with my former zest. Do not you and your brother suffer any person but one of
you to buy the ancient residence[14] of your Father for it would affect me to see
it in the possession of a Stranger, but let not this determination be known or
it may cause you to be imposed upon, nor do not suffer it to go under its full
value. Remember me to Charles & tell him how weak & low I am in health &
spirits.

Adieu D[ea]r William, believe me your sincere tho' afflicted friend
James B. Richardson
William Sinkler Esq[uire]
St. Stephen's Santee

[Addressed to]
William Sinkler Esquire
at S[ain]t Stephen's
P[e]r Sam Santee
[Note on envelope]
Make Adam Set off by Day light with this Letter—It must Reach William Posi-
tively tomorrow night it is of consequence, & he must put it in no hands but
William Sinkler's—for JBR—

[SCHS 73-VI-19]
JAMES B. RICHARDSON TO WILLIAM SINKLER, ESQUIRE
[AT BELVIDERE, SANTEE]
JAMES VILLE 3. NOVEMBER 1805

My Dear William,

It is the intention of your <u>Mama</u> to send down tomorrow to Bellvedere [*sic*], I
write you by the opportunity, after a night and great part of this day being spent

14 It is unclear whether this refers to Belvidere Plantation on Eutaw Creek, built about
1800, or to Old Santee, south of St. Stephen, the former residence of James and Margaret
Sinkler. As this letter is addressed to St. Stephen and refers to it as "the ancient residence,"
it seems most likely that he was referring to Old Santee.

in much pain, & sorry to say no prospect of getting better short[l]y—The rest of the family thank God are in good health, & I trust will long continue so, with yourself, but this warm change in the weather has a very unfavorable tendency, & I fear the well will experience it, if it continues long. I have to request of you my William & Benjamin[15] that you will see every possible expedition used in harvesting the Cotton & that you will give orders that it is taken clean out of the field. I will get C. Richardson to come down, take a view of thing[s], displace the old man & give you quiet possession; this I expect will be in the course of three or four days. If the potatoes are done, have the Pease trash'd & let the hands allowance first on them; Benjamin will give out mine, & corn is far better towards spring, but leave enough for seed. I request you will put the Waggons to drawing in the Brick wood as fast as they can, that they may burn them before the weather becomes freezing, which will injure the bricks some, & as soon as enough to begin, let Quaccoo have assistance, & tell him to commence it, & charge him from me to use all care to have them well burn'd, for good work cannot be done without the brick are good.

Remember me to Benjamin & tell him I have sent him Polly Thomas. Adieu D[ea]r William I can sit to write you no longer—believe me yours very truly,

James B. Richardson

William Sinkler Esq[uire]

Bellvedere—

NB. Your Sister & the girls all say howdy'e.

[Addressed to] William Sinkler Esquire

Bellvedere [*sic*]

Santee

Per Servt.

[SCHS 73-VI-19]

JAMES B. RICHARDSON TO WILLIAM SINKLER, ESQUIRE
    [AT ST. JOHN'S, SANTEE]
JAMES VILLE, NOV.R 23. 1805

Dear William,

I received by the boy yesterday evening your letter of the 22d. ins[tan]t and was glad to find it left you in good health. I do not recover as fast as I expected, & I have been some alarmed from my feelings of yesterday, that perhaps I will

---

15 Probably Benjamin Walker (1786–1845), JBR's friend and overseer. As the son of Charlotte Cantey, a half-sister of WS's mother, Margaret, he would have been WS's first cousin.

require another operation before I am thoroughly restored; God I trust of his infinite goodness will [a]vert it. It is pleasing to see you engage with so good a resolution in the care & management of your business, persevere in it, and I doubt not you will be successful; I well know the inconvenience from your distance that you labor under, & for that reason combined with others, I would recommend you to remove your situation as soon as possible. Benjamin Walker wrote to me for twine but I thought there was enough there among us, to do for some time yet, if you have any, as it was allways kept together, divide it with him, untill what I have written for to Ch[arle]ston should arrive, which will be in a few days; for I have none to spare him from here.

The mules I bought were not very large, but good size enough, and I have reserved four for you, & the six for my Plantation down there, but they are all unbroke & very unruly, & I know not how to contrive them down to you & Benjamin, you had best send up for them in the course of next week, but it must be a very carefull hand. I am sorry the Boat is going down so suddenly, as it does not give your Mama an opportunity of geting her furniture up,[16] particularly as the obsticle remains—but she is going down this morning, <u>needs never my contrivances</u>, and I doubt not but will devise a good scheme for the purpo[ses] to be obtained_____ Adieu Your friend with sincere affec[tion.]

James B. Richardson

William Sinkler Esq.

NB. I wish you much pleasure at the return of <u>Miss A W to the old place</u>.[17]

[Addressed to]
William Sinkler Esquire
St. John's
Per boy Santee
Peter
[Note on envelope:] Do send up the 4 bags by the boy to send things down to Bellvedere [*sic*].

16 It is unclear whether Margaret was having furniture moved from Charleston to Belvidere, or from Belvidere to JBR's, where she visited frequently. Perhaps she was planning to visit over Christmas.

17 This could refer to WS's first cousin and contemporary, Ann Walker, sister of Benjamin Walker. See n15.

JAMES B. RICHARDSON TO WILLIAM [SINKLER]
JAMES VILLE, 10 FEBRUARY 1806

Dear William,

I have sent you down Frank as you appeared so desirous he should go, & would have sent him the day after you started, but he never came to me untill the day following. I received your letter by Robert and was glad to hear you continued well, except the vapors, which your good reason & hope of <u>succeeding with her</u>, must dissipate. I wish indeed my health was good, & those I love so tenderly & all would be made pleasant with me, but at present I feel the necessity of some want, which expression cannot tell, and makes me low in spirits too. I wish you had mentioned the situation your Mama's health, I trust it may be better in consequence of your silence. Nancy[18] has continued very sick since you left this, tho appears some more at ease this morning than any time since she was first taken, and may perhaps derive benefit from the assistance of the Doctor who has attended her since Sunday. I expect you have sent on your little mare to Charleston, if I should come, I must share her success as I shall allways feel interested in her wellfare on acc[oun]t have been handed down from Augusta very incredible & unfavorable to the Co. It states Nancey Air having been beat by Dungannon; Gallatin winning 2d & 3d days & sold for $3000. & the Gourdseed beat easily by Gabriel, & return'd to Singleton's with extreme swell'd hocks. The former of this intelligence carrys but little probability, but the last part is too true; yet it may be all correct. I have really intruded upon my mind, to afford you some information, for I am sure neither my health, spirits, situation or inclination, tends the least to regard at this moment, the subject of which I have treated. Adieu William, give my love to your Mama & tender a kiss for me, and believe me with much sincerity. Yours very truly.

James B. Richardson

18 Nancy Air was a racehorse listed in *The History of the Turf* as belonging to JBR's younger brother, John Peter Richardson. She is described as being "6 yrs. 126 lbs." On Wednesday, February 19, 1806 she won the Jockey Club $800 purse, run in four-mile heats.

[SCL: Sinkler, Coxe, Fishburne, Roosevelt, and Wharton family papers]
James B. Richardson to William Sinkler, Esquire [at Springfield, Santee]
James Ville, 9 April 1806

Dear William,

Yours of this morning I duly received by Prince, and regret sincerely that your Potato seed has fallen short of your expectation, as I fear it may so happen, that Mr. King have used his for provisions, as he wrote me if they could be done without at Belvidere, they would prove an addition to his provisions, & that if he did not hear from me immediately, they would be applied to that purpose; knowing they were in want of some substitute, & not having the most distant Idea of your wanting seed, I did not write him on the subject, as I had concluded to purchase for myself, and let those be used in the plantation. It is nevertheless well worth your trouble of sending a boy down to see if they are consumed, and if not, certainly send for them, as any Thing is preferable to buying them [in] scarce times, but it is out of the question that Mr. Kings cart can be spared to bring them up, as he is using every endeavor to recruit his oxen sufficiently to waggon his Rice to a landing, expecting from the uncommon dry spring, to be obliged to send it to some Toll machine to pound out. I shall write Mr. King to let you have the potatoe seed (if there) whenever you send for them, & I expect myself to send in that neighborhood for some as I spoke to Col. Sinkler & Mr. Cooper[19] for what they might have to spare, as I very much fear Benj[ami]n Walker has not taken proper care of his Seed, & will want some.

I rejoice to hear you continue to have good rains, nothing is to be had up here but dry weather & frost, yet all are pert and cheerfull, tho' poor and needy, & matrimony the theme of the day, so it behooves you to have a feeling for your future prospects, which you have once painted in imagination for yourself. You are always too slow & tedious in your determinations, & will in a little time loose the finest Girl (thought to be) in this neighborhood, and who seated by your fireside in your homely house, would have strove to make your days more than happy & been quite happy to have shared the events of time with you, but alas! the die is cast, & her fate forever sealed, she now becomes anothers, & is to bless the arms of your inveterate rival. Oh! William, 'ere that important period arrives, take one look more at the charming hue of her cheeks, that the impression may

19 Colonel Sinkler was probably William Sinkler's older brother, Charles (1780–1817), who inherited Lequeux, Mattasee, and Flower-Canes plantations from his father. The legislative directory lists him as having been a militia colonel. James Sinkler's older sister, Jane, was married to Thomas Cooper, so Mr. Cooper may have been a first cousin.

be indelible, & live in your remembrance for life. I am sorry to hear you have been indisposed, you best trip up here, & peep at the times, I think you will have some emotions & perhaps better your health. Thank God my Mrs. Richardson & the little children are all well, myself much as when I seen [*sic*] you.

> With sentiments of affection
> Dear William
> Yours very truly,
> James B. Richardson
> William Sinkler Esquire
> Springfield

[Addressed to]
William Sinkler Esquire
Springfield
Santee
Mr. Prince with wagon

JAMES B. RICHARDSON TO WILLIAM SINKLER, ESQUIRE
[AT SPRING FIELD, SANTEE]
JAMES VILLE, 17 JUNE 1806

Dear William,

Your favor of the 16th ins[tan]t has this morning come to hand the contents observed, and your apology for not writing me readily admitted. The Plough moulds will have immediately made, and on telling J[oh]n Smith what you said respecting them, he observed that each mould would make a good Plough, & it would be a pitty to injure them in attempting to make two. I have some Ploughs by me ready made and if Frank can conveniently take them with him today, will send you down three for the moulds. I am indeed sorry to hear that crops are so much infested with grass, altho' a prevailing evil attending almost every person, and some, completely overwhelm'd, yet none so situate just in this neighborhood, but difficulties sufficient to contend with, and none more than myself however the promising prospects give encouragement for strong and arduous contention, & I must exhaust every mite of strength, before I can reconcile to relinquish any portion of it. I have sent you down the horse and beg you to use him as you please and as your own; & I should have sent your chair[20] (for the use of which I am greatly obliged) but thought as you would be up, you could then ride down in it.

I regret exceedingly that you did not mention the health of your good Mama, I presume she is well from your not making mention, because I wish it, but this

---

20 A chair, sometimes called a chaise, was a two-wheeled cart pulled by a single horse.

an ordinary cause for consolation, when it was in the power of circumstances so easily to have afforded better, yet it is perhaps as much as I <u>am entitled</u> to, and it becomes my duty to <u>court content</u> with whatever falls to my lot. Your Sister desires me to assure you of her acceptance of your love, tho' reserved for a postscript & blended with the ploughs, yet it is pleasing to know you think of her.

Adieu my Dear William, believe me with good wishes and affection. Your friend very truly,

James B. Richardson

[Addressed to]
William Sinkler Esquire
Spring Field
Santee

James B. Richardson to William Sinkler, Esq[uire]
Asylum 20 Sept[embe]r 1806

My Dear William,

I have to acknowledge the rec[eip]t of your two favors which came duly to hand, and that of the 19. ins[tan]t now before me; the former I should have replied to by the opportunity of Peter, but indisposition destroyed both inclination and ability to commune with you; I am happy I can say I am something better, & hope now for a thorough restoration, but alas, how fruitless are the most sanguine expectations of man at sometimes, and things as they occur through life at sometimes has strongly a fortuitous appearance. I have not been able to contract with Mr. Slater for the Gin, in consequence of his not informing me, agreeable to promise, the stated period in which he could accomplish it. I shall therefore, as you would prefer not to part with your carpenters Time, repair to Mr. Fordham and endeavor to obtain one from him, and the result of my application, I will advise you by the first conveyance. Mr. Slater said when with me, that he could complete you a Gin by the 1. Dec[embe]r next, but that I thought, a too distant period to contract for, & he parted on the promise, of endeavoring to make earlier arrangements and apprizing me of them. I have not the least objection to your using the swamp land, whether it should prove in your allotment or not, as the lands are undivided, 'tis highly improper to delay work for the Survey to be made, besides, if it was known to be mine, you shall be perfectly welcome to the use. I received a letter from Mr. King, St. Stephens, he mentions that he is greatly in want of the Carpenter you have but he does not mention in particular for what, you best send him down as soon as you poss[ibly can.]

I hope 'ere this, that the health of your Mama, my esteem'd friend, has much amended, my sensations are alive when aught assails her, and my orisons are offered to the throne of Mercy, for a thorough establishment of her valued health; Present my affection to her. Your Sister had another Stout Daughter[21] on Wednesday morning last, William is luckey to preserve his station secure so long! Adieu, the family unite in the offer of their love to you: and I request you to accept assurances of being your friend and affectionate.

James B. Richardson

William Sinkler Esq[uire]

JAMES B. RICHARDSON TO WILLIAM SINKLER, ESQ[UIRE AT SPRINGFIELD] JAMES VILLE JANUARY 25, 1807

Dear William,

I have just had the pleasure of receiving your affectionate letter of this morning which affords me much satisfaction in the account you give of yours & your Mama's health. I trust and hope that hers will continue to improve, untill a thorough restoration is affected; I shall however fondly wish, that with her improving health, her inclination to write may not decline, for in ill health she wrote me but little, and if even that should lessen, soon I fear none will be my portion; for it is indeed but little better than that now; tho' I cannot but think this opportunity she was misapprised of, or I should undoubtedly have been the better of a line or two. It is said, and perhaps correctly, that prosperity & good health, sometime make us mortals forget ourselves, and neglect those, who in reversed situations, would be the first sought after, but what can ever make us forget, or even for one moment neglect the being who from coincident of sentiment is found to possess a mind congenial with our own, and with whom to converse is the "feast of reason & the flow of soul"? I am extremely sorry to hear of the continued ill health of my little Anna,[22] and at her reluctance in leaving her Mama to pursue her studies, no doubt it would be a considerable alleviation to her depression of spirit to have the company of her school companions; prevail upon your Mama to let her remain until those come down which will be Tuesday or Wednesday next & she can accompany them. I am very much obliged by your kind offer in attending the Children to Town, your business, like my own appeared deranged, or I should have solicited the favor of you. This may perhaps continue and I had concluded to go as far as your Mama's with them, and send them on from thence, as it met the period designed for my being there. Yes, I soon heard of your trade

21 This would have been Matilda Mary; William was the next older child, born on December 19, 1804.

22 William Sinkler's younger sister, Margaret Anna, was born on February 2, 1793, so she would have been nearly fourteen years old. A family memoir says that she attended Madame Talvande's School in Charleston.

on your way down, and wish it may answer your sanguine expectation. The vehicle is gone to Augusta with two race nags, Kermit has returned quite crippled. I am quite obliged to you for sending the saddle, but sorry you should have taken the trouble of it, as on my coming down, it would have answered every purpose for my use then. We [are] all in tolerable health, except myself from a sore throat, which I contracted on Monday last, and was for two or three days exceeding bad. Tender my sincere love to my valued friend (your Mama) and assure her of my best orisons for her good health and accept the united affection of all here & the little William[23] in particular, who is unruly beyond controul.

Believe me D[ea]r William with regard

Yours very truly

James B. Richardson

[Addressed to]

William Sinkler Esq[uire]

Springfield

JAMES B. RICHARDSON TO WILLIAM SINKLER, ESQ[UIRE AT SPRINGFIELD]
JAMES VILLE SUNDAY MORNING 15. MARCH 1807

My Dear William,

I have been constantly in the hope since my last to you, of the pleasure of seeing you up here, and regret extremely the cause that has prevented you, as I am sure after my particular request for you to come, that if it had possibly been convenient, you would have done so. I hope you continue in good health, which blessing myself and little family participate, and I hope may long be in the enjoyment of it.

I expect you are in great forwardness for planting, & that your desire to be foremost has caused you to attend so closely to your pursuits. I never was more backwards in my life, so much extreme bad weather that scarcely any work could be done. I expect to send a Boat down in a few days, write me how many Bales of Cotton you have ready, & desire Benj[ami]n Walker to write & let me know also, and the situation of his business. There is nothing yet planted up here, tomorrow or next day I shall plant some corn as a begining [*sic*]. The Cotton baging you wanted will be up in Mr. James Boat which Mr. Carson mentioned had left Town.

Adieu Dear William believe me with every sincerity[.]

Your affectionate friend

James B. Richardson

23 William Henry Burchell Richardson would have been two years old.

[Addressed to]
William Sinkler Esq.
Springfield

JAMES B. RICHARDSON TO WILLIAM SINKLER, ESQ[UIRE, AT SPRINGFIELD]
ASYLUM 3D AUGUST 1807

My Dear William,

Altho' I have scarcely one moment of time now to address you, and quite indisposed from a very violent cold, I cannot omit doing so, in the most laconic manner possible, saying that I am sorry to inform you my little William & Marg[are]t have both had their fevers to return since Friday last, but has intermitted, & become every second day. I hope your dear Mama (my beloved friend) continues well, as does yourself, and that my dear Anna is restored to as good health as can be expected at this season, and after so long a deprivation of that blessing. I do indeed wish that <u>we</u> were <u>all</u> together through this summer, for the short time I shared your society, rendered the deprivation weighty, and very sensibly & generally experienced, to me I believe it was more particularly so, whether because you were going where I desired to accompany you, and whither my wishes ha[words missing]ously gone, or the loss in society intrinsically felt, I cannot [word missing]ibute, but I believe the causes were combined. I th[ank you] for the use of your Waggon which I now return & hope you will receive safe. I inclose you an advertisement to which I have affixed my name, thinking you might not wish to put yours. You must write others from it, and if you can recollect any more accurate description of them, insert it in those you draw, & place your name if you prefer, & to the pap[er] too.

Adieu I am off this moment to meet the Commissioners of Roads and hope in a very few days to see you.

I am with unfeigned regard
Your affectionate friend
James B. Richardson

[Addressed to]
William Sinkler Esq[uire]
Springfield

~

James B. Richardson to William Sinkler, Esquire
[at Spring Field, Santee]
Asylum, August 19, 1807

My Dear William,

On my arrival yesterday I found my Mrs. Richardson, my sweet little William, and Margaret and Matilda all sick, my William in particular was extremely sick in bed, & had been for two days previously, my heart bleeds for the welfare of this only boy of mine, and when I view his pallid cheeks, & feel the violent fever with which his little slender frame has to contend, the feelings of a tender father is wound to the highest pinnacle of sensibility, but my trust is in the mercies of my good God, who has overflowed my cup and bow'd me down with obligations for his daily mercies, and I hope will help my Son, my darling boy, with length of days and noble mental qualities.

I found Moses here, who had returned the day before yesterday, after a fruitless travel, all towards the Southward from you & then to Georgetown and he had no traces of any tiding, that could induce his longer continuance and I shall send him down tomorrow with the Colts, when he can inform you of every place he has been, and you can draw your conclusions of what direction you think those Africans may have taken; I am however of the same opinion as when I left you, that the most probable place to find them will be in Orangeburgh where you had better send, if you have not already done so. It will always give me pleasure to see you at my habitation, which I trust cannot be necessary, for me to remind you, and I hope my D[ea]r William you will not let it be long before you afford me that satisfaction, and were it possible to bring my beloved friend (your good Mama) and Anna, I should feel myself forever, under obligations to you. Adieu My William, believe me Y[ou]r Friend very truly

James B. Richardson

[Addressed to]
William Sinkler Esquire
Spring Field
Santee
Per boy Billy

James B. Richardson to William [Sinkler]
Home Pence. 2 O'clock p.m. August 24. 1807

My Dear William,

Your favor of yesterday this moment has come to hand, and I hasten to reply as you express a desire for the return of the Serv[an]t immediately, but I fear much he may not find it possible for him to reach you tonight. I sincerely thank you for your tender enquiries and good wishes towards my family, & in particular my little William who I trust in my good God may be restored to health, and in maturity meet my fond hopes for mental acquirements, and benevolence. He is extremely weak & poorly but is some better one day than the other, and I have persuaded his Mama to ride home with him a little while today (as the Doctor has recommended exercise whenever he is able to bear it;) in the hope that it may prove serviceable to him. The rest of family some better. You know not my Dear William how extremely concerned I am to hear of the sickness of your good Mama (my valued friend) indeed it writhes my soul to hear she is so sick. I pray my good God to restore her & my little Anna soon to health, for I am rendered unhappy whenever aught assails my friends. I trust my dear William that you will urge every application that may be thought serviceable to her, and in a continuation, do not fail getting the assistance of the Faculty, which she promised me when I left her of sending to Dr. Thomas, if she was not better. I am concerned that you should have so much trouble with these Africans, it was foreign I assure you from me when you first had them that they would have made a second attempt, but I hope you will do with them as you please, and I pray teach them better, than ever to repeat the like offence and may be the last trouble you will have with the villains. I would send you down the money to pay the fees but I have not as much small bills by me, having to pay away some that I mentioned to you when down, and here I happen to have none, but I will certainly repay you some short time hence; tho' I think as you do, that the expences are enormous if they are as you state to me, he will however make a bill out from the time they were committed which will enable you to detect any overcharge, and as for Cato I think you had best advertise him at Orangeburgh where it is more than probably he may be brought, and request some of them start on towards Edgefield. You may be assured I shall attend to Dr. Boyd respecting the land and have very little doubt, but you will have the refusal and as it regards myself, there shall be [e]very thing done which I possibly can for your accommodation.

I intend to be down in two or three days to see your Mama and hope in God to find her in much better health than when you wrote for I am very much concerned to hear she has been so sick since I left her. Do give my love to her and say how ardently I hope for her restoration, and all beside which an affectionate heart can dictate. Adieu my D[ea]r William your desire for the serv[an]ts return hastens my conclusion, accept the united love of all the family, & particularly little William, and believe me with much sincerity. Dear William Your very affectionate

James B. Richardson

NB. I sent you the Iron by Moses yesterday, he could not carry the bags but will send them by this boy. adieu The letter I wrote to Mr. Carson to go by Moses, which do give him if he has not gone

JAMES B. RICHARDSON TO WILLIAM SINKLER, ESQ[UIRE,
    AT SPRINGFIELD, SANTEE]
JAMES VILLE 22D JAN[UAR]Y 1808

Dear William,

I did not receive your esteemed favor of the 20 ins[tan]t untill yesterday evening, and the cause of delay the boy said was owing to the badness of the road. I am extremely obliged to you for your sending the letter up from Mr. Gourdin but it is not an offer of land enough to induce me to embrace it, as you will have an opp[ortunit]y of seeing when you peruse the letter. I sincerely thank you my William for your desire of entertaining me with good sport, but my time is so limited, that I shall be obliged (however reluctantly) to decline it. It is very unfortunate that today should be so bad, as I am desirous to set off my race nags, in order to give them one days rest before the performance, but I must do my best, and hope for the rest. They will be with you this night or tomorrow. Do tell Benjamin[24] to drive with the business, this poor fellow here is on the mend slowly & will be down soon as he can, that I am burning up all his logs have got his rails maul'd, his kitchen & seven negro houses compleated, & his dwelling house done on Monday next so that he will be sufficiently forward here, & I trust will have things so down there. I have deliver[ed you]r letter to your sister who will attend to your request and adjoins me with the Girls & your William, in best wishes toward you, and sincere affection.

Believe me Dear William

Your sincere friend & very affectionate

James B. Richardson

24 Benjamin Walker, a St. Stephen planter, appears to have managed some of James B. Richardson's property in Upper St. John's and apparently was in frequent contact with William Sinkler. However, Benjamin King was a friend of JBR's and had signed a contract with WS in March 1808 for construction of Eutaw Plantation. It is possible that there was a verbal agreement, as WS had talked about having Benjamin King build him a house since 1801.

William Sinkler Esq[ui]r[e]
Springfield
I have sent you my Dear William your sausages which hope will please you
also all the garden seeds I have. I am glad to hear you are well.

[On reverse]
169 pieces of sausages and a list of garden seeds
    Pease [*sic*]
    Cabbage
    Raddish
    Lettuce [fine] cabbage
    Lettuce
    Celery

[Addressed to]
William Sinkler Esq[ui]r[e]
Springfield

ANN C. RICHARDSON TO MR. WILLIAM SINKLER [AT SPRINGFIELD]
APRIL 8, 1808 JAMES VILLE

My Dear William,
    I have just received your letter by Saby I am very sorry to hear you are indis-
posed[.] I trust you will soon be restored to health, which blessing I hope may
long be yours. My beloved Richardson left me to day for Belvidere e'er this I hope
he has arrived safe. My little flock thank God are well and myself in tolerable
health, but my Brother my spirits are extremely low. Oh, my Dear William the
thought of an event[25] that may take place the last of this month wrings my very
Soul and fills my Bosom with pangs almost insupportable, oh poor me and my
little helpless family what will become of us. Join with me in prayer my William
to the throne of mercy, to avert such an event and spare to us our protector and
our all. Pardon me for the subject but it is all that occupies my mind and it is an
invitation to a disturb'd mind to unfold it to a friend, so I trust you will excuse
me. William received your help and said thank you he says you must come see
him[.] Adieu my Brother may you be happy prays your affectionate Sister.
    Ann C. Richardson

25 This may refer to the property dispute caused by the lawsuit over James Sinkler's will,
which took a long time to settle.

[Note on reverse]

Do tell my Richardson, I would have wrote him but Saby arrived so late, that defer writing till he sent up my love to him in the most affectionate manner. Do not forget to tell him my William

ACR

[In left margin]

I received the Jar safe and thank you for the eggs—

[Addressed to]
Mr. William Sinkler
Spring Field
by Servant Saby

JAMES B. RICHARDSON TO WILLIAM SINKLER, ESQ[UIRE, AT SPRING FIELD]
JAMES VILLE 7TH MAY 1808

Dear William,

I duly received your very affectionate letter of the 5 ins[tan]t and was happy to hear of the safe arrival of yourself & the Colonel[26] at your habitation, and more particularly that you found my dear friend (your Mama) in better health than you left her. I sincerely hope she may once more experience the perfect enjoyment of that invaluable blessing of which she has been so very long deprived. I thank you sincerely for your kind inquiries after the health of myself and family, we are thank God as well as when you left us in general, and myself in particular. Some better of my cold. Your representation of the Crop I am sorry is so very unfavorable. I trust however, that you may not be as bad off as you have stated. Tho' this very unseasonable weather is indeed much against the recovery of any tender vegetation, after undergoing the effects of a Frost.

I was much in the expectation of being with you my Dear William, on Sunday next, but I shall be prevented from that pleasure, for at least a few days longer, in consequence of the renewal of this old disputed affair,[27] of which I knew nothing untill yesterday about 11 o'clock, how it may yet be brought to issue I know not. When here, you very kindly said it was your wish to return in the event of such a thing, but my young friend, spare yourself any uneasy emotion at a hazard of this kind, and trust in the goodness mercy of divine providence who orders and directs all things for the best, tho' at the moment it may be difficult to believe so;

26 Probably William Sinkler's brother, Charles (1780–1817), who was also involved in horse racing.
27 Probably the lawsuit over James Sinkler's will, but not certain.

Yet whatever arrangement my friend may make, I shall feel it my duty to comply implicitly with. Adieu my Dear William, accept the love & affection of my D[ea]r family adjoined with mine, and believe me with much Sincerity.

Your friend very truly,

James B. Richardson

[Addressed to]
William Sinkler Esq[ui]r[e]
Springfield

NB. I have delivered the mare to your boy for you to send to Col. Sinkler with my best wishes . . . .

JAMES B. RICHARDSON TO WILLIAM SINKLER, ESQ[UI]R[E, AT SPRINGFIELD]
ASYLUM JULY 28 1808

My Dear William,

I had the pleasure yesterday evening to receive your favor per your Serv[an]t which was materially heightened by the information of your good health; which blessing I wish you long in continuation. With respect to the health of all in the Asylum, I must refer you to mine of yesterday, only that your Mama having entirely lost her fever is recovering her health as rapid as can be expected, and I hope will 'ere long have it thoroughly restored.

I am very much indebted to you for your attention in this business[28] with Mr. Davis. I cannot conceive the objections he could adduce to giving a statement of the demand, and surely it was necessary in arranging the amount to be answered by each heir, to assertain the particular property assess'd, however he may yet have the same business to arrange with me, if my letter should arrive in possession previous to the presentments of my order, when I shall not fail [to] make such representations to him, as perhaps he may find some satisfaction from.

Your representation of my crop is extremely flattering. I hope my Dear William you would desire to elevate the expectations of a friend, that you should be furnished with an opportunity, of beholding another instance, among the very many in human life which Presents, of the important effect, of disappointment on the firmest mind. ___ Your request of my writing to Mr. Carson shall be immediately attended to, and I will request the Post master to speak to the rider & get him to bring up the brads. I was so impressed with your intention of sending to Town, that I committed to your care a letter for Mr. Carson, but should you not

28 This probably relates to the lawsuit regarding the intestate status of James Sinkler's will.

send down, I will likewise avail myself of the opportunity by Post. I send you by the bearer the rivets for the window hinges, but I have not any whitelead, if there was the least particle of it, I would certainly send it to you; I have sent you some glue which I believe will answer every purpose.[29] All the family unite in love and best wishes for you and accept I request you the assurance that I am very sincerely

Your friend

James B. Richardson

[Addressed to]
William Sinkler Esq[ui]r[e]
Springfield.

My Dear William,

I confess to you that I have been much disappointed in not finding you here on my return, more has it been important as I have much to say to you, and some not unimportant to you as respects your present and future advantage, you must therefore hasten to me, that I may unburthen my mind, and allay that little curiosity which I necessarily must have created in you from the foregoing intimation, you must not then disappoint me in the pleasure I promise myself to find in the relief, and such as the communication will afford you and my Dear William I earnestly request you not to fail in using your utmost endeavors to prevail on my beloved friend your good Mama, & sister, to accompany you, which in addition to my entreaties with her, if you can effect, will place me under singular obligation to you, which will in gratitude be indellibly impressed on my recollection. I have sent down a Servant with the horses & the Chair, and again beseach you to leave no means unapplied, that our entreaties with my friend may obtain; and in the unfortunate event of her absolute refusal you must endeavor to bring Miss Anna, and come to me, that we may mutually bewail the misfortune I shall sustain in my friends not coming.

I am indeed sorry to find that you have been kept out of the use of your Cotton Gin so long, from the irregularity first of the workman, and then fr[om] unavoidable circumstances. I hope however she may [w]ork to your approbation, and by February when the commercial world will become active, will have your crop ready to embrace the advantages then presenting. Adieu my William, my Horses are on the turf draped for sweating to which I must attend, & Sawney

29 William Sinkler was building Eutaw Plantation.

in such good order that I wish you could see him, holding in readiness for Manchester,[30] where I enjoin you to be & see him retreive his long lost fame. I hope you continue in good health. I wish you the blessing very long, & am sorry to observe that this morn[in]g I feel indisposed, all the rest thank God very well & your William says come & see him on Saturday next. Adieu again and accept the assurance of love and esteem from my Dear William

    Your friend very truly

    James B. Richardson

[Addressed to]
William Sinkler Esquire
Springfield
Santee

[SCL: Richard Irvine Manning and Elizabeth Peyre Richardson
    Manning Papers]
Margaret Cantey Sinkler to Elizabeth (Betsey) Richardson
[Belvidere] 24 of October, 1809

I am pleased my D[r]. Betsey to hear that the Little invalids of your house are on the recovery. I hope they may continue so—& the rest of you a continuation of the good health you now enjoy.

    I am at present all alone, Anna has accompanied her Brother to Pineville—& I have been here since Sunday without a white Soul on the plantation but myself—not even the overseer at home—do you not think it requires some fortitude to live so lonely a life. There is no telling how much I have miss'd my Anna—only to know she is with me, is a satisfaction tho' I do not see her all the day by this opportunity I send the children some Pomegranates meaning the best for yourself adieu my Dear

I believe ever tenderly your

    friend MS _ _

    My love to all with you

[This was attached, but appears to be a separate letter]
It is with pleasure I received my Dear Betseys [*sic*] affectionate Letter with the home spun sent. I return your Mama many thanks for the favors; I am glad to hear you have all enjoyed health it [is] more than I can say. I have been very sick with the fever & ague, for several days past—& just began to take medicine— which I hope will assist me. My good girl you must excuse me just as I sat to

---

30 Racetrack nearby, probably on JBR's property.

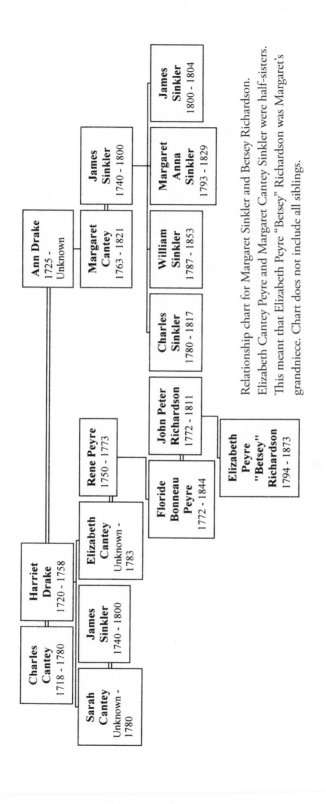

Relationship chart for Margaret Sinkler and Betsey Richardson. Elizabeth Cantey Peyre and Margaret Cantey Sinkler were half-sisters. This meant that Elizabeth Peyre "Betsey" Richardson was Margaret's grandniece. Chart does not include all siblings.

Charles Cantey
1718 - 1780

Harriet Drake
1720 - 1758

Ann Drake
1725 - Unknown

Sarah Cantey
Unknown - 1780

James Sinkler
1740 - 1800

Elizabeth Cantey
Unknown - 1783

Rene Peyre
1750 - 1773

Margaret Cantey
1763 - 1821

James Sinkler
1740 - 1800

Floride Bonneau Peyre
1772 - 1844

John Peter Richardson
1772 - 1811

Charles Sinkler
1780 - 1817

William Sinkler
1787 - 1853

Margaret Anna Sinkler
1793 - 1829

James Sinkler
1800 - 1804

Elizabeth Peyre "Betsey" Richardson
1794 - 1873

write, a Carriage has arrived with 3 ladys [*sic*] from Pineville adieu then my Dear
Betsey & believe me always thy sincere friend M Sinkler—

$\sim$

JAMES B. RICHARDSON TO WILLIAM SINKLER, ESQ[UIRE, IN CHARLESTON]
   JAMES VILLE, JULY 8, 1810

My Dear William,

I had the pleasure to receive your friendly and affectionate letter of the 21
ult[imo] previous to my leaving Belvidere and fully intended to reply to it long
'ere this, but a variety of causes have interposed, and the most important has
been my various engagements in some pursuit or other, which always brought
with it a pressure wh[ich] imperiously demanded my immediate attention. It
may reasonably be supposed that they could not so wholly have occupied my time
as to preclude me from writing a line to a friend I revere, and think of as often
as I do of you; but it prevented I should do so to my satisfaction, and I have in
every respect, no great objection to present my friend with what I am displeased
with myself such cogent reasons operating in my behalf your liberated mind will
doubtless accept my excuse and pardon the delay of my answer. I flatter myself
that you and your Eliza will continue to enjoy your health through this unpropitious season of the year, which has caused us to divide and seek a refuge for the
preservation of our healths with the blessings of Divine providence, which I hope
will continue with us, and afford us a happy meeting again at its conclusion. This
blessing we share abundantly in our Asylum and live in the hope that throughout
the summer it may be our happy situation to enjoy it. You know not how much
your society is miss'd among us. The recurrence to very many events of the last
year add to the number of times you are brought to my recollection, and while
I yield the treasure, I am alone to derive pleasure from wishing you ten thousand times happier than this place with all its inhabitants could possibly render
you. I thank you kindly for your good wishes of my success of the prize in the
Lottery,[31] the fate of mine are known to you as respects the prizes I had in view,
how far they may still be successfull will be yet to determine, it would have been
unreasonable in me to have expected your prosperous wishes, where your interest
was in question, but I fully calculate upon the second place in your wishes, as
you might feel me [en]titled to it from affection, and as you observe, my known
generosity, from whence some good purposes would emanate.

   With respect to your offer of the Filly Corinna, I feel sensible you intend it
as a favor, and I should with pleasure embrace the offer upon any reasonable
terms, but your attaching to the contract this other Filly, renders the conditions

31 Although the Charleston race records do not specifically list a lottery in the 1811
schedule, it is quite likely that this refers to horse racing.

objectionable, as it is against numbers in horses, that I am so warmly opposed in bargaining, if you will make any proposition as respects the first in the way of a mixed trade, such as life for life and the difference, I think it may then be made to answer: altho' I assure my William, one of the principle objections to my gating[32] this Filly would be that of destroying your interest on the Turf, which perhaps you might never again renew with so genuine a Stock.

The distance which divides us must not prove a cause to prevent me my Dear William the pleasure of hearing from you it is to be recollected that the Post fly's to & from us twice a week and I hope you will indulge me with your communication whenever you possibly can make it convenient. I promise you in future a better and more ready return than you have derived from your last, and short of the enjoyment of our friends society; that of their communication is most desirable.

My Dear Mrs. Richardson and family unite in affection to yourself and your Eliza, and little William in particular, offers you the assurance of a constant remembrance during your absence and a tender of his love. God bless you my Dear William with health and happiness, and grant us a happy meeting are the humble orisons to divine providence of your friend very truly

James B. Richardson
William Sinkler Esquire
Charleston

NB. I shall send my Boat down next week and by her our corn and fodder, which I have been uneasy I did not send before, but I assure you our people [words missing]portant in such an unpropitious year to [words missing]ices any earlier. The freight of the Cotton you mentioned, you can put at the rate you mention, if you think the former too high, but it has latterly been customary and formerly was much more.

JAMES B. RICHARDSON TO WILLIAM SINKLER, ESQUIRE[,] IN CHARLESTON ASYLUM. AUGUST 11, 1810

My Dear William,

I had the pleasure of receiving on the 9 ins[tan]t your very friendly and affectionate letter of the 30 ult[imo] in which I found a twofold gratification of the first, and very many of a secondary consideration. Your delay in writing me, has been fully and amply compensated by the pleasing formation that your indisposition was not the cause of it, and from the flattering and affectionate tenor throughout. The first, believe me sincerely to you and yours, to wish a series of

---

32 Gating likely refers to racing the young horse. It has been suggested that starting a horse too young to perform well could be damaging to her reputation.

time in continuation, as the best gift of heaven, for health alone enable us to participate (with a due appreciation) of all those other blessings which await man, through life: and the second, I am fondly made to believe emanate from too pure a source to issue, but to delude and beguile the unsuspicious heart, which confidence in your sincerity has always been unbounded, and unshaken, and never can be pursuaded to any variation, but from the most indubitable and incontrovertible testimony. Yet in the excess of our affection and from the high ideas we entertain of our best friends, how oft are we to overvalue their worth, or but dimly see their imperfections, through the thick veil which friendship carry over the object of our regard and too often leads us to believe with the utmost sincerity that they really are what our fondest wishes would make them. This to be sure, has some inconveniences in society awaiting it, because it induces us to desire to impose upon it at sometimes a character undeserving its attention, and not worthy of what our regard and friendship would make us believe: but indeed in the chain of society, and the interchange of good offices between man and his fellow man, it has very many good consequences attendant thereon among which is the establishment of confidence in whatever is said or done, a strong propensity to every beneficent act to the relief of distress, with a steadfast faith in the promises of remuneration, and above all, the best ingredient to root out jealousy, suspicion, and envy. Those huge and corroding masters to the peace, harmony & prosperity of society for without that faith and confidence subsisting among us, what a deplorable situation would be that of man's, the world would not be worth inhabiting[;] hence the rule of society justly proscribes the man, who possesses not those essential qualifications to nurture and cherish its existance. May not then my Dear William possessing the most affectionate heart, and the fallibility attendant on human nature, have too supercilliously spoken of his friend, and believes more highly of him than he can possibly deserve? I fear it is too much the case, tho' I do not question your sincerity, when you express your belief, and am confidently impressed with the idea, that if your good wishes could prevail, you would have me the excellent orator you have so happily described. Then I should embrace with avidity the tender of every distinguished appointment in the giving of my country, and boast of being the Richardson of Carolina.

Our political horizon continues still to be overcast with lowering appearances, as respects our commercial interests and the leading powers of Europe seem equally disposed to violate the right of nations, and intercept the user of the Ocean that common highway which God has designated for the enterprizing mind of man. These outrages against our natural rights, and the purloining of our Citizens treasures, demands a firm & decisive conduct in our government; but nothing [is] to compare with the insult to our flag, because our Citizens when they embarked in the commercial world, they were aware of the perils they must necessarily encounter, and of the allurements they were about to discover, to avaricious and unprincipled powers wherin laws were perverted at all times to meet their advantage and satiate their mercenary designs. No delusion from credulity has been the means of marking out the Conduct which America has persued for no Citizen whose mind is sufficiently capacitated to comprehend the relative situation of the beligerents, as respects us, but must be sensible that their interest and no regard for those rights of neutrals guaranteed by the laws of nations, is the main spring of all their actions. But under every circumstance which can possibly present on this momentous point I would ask, what could America have done more than she has except an open declaration of war, and pray what would that have avail'd were the means ours to coerce than British or French on the high seas to respect our rights, as a sovereign & independent nation? No! And I think you will not hesitate to subscribe your assent to the declaration: and those means which were in the power of our government, such as the Embargo & non intercourse were used, but proved ineffectual from the alienation of our eastern Citizens to the support of our government, view the correspondence of Erskine to Canning[33] and observe his demarcation of the different interests in the union. Upon this subject however, you must excuse me from saying more; it is one I am sure you & myself do not differ essentially; I will therefore only observe, that of all beings whose situation is pitiable, & with whom I commiserate, are our present members of Congress, if they have feelings of sensibility they must be harrowed and their Bosoms lacerated with wounds of reproach, for what I consciencously believe, they had no window to avoid. Can public favor be worthy an endeavor to maintain, when it is manifested so capriciously, that those who are all with them today are nothing tomorrow? You as well as myself can remember when several of those very members, were boosted in whole columns in the Gazette, of what they merited from their literature, & some, the atcheivements [*sic*] of their ancestry, & so raised to the very summit of the emminence when now behold them prostrate at the very base & none to support them, no one to give a solitary word of comfort in their decline of popularity. My heart sickens at the recollection, and a thousand imaginary scenes play before my mind, sufficiently great to frighten me from the stage, 'ere their fate becomes mine.

Since I have had the pleasure of addressing you, I have experienced great inquietude for the safety of my Dear Dorothy, who has been seriously[,] seriously-ill, as well, from the first attack, as from something of a relapse. Alas the anxieties that came on such an occasion possess the paternal bosom were familiar to mine

33 David Erskine was the British minister to the United States, who, opposing war, attempted to work out deals affecting trade with President Madison. George Canning, the British foreign secretary, replaced him with a less cooperative minster. James B. Richardson and William Sinkler had serious interests in the outcome because their livelihoods depended on the crops they exported.

and between hope and fear preponderated the trust in the all wise, and mercifull creator, whose mercies has preserved her yet as a blessing to us; fairly now I hope in the way to restoration after a confinement of five weeks, to her bed & chamber. You are now my friend approaching to that particular state, when a parents care will become yours;[34] may your portion of the bitter cup of inquietude be drained to the dregs, 'ere you taste thereof, and may you have peace & happiness to encircle your few, and be bless'd with a chosen friend at all times, are the wishes of my heart. Your prudence I know dictates to you the choice of but few, let them be made so from their worth, and be carefull to preserve them, great confidence is not always to be found in a plurality, and is most difficult in their preservation. It is very pleasant to me to hear that altho' within the vicinage of a gay City surrounded by the best blessings the heart can desire, that this humble, rural little spot, is not wholy erased from your recollection; that its inhabitants should be so, would be unnatural; but that those pleasures in which you used to participate, should not be obscured by brighter objects, is a just manifestation of your taste for the rural enjoyments which this place is calculated to afford, & amidst the society of those most dear to me, I share very many comforts of life, and envy not that being on Earth. You will doubtless say, then I must be happy, so I am my William, as much as falls to the lot of mortals, or as much as my nature & disposition will admit, but even this happiness is heightened by hearing from you that you are likewise so; tho' I cannot divest myself of that selfishness, of wishing you sometimes deprived of them, for the benefit of your society here.

I am truly gratefull for the flattering terms in which you have expressed your sentiments of this proferred bargain in your valuable animals, the circumstances are so pleasing, that I can scarcely withstand it; your discerning faculty and ready perception has discovered my frail part, and you have almost brought it to the purposes you intended, but on this subject I shall say more to you in my next.

I would that I had it in my power to entertain you with any thing new from this place of retirement, the amusements you have often witness'd, they continue the same with but little variation, tho' they have great endearments for me. Politics are scarcely mentioned, & only within a few days, has a word been said on the subject of ensuring elections; which peril you know I must encounter too, & trust to fate and a fickle public for my success, which to confess the truth, I am very regardless about. Shall I not ask of you the favor you did of me, that for the eye of friendship alone were these lines dictated, and to none other commit its perusal, your example if good as it respects you, is worthy of my inclination, and you will I trust observe it.

34 WS was about to become a father.

It is now late at night (my usual time of writing) and Somnus[35] has nearly overpowered me with his opiates, therefore I must yield to its influence, and hasten to assure you of the tender of the united love to yourself and your Eliza, and of the affection and good wishes for your health & happiness, by every individual (your little William[36] in particular who says he never will forget you) and by [word missing] by him who subscribes himself [word missing]eigned sincerity, my Dear William

    Your friend very truly

    James B. Richardson

    NB. My boat leaves this on Thursday next, she [has been] detained thus long, by a combination of [word missing.] She shall certainly take down every thing [di]rect, and the corn I shall attend to myself.

[Addressed to]
William Sinkler Esquire
Charleston
South Carolina

  〜

JAMES B. RICHARDSON TO WILLIAM SINKLER, ESQ[UIRE, IN CHARLESTON]
JAMES VILLE, NOVEMBER 23[R]D, 1810

My Dear William,

    I had just returned from the sports of the Turf in Pine Ville[37] when I had the pleasure of being put in possession of your esteemed favor of the 9th ins[tan]t with many others which demand my reply, and at this time, upon the eve of my departure for Columbia the pressure of business, some Domestic, and much for mankind occupy my whole time, but the inclination to address you, supercedes every other consideration, and has allways preeminent claims upon my time. It is indispensible that I should say something in extenuation for my apparent neglect of your valued favor of the 3rd of September last, previous to making a reply to the latter, which I trust your liberal mind will deem to be an adequate excuse; and should a hesitation lurk in your bosom afterwards [not] extirpated, deeming the excuse not sufficiently cogent, let our former friendships, and reciprocal kind offices, plead in my behalf, and the benevolence of your heart, will surely produce an acquiescence.

---

35 Roman god of sleep.

36 This is actually James B. Richardson's son, who most likely was named for William Sinkler and may have been his godson.

37 Pineville is in western Berkeley County and had an active racing history. As a result, many people associated the name "Pineville" with horse racing.

When that letter arrived, it was at a time when the minds of the people were greatly convulsed with the approaching biennial election, in which was deeply concerned the interest of your friend, whose every effort was call'd forth to repel the wicked, envious, and malicious, machinations of his enemies, endeavoring to sap the foundation of that public eminence which the faithful service of years, had enabled me to attain. Thanks be to that kind providence, who controuls [*sic*] all things, and never fails to regard truth and justice, their evil designs did not obtain, their wickedness recoil'd twofold upon their own heads, and "I fought and conquered," the victory[38] was sovereign and truly gratefull. The exultation then (which I cannot but in a case of this kind think was laudable, for with the noble mind, conquest alone is sufficient exultation,) was great, and among our friends become general, and for the moment, made me forget my attention to your letter; in addition to this, I had heard of your arrival at Belvidere, and did then indeed expect to have had the pleasure of your company, and answered your letter in person; surely I said, my William will dedicate a few hours to me, when we might participate in the "feast of reason and the flow of Soul" and occasionally disseminate the attic salt,[39] that seasoning to society. But alas! I was soon informed that you were on the wings of the wind, riding with unparaled [*sic*] velocity to your Treasure, forgeting, (but not forgot by) all you left behind you. This certainly did create some compunction in my feelings, that I had not written you before, and given you cause thus to slight me; but yet I could not avoid thinking hard of your being so near me, after an absence of long, and then omiting to see me. It did not however cause me to value your letter less, or be less determined to answer it, but one occurrence or another allways interposed to preclude me that indulgence, which I even derive pleasure from.

Yours of the 9th demand my warm acknowledgements, because it convinces me you do not act ceremonious in writing, which your time now admits you to do, with far more convenience than I can, and because your goodness makes so many allowances for my delay, which suffer me to assure you in no instance ever proceeds from intentional neglect. You cannot for one moment, indulge a suspicion that secrets itself in your affectionate bosom, that at this period of your life without meriting it, that I should cast you away from my attention and regard, when in your infancy, and your probationary state for the Theatre of life, left destitute of a better dictator, my mind guided and my hand pointed you to the way to goodness & to greatness, and fostered your daily improvements with my aid and tender care: now is it probable, that when that scion has become a Tree, its foliage expanded and the fruit rife, sweet and delicious, that I should reject the comforts it afford, no! nor will I, but under the severest pangs, cumpulsion can

38 James B. Richardson had just been reelected to the state senate.
39 Another term for "wit," referring to verbal salt, produced in one's attic, or head.

enforce and now, what consideration would be too great, for about three hours conversation with you before I leave this for Columbia, where I embark in the duties of my public station, under the kind influence of hope, that the services of my good God will await me, and prosper my endeavors to clothe us with honor and virtue, and to benefit mankind, which has been the summit of my wishes and exertions, through a long career of public service.

With respect to business upon which you have claimed my attention, and the purchase of the land in particular, I have to observe, that I am perfectly disposed to let you have it with the exception of a way through it, for five hundred pounds with any reasonable indulgence you may require, and if you choose, take your filly at $250 in part. I do not believe you will hesitate at the proposition, and assure you I am induced to it, from motives of obliging you, as you say it was what I had promised you. I have been engaged in the resurvey of the Swamp Lands, which I have indeed found difficult and fatiguing, but have accomplished all to the division lines, which as soon as the lots are drawn, can be completed at any time at which I hope on my return from Columbia you will be able to attend to it, or depute some person to act for you.

The sports of the Turf are reviving in this place and at St. Stephens. The subscribers increased rapidly at the races, and I have no doubt on my mind, but that the violent opposers will all become members before the next races. The liberal hospitality of the place was greatly manifest'd in the President of the Club, who suffered nothing to be wanting that he could bestow, and indeed <u>others</u> of the inhabitants did likewise, but their efforts were in <u>miniature</u>. John[40] & myself did all in our power to compensate their goodness, by giving them sport, in which I trust we acted well our parts; if appearances were good grounds for conjecture, but I am forbid by the <u>present</u> <u>custom</u> of the <u>times</u> to <u>praise</u> <u>myself</u>, let me act never so <u>praiseworthy</u>. You I wanted much there, in the field you would have been conspicuous, but in the floor resplendently transcendent, and I fail'd not to represent it to <u>those</u>, whose appearance I thought would have made the <u>information</u> <u>desirable</u> to you.

You desire some information respecting my race Nags. I assure there are some excellent, but my favorite, Precursor is a <u>villain</u>, and I fear will come to very little consequence. Doo [*sic*], my William visit us this Xmas & with your Eliza and friends, and see this great Sweepstakes run, your presence there will greatly heighten my pleasure, and I hope you will comply. All your good wishes toward me through life, I sincerely reciprocate with you: and request you to tender my love to your Eliza adjoined by all the family (and my little William in particular) and for yourself, to accept the unfeigned assurances of affection from My Dear William[JBR's son].

40 John was most likely JBR's brother, John Peter Richardson, who also had racehorses.

Your friend very truly
James B. Richardson

[Addressed to]
William Sinkler Esq[uire]
Charleston

NB. Do get me a good saddle of Mr. Grant, the most fasionable with low cantle, and Major Phelon will give you the money to pay for it, you know I dislike a saddle high in front; and your choice I am sure will please me.

[SCL: Richard Irvine Manning and Elizabeth Peyre Richardson
    Manning Papers]
Margaret Cantey Sinkler to Elizabeth (Betsey) Richardson
Belvidere February 21, 1811

It was with great Pleasure my Elizabeth that I received your little note by Bob—which convinced me you thought of me & afforded me gratification to hear you were all in tolerable health—I shall, my good girl with [peculiar] satisfaction hold communication with you at all times, & hope my Betsey will always view me in the light of a tender friend & affectionate relation. there is nothing in my Power wherein, I can serve you, your Mama, & Family—But I will do with willingness—Affliction is the time to try our friends & I have felt, & known too much of it myself, to neglect those I love, in so trying a situation, you have all become doubly endeared to to [*sic*] me from your recent misfortune, & I hope you will never hesitate to call upon me at all times as a friend that never will desert you. I always loved your Lamented & respected Father,[41] whom I knew from a boy—& always lived with him on the most friendly terms—can I do otherwise my Dear than love these he has left behind—which he doated on with truly parental fondness—oh what a loss have you not all sustained, in the press & support of your tender years—you have now but one parent left—Pay the strictest attention to her commands—Set an example to your Sisters & Brothers, worthy of imitation from your exemplary conduct—endeavour from your Duty to prolong her valuable life to you all. Console her under this weight of affliction, & let the love of Duty & her Children in Some measure alleviate her sorrows for loss of the Partner of her heart—Respect age where ever you meet it. That God may bless you with length of days—& you may expect then, that reverence which you have showed to others—in the helpless years of infirmity & misery your good sense will teach you never to forget your Duty to your God—bless him for his daily

41 John Peter Richardson died on January 30, 1811.

mercies & ask his protection in your Fatherless situation & he will be all, you wish, to you[.] Read my Child instructive Books & improve your mind—among them your Bible it is worthy your attention—& will give you that proper knowledge of our Maker. That we cannot be made too early acquainted with. Think me not Presuming my Dear Betsey that I thus advise you—your Mama is fully capable of doing so but I feel so lively an interest in your behalf that I write you, so I do my Anna & I am convinced one of your amiable disposition can never take offence, at what was never intended to give you pain.

I send your bag which I have at last finished. I hope you will like it—I have not put the tassels to it expecting you could do it much better yourself & more fancifully—within it you will find a peice [*sic*] of cambrick for a cap for Eliza's little boy. I cannot prevail with Anna[42] to finish the one she has or I would not impose the task on you my Dear. It was sent her, by my request and I feel not a little hurt that I should be the means of work being sent her, which she will not be persuaded to complete. Pardon me my good girl this freedom, I know no other that I would make the like request of—endeavour to complete it as soon as possible, & I will do any other kind of work for you—in turn while you are thus employed for me & at other times when you require it.

Your good Mama offer'd to have some Weaving done for Charles & myself. Tell her I accept it with gratitude & send her a peice <u>for each of us</u>—one peice coarse for myself & a peice of finer for Charles. Such as will run 5 yards to the pound—he wants it for Common sheets—beg her to have it wove wide or it will not answer for that purpose. Kiss your Mama for me & tell her exert herself to support what it has pleased God to take from her. She has yet many blessings. Live for their sakes & endeavour to bring up her children in the fear & love of God. Adieu my Dear Elizabeth—write me often & believe me with tender affection your friend most Sincerely.

M. Sinkler

The top piece of homespun in the bag is for C. Sinkler—

[SCL: Richard Irvine Manning and Elizabeth Peyre Richardson
    Manning Papers]
Margaret Cantey Sinkler to Elizabeth (Betsey) Richardson
    [Belvidere?] 14 of April, 1811

A tedious & long indisposition my Dear Betsey has prevented my replying to your Letters by your Sister, & thanking you a thousand times for your ready compliance with my request in Working the Cap for my little James.[43] It has been

---

42 Betsey was a year older than Margaret's daughter, Anna.
43 William Sinkler's son (Margaret's first grandson) was born on December 29, 1810.

much admired, & the work acknowledged to be extraordinary[l]y fine. I told Eliza it was done by you, at my particular request—therefore She must accept the favour Thru me to conceal your Name my Dear Betsey would not be doing justice to your hansome [*sic*] work. I therefore took care, to tell them it was done to oblige me—I hope your Mama & all of you are quite well, I wish my good girl I could say I was well too—but I yet have very warm [fe]vers every Night. I have been taking the bark this day, for the frost—my stomach has got so weak that I could not admit it afore—I long to see you all, & was it not for my bad health—I would endeavour to ride that far & see you but God knows when I shall be able—Stand not my Dear upon idle ceremony with me—I shall be always glad to hear from you—therefore write whenever you have an opportunity—you should remember I have a thousand things to do that you have not—adieu my Dear Betsey give my love to your Mama, Sisters & Brothers—& excuse this short letter—as my health does not permit me to fatigue—& accept of me warmest affection of
> your truly tender & Sincere friend
> M Sinkler

I enclose a bag & thread case which please give to your Sister Anna for me & tell her she must learn to Work—

JAMES B. RICHARDSON TO WILLIAM SINKLER, ESQ[UIRE, IN SPRINGFIELD] JAMES VILLE, 27 AP[RI]L 1811

My Dear William,

I received your favor of yesterday by your Servant who had in charge Belvidere, to whom I gave three amorous embraces of Virginius, her ready assent heightened the gratification, and caused the business to be [well] done & I trust will be effectual; as an adept myself in the works of procreation, I feel capable in pronouncing her to be faithfully treated; and in no other matter could you be more certain in trusting to my judgement and skill, than the present.[44]

I shall be sure to have the necessary papers you requested carefully drawn out ready for execution when I come down, and which I trust will be the early part of next week, when I shall hope for the pleasure of seeing yourself & family in that good health, I am happy to find you at present participate. I communicated to your Sister the message relative to the visit you mentioned, when she assures it would give her much pleasure to see you at your habitation, but can look forward to no period should [words missing] promises herself the pleasure with any certainty does indeed appear of late as tho' all that familiar intercourse with our

---

44 Horse breeding details.

dearest and most valued friends formerly so frequently exercised, is by some occurrence or other obstructed; and that, that pleasure and happiness once enjoyed in reality can now be only experienced by an indulgence of sweet reflection upon the happy times that are past. The indulgence to me, (when I can steal a moment from the busy cares of the world) is a source of melancholy pleasure, which I never fail to enjoy with that peculiar delight it is calculated to afford; in the rotatory revolution of which, your juvenile days my William often occurs, when the important charge of expending your youthfull mind, was left to my direction and care; I rejoice to view the fullness and perfection of it, and have only to regret I am not oftener with you, to partake the benefits thereof.

With respect to the fellow of the Estates, I cannot at this time give you a positive answer, as I know not what engagements Charles[45] may have for him. I rather think some of consequence, as I told him that I wanted myself to hire the fellow, whenever he was unoccupied on the plantation, not hearing from him on the subject, I have concluded that he was still wanted there.

I am sorry to say that my Dear Mrs. Richardson has had some very warm fevers since you went down & still continues every other day; my little John,[46] too has been quite sick, & myself far from being well. Tender my respects, adjoined by the family (& by William in particular love to you) to Eliza & the family, and accept yourself the assurance of affection from my Dear William

Yours very truly

James B. Richardson

[On margin]
NB Why did you not let your Mama know of the opportunity that I might have been favored with a letter.

[Addressed to]
William Sinkler Esq.
Springfield

[SCL: Richard Irvine Manning and Elizabeth Peyre Richardson
Manning Papers]
Margaret Cantey Sinkler to Elizabeth (Betsey) Richardson
[Belvidere?] 20 of August, 1811

Your [two] affectionate letters, my Dear Betsey have been Duly received and I hope you will not think I neglected you by not immediately replying to them,

---

45 Charles Richardson, younger brother of James.
46 John, born in 1809, died in 1812.

each time they came to hand I was very busily employed—and trust your good nature will readily pardon my Silence. I set too great a value by them ever to over look them & will always write whenever I can—

I am highly flattered my Dear at your expressing a value for my friendship & [a]dvise. The latter, you never can want when you have Such a Mother & other very valuable friends who loves [*sic*] you, too much, ever to neglect bestowing in when ever it is necessary—tho, one so prudent as you are, can Seldom have occasion to call forth the admonition of your friends, yet they are none of us so perfect but are better for the Counsels of a friend whose years & experience qualifys them to guide the thoughtless and giddy young creatures through the intricate paths of life. My friendship my Dear Betsey you may always calculate upon. I say always for I hardly think you will ever forfeit it, & I shall be as ready to serve you as any friend you have. My Love to your Mama, Sisters, & Brothers & believe me with the tenderest affection my Dear. Your Anna's love to you all— Sincere & warm friend ever M Sinkler

I send by the boy a little Piggin for Thomas & Anna[.] Beg your Mama to send me some Mustard Seed if any to Spare—

∽

JAMES B. RICHARDSON TO WILLIAM SINKLER, ESQ[UIRE]
ASYLUM, SEPTEMBER 28. 1811

What shall I urge in atonement to my Dear William for my long apparent neglect in not writing him a single line throughout the dreary season of Summer were I to resort to the busy cares of life, and say that its multiplication upon my already burthened mind, was my adequate excuse, you would be entitled justly to reply, it is what every person in life could with propriety make, for all have their calls & their cares, & ought not therefore to be admitted in extenuation with propriety too, may you more forcibly urge the inadequacy of such an excuse, when you have witnessed yourself, my repeated communication amidst the throng of care incident to my Domestic and Executive life. It will however readily present to your observation, that in doing so, it was answering the imperious call of necessity, it was discharging an important duty which then devolved upon me, to point to you the obligations which you were under to your friends & your country (& those in particular who had in immediate charge your education) to use that time to the best possible advantage, to become an honor to your parentage, an ornament to society, and a valuable instrument in the hands of your Creator. Now that those objects are answered, which my fond wishes lead me to hope I was in some measure instrumental to, that imperious necessity ceases with it to exist, and my like cares and attention are summoned to another source, awfull indeed was the event which has drawn again upon me, the tender and important offices of a Second parent,[47] not less important my Dear William than your own was. Yet with weekness [*sic*] & humble submission I bend to the Almighty hand that imposes the weight, and humbly supplicates his aid and support in the discharge of so arduous an obligation: which tho' painfull and oppressive I endeavor to bear without a murmur to the world, & but seldom lament to my most in[ti]mate friends, knowing it the dispensation of a divine providence.

This world my William appears to be calculate[d] to daily involve mankind in some new care or other of life, and indeed it does often times alleviate the burthen of affection, which all are more or less liable to, some indeed experience but little, compared with that of others; and many have a long career of bliss & pleasure without having the heart once wrung for the loss of a beloved child or a friend; but it does not follow that the bitter cup has been drain'd to the dregs, & nothing falls to their lot, when once the calamity commences, it too often happens that a long catalogue of ills succeed; it therefore becomes us well to commiserate with the afflicted, & dwell upon the thought of our own to hereafter follow, nor to complain of the accumulation of those cares in life, since they are calculate[d] to delude our minds from trouble, and discharging that duty for which the Creator designed us. I have indeed had much business upon me since I have had the happiness to see you, and may indeed with some propriety have offered it as an excuse for my not replying to your acceptable favor, but it was not to that alone it was ascribable, for truly I might have found time to have thus indulged my wish, & to have gratified you in another proof that I often thought of you; but it was that your Sister (who I aver is no bad scribe) continually corresponded with you, & that from her I would allways have the good tidings you afforded, & that doubtless I was of too much consequence with her, to be wholy omited in her letters to you, so that you would at least hear from me indirectly, & that your extreme goodness of heart would induce you to make a thousand apologies for my remissness, was indeed the cause that did not make me break down the barriers which business created, to indulge the pleasure of drawing from you some account of yourself. In a reversed situation, nothing would, nor could have compel'd me to silence; I should have so imposed my epistles, as in self-defence, would have precluded you from withholding a reply. Surely after this honest confession, there will not remain to be found in the bosom of my Dear William a single reproach that will not have lost its sting of asperity, or be softened into a reproof of the most delicate kind, for thus long having neglected to address him.

I rejoice to have heard that yourself, family & friends have all enjoyed good health this summer, & yourself & little boy in particular whose constitutions

---

47 This may refer to the January 30 death of James B. Richardson's younger brother, John Peter, of whom JBR would no doubt have been quite protective.

have not been assimilated to a City life. That blessing has been exuberantly participated in our Asylum, myself the only exception in my family, & I have been much afflicted occasionally for two months past, with a pain in my tooth, back of my head & side of my face, from some cold which I suppose I must imperceptibly have contracted, in the too zealous pursuit of a faithfull discharge of duty, and last night was in much anguish, & write you now in considerable pain, but as this was the dernier resort, tomorrow's post or none before I hope the pleasure to see you, either here or at Belvedere [*sic*], I was determined to embark in the good cause, & trust to favorable circumstances for a happy conclusion.

The tornado[48] which was so violent with you in the City, & which did such manifest & considerable injury to to [*sic*] so many individuals, was considerably experienced here, & did some injury to the crops of Cotton & Pease but good God how thankfull that we were without the vortex of its violence, which would have hurl'd in its devastation our little all in a moment, & left us destitute. I hope my Dear William to see you soon, & flatter myself that you will always fullfill your promise, that you will visit my mansion whenever you can. You must not loose the recollection that it was once your second home, nor forget that within its walls you had some good counseling, & pleasant conversations, & above all the first to <u>her</u>,[49] who is now to you above the price of rubies, & therefore ought to venerate & esteem the place & visit its inhabitants whenever you can; they have among them, if nothing costly, much happiness prevailing, and an invisible something, which bespeaks a pleasure and tranquillity emanating from a comfortable source.

Very many places bring you to my recollection very often, & many amusements often occur that we have had together, but alas! I view them as past never to return, and when I think of you, it is like one having flown his post, and is far, very far beyond my reach. Adieu my Dear William I must surely have worried your patience, tho' as I have began I confess I have not said half I wish, yet amidst the conflict of pain & desire, you must accept the will for the deed, & flatter yourself with the reception of one approximating more to my wishes for the next letter. Accept the Love of my D[ea]r Mrs. Richardson & a fine family of children (& two fine boys in particular) to yourself & your Eliza & fine Son, & believe me Your sincere friend & very affectionate James B. Richardson.

NB. I request that before you leave town that you will request Mr. Carson to let you have the papers that I desired him to forward by you. You know how dilatory he is with papers, therefore urge him often, & doo [*sic*] I beg you would not leave them, as they are papers of importance.

48 A hurricane of September 10 is said to have spawned tornadoes in the lowcountry.
49 This suggests that James or Ann Richardson might have introduced William Sinkler to Eliza Broün at their home.

James B. Richardson to William Sinkler, Esq[uire, at Santee]
Asylum, June 25, 1812

Dear William,

I was yesterday evening put in possession of your favor of the 22[n]d ins[tan]t and acknowledge with pleasure the gratefull obligations for your early & kind enquiries after the health of myself & family; and your good wishes for the enjoyment of so invaluable a blessing. Suffer me to assure you, be it ever so extensive, it is reciprocated towards you, and that I enjoy an honest & sincere satisfaction to learn you & yours are well. It cannot be questioned by your friends, who know you best, the sincerity of your kind expressions, & of your best wishes for their prosperity & happiness; both of <u>which</u> I am sensible your exertions would with alacrity be exercised to advance.

The times present an aspect rather unpleasant as to pecuniary considerations, but promise a fine field for such young men as you are to manifest your importance to your country, and establish an exalted standing in society, & an immortal place in the pages of history, and make you to America, what the armless Nelson was to Britain. War is indeed a calamity to any nation, even Rome whose confined limits excluded ten thousands emplo[y]ments for the mind of man, experienced its weighty effects; how much more to be deprecated by a country like this, which growing rapidly in wealth & prosperity, opens to the aspiring genius, a field so beautifully & profusely spread with alluring engagements, to the pursuits inclination may dictate. As it however respects myself, if it is to occur at all in my time, it cannot be at a more suitable time than the present, when I am able & willing to render my services, & through my little might in the national scale, to aid its favorable preponderance. Yet I wish, sincerely wish that all who are now clamoring for war; may not in the time of trial be found wanting.

I am sorry you sent the watch, as I have really no use for such a one, having one that I would not give for all the watches in Charleston; besides I only thought a conditional bargain had been made, "that if I approv'd of her when repaired that then I might take her." If it had been a possitive bargain, & I was under that impression, (as usual with me) nothing could induce to retraction. I shall however if on trial take the watch, beg you to believe that it is soley [*sic*] for your accommodation, for I have no want of such a one.

I regret that your time is so restricted as not to afford me the pleasure of seeing you in this homely habitation, where you have been, & now would be, most heartily a wellcome guest. But I am one of those who are allways happy to see my friends, and stifle compunction of feeling, where it is incompatible with their convenience to see me, and strive to be to them, as they are to me, in spite of every sacrifice of feeling. I know not when I may see you again. Suffer me in this interim to give you an assurance in addition to all those I have already given, that I am with sincerity of affection

Your friend very truly,

James B. Richardson

NB. William tells me to say to you that he loves you & will never forget you, which he fears on your part. All the family desire (with me) to be remembered to your Eliza & James. I send you herein the statement of our little transaction in d/c.

[Addressed to]
William Sinkler Esq.
Santee

[SCL: Richard Irvine Manning and Elizabeth Peyre Richardson
    Manning Papers]
Margaret Cantey Sinkler to Elizabeth (Betsey) Richardson
[Belvidere? April 25, 1813]

Your affectionate letter, my Dear Betsey I received Safe it afforded me pleasure to think you thought of me, & have renewed our correspondence again. I shall at all times Be happy to hear from you & will Chearfully [*sic*] answer your Letters when you favour me with them.

I have too great an opinion of your Sincerity to Believe you could profess a regard where you felt none. It is only the friendship of Such Character that I Covet deception I really despise, & wish to hold no entercourse [*sic*] with those who are not at all times the Same. A Sincere a [*sic*] friend is a jewel beyond Price, & a deceitful one we cannot too soon get rid of.

I am Sorry to hear my Emma [Betsey's younger sister], has been Sick again. I was in hopes her journey would have restored her to health. Your Mama had better take a ride to see John. The excursion would be pleasing & Beneficial to you all particularly Emma. I wish it were in my Power to accompany you—I Should like to take a travel very much, but it is impossible for me to Leave home.

On Thursday next, there is to be a Grand Ball, & Dinner given in Pineville—the Ladies are all in this Neighborhood invited—I do not Believe Anna Will go, as she has no one to go with her—her Brother Charles is obliged to Attend a Court Marshall, at Strawberry & William's family does not go. Mrs. Robert Deas they have just heard of her Death—Miss Broün Cannot go on that account you see my Dear Betsey. I have given you some little of the News in circulation here. Remember me to Emma & the Children. & believe me My Dear Betsey your [lo]ving affectionate & Sincere Friend

M Sinkler

April 25, 1813

∾

[SCL: Richard Irvine Manning and Elizabeth Peyre Richardson
   Manning Papers]
Margaret Cantey Sinkler to Elizabeth (Betsey) Richardson
[probably Belvidere, n.d. but probably before July 30, 1813]

My Dear Betsey—

I Received the Wool sent by your Unkles [*sic*] Waggen & ask [torn] your
Mantles as soon as Possible, as it affords me pleasure to do any thing for one
I think so highly of—Your Mama was so kind as to promise to have a peice of
Cloth Wove for your Cousin Charles, which I now send her. If it is Convenient
for her to do it. If not, do my Dear Betsey beg her to give it to any one that will
weave it faithfully. They [*sic*] are no doubt [a] good many Weavers about; that
will take it for her—have it wove <u>Wide</u> & fill'd <u>in thickly</u> it is for his house Servants & he wishes it wove well, I think it a good 4 yd thread, it is to be fill'd in
with Wool—which is in age & I will Send it a [*sic*] Monday to you. I hope you
are all well[.] Anna & myself enjoy a tolerable Share of the Sweet blessing[;] my
love attends you all & believe me ever your friend
   affectionately M Sinkler

12 pounds of Warp—48 hanks

[Addressed to]
Miss Elizabeth Richardson—

[Note 1]
by Servant with 48 hanks of yarn

[Note 2]
The bag which is for your Mama has her Name, Written on a peice of paper—

∾

[SCL: Richard Irvine Manning and Elizabeth Peyre Richardson
   Manning Papers]
Margaret Cantey Sinkler to Elizabeth (Betsey) Richardson
[Belvidere] July the 30, 1813

I received your favour My Dear Betsey & Should have earlier replied to it—But
have been very much engaged. I am happy at all times my good Girl to hear from
you & your Mama. I was indeed glad to hear you were all well. I trust this happiness you will continue to enjoy during the inclement Season of the year. Our
most Sickly month now approaches & is much to be dreaded—

Will you My Dear Betsey beg your Mama, to Let David make a Set of Harness[es] as Soon as Possible for course homespun for me. I have got a Woman to come & teach a boy for me—& I want to put up two Looms at once. Nancy has Promised to make a set—I have been long a trouble to my friends to do my Weaving. I hope I shall have it in my Power in some Way to return the favours I have received—adieu my Dear Betsey. Offer my Love to your Mama & the Girls & kiss the Little boys for me & believe me my Dear Betsey your Sincere & affectionate

Friend M Sinkler

[Addressed to]
Miss Elizabeth Richardson
by Hercules

[SCL: Richard Irvine Manning and Elizabeth Peyre Richardson
   Manning Papers]
Margaret Cantey Sinkler to Elizabeth (Betsey) Richardson
[Belvidere] August 25, 1813

This small peice of paper I have only left <u>one here</u> my Dear Betsey—But I will use it in for the purpose of enquiring after all your Healths, which I hope is as good as when I parted from you—We arrived here in good time the day I left you not without some Rain—which we have had both Tuesday & Wednesday a plenty of [.]

I hope my Dear Betsey your feeling heart—will induce yourself & Sisters often to visit, the house of Manning <u>your Cousin</u> has been Peculiarly unfortunate & everyone must Sympathize with her. You know my Dear Child we are all of us Subject to the Like misfortunes in our Families & know not how Loving God may Bend his rod over our Shoulders which we are obliged Submissively to Support. She is young & you have all been Companions & I have no doubt but your Companies would be more acceptable than any others. You are too amiable a girl to Let So favorable an opportunity escape to distinguish your friendship in the time of trouble—then it is that Friends become doubly valueable, & no heart but must be grateful for attention bestowed at that house of Bitter distress.

Will you tell Flora that I beg her for the Silk yarn She Spins to form the <u>Cord</u> of her Counterpanes & when David is at Leisure, I will thank her to Weave some for me—ask her if it would be convenient to take a boy for Charles Sinkler—he wants one instructed & thinks David fully equal to the task—

She will confer a favour if she will have a Block made for me, for the purpose of making harnesses. I could easily make my Carpenter do [it] if I knew how to Direct him. But I really cannot do it, or I waver to not trouble her. The boat is coming down & She can Send it in her—if She will be so obliging as to have it made—

Remember me affectionately to your Mama, Sisters, & Brothers—a kiss for Thomas. I hope you have heard from John & he is Better—adieu my Dear Betsey & believe me most tenderly thy Friend

M Sinkler

ANN C. RICHARDSON TO WILLIAM [SINKLER]
JAMES VILLE NOVEMBER 26, 1813

My Dear William,

I received your affectionate letter last night and thank you for your good wishes, it ever has been my opinion that we should always believe and be satisfied that whatever is, is right and I have ever endeavored as much as frail mortal could, to be content with my fate[50] and resigned to the will of my Creator. I acknowledge I did wish for a Son, more on account of my beloved Richardson than my own, we have but one poor little fellow who does not look healthy, and every Summer has a severe attack of the fever, that should we be so fortunate as to raise him his constitution I fear will be very weak. I can my Brother from experience say that daughters are great comforts; we are bless'd in ours for they are indeed good and dutiful Children. I do not believe they would do any thing to disoblige us and more attentive children no Parent could wish for. To you my William I have been very candid in expressing myself about my girls it is only to a friend and to you who know them as well as I do. My Matilda is still poorly but I trust will soon be restored to health, she has been extremely ill she had the fever 14 days that was never off. I am very glad to hear yourself and family are well[.] I hope you may long continue to enjoy that greatest of all earthly blessings health. I received the Ducks quite safe, beg Eliza to acc[e]pt my sincere thanks for them[.] she is indeed very good[.] I will take good care of them and hope I will be lucky with them. Dorothy and Margaret leave me to day for a fortnight. Sarah Hermione and the little ones beg to be remember'd to Eliza and yourself[.] William begs his love to you and thanks you for your particular remembrance of him. Give my love to Eliza and kiss your little boys for me[.]

Adieu my Dear William and believe me ever

Your fond and affectionate Sister

Ann C. Richardson

50 Genealogical records indicate Ann's having had a daughter, Julia Anna, on November 29, 1813, but the letter is clearly dated November 26.

~

[SCL: Richard Irvine Manning and Elizabeth Peyre Richardson
   Manning Papers]
Margaret Cantey Sinkler to Elizabeth (Betsey) Richardson
[Belvidere] February 22, 1814

I received the Netting my Dear Betsey & beg that you & Emma will accept my
Warmest Thanks for them—I Shall often view them & think of the Hands that
So ingeniously completed the Work—I hope your Mama, & all of you are quite
Well—give my love to Flora & thank her for the Pigs. I wish it was in my Power
to return her the many favours She bestows on me. She must accept the tribute
of greatful heart & a Willingness at all times to oblige her—

   I hope you got the red Rose trees Safe, Sent by Charles Richardson['s] servant
any other flowers I have you Shall be Welcome to—that you have not—adieu my
Dear Betsey Accept my love—to yourself & Sisters & believe me in Truth your
Sincerely affectionate M Sinkler—

   Kiss Thomas & James for me—

[Addressed to]
Miss Elizabeth Richardson

~

[SCL: Richard Irvine Manning and Elizabeth Peyre Richardson
   Manning Papers]
Margaret Cantey Sinkler to Elizabeth (Betsey) Richardson
[probably Belvidere] n.d. [one of two][51]

My Dear Betsey's affectionate favours came only to hand. I was indeed glad to
hear you were all well. I hope you enjoy all this time The Same Blessing. Anna
& myself are tolerable well, tho' I feel that I shall be obliged to take medicine
from the quantity of Bile on my stomach—I suppose by this time Bob has returned. I trust he has brought you good news with respect to John['s][52] Health &
Welfare—no doubt poor Fellow he longs for the time to return to his home, to
meet an affectionate Mother & Sisters—it requires no little resolution in a youth
to make up their Mind to stay so long from their friends with contentment—She
is So very far that it makes it worse—

   I send your Mama a Small Lump of Indigo. I made but very Little, but
cheerfully devide that Little with my friends. adieu, my Dear Betsey offer my

---

51 Although this letter is undated, its content suggests that it would have been written
during this time period.
52 Probably John Peter Richardson II (1801–1864), Betsey's younger brother.

affectionate love to your Mama & Sisters—not forgetting the Little Boys & believe me Sincerely & truly thy affectionate Friend

M Sinkler

ANN C. RICHARDSON TO MR. WILLIAM SINKLER IN CHARLESTON
ASYLUM. SEPTEMBER 18, 1818

My Dear William,

I should long since have replied to your very affectionate letter, but a variety of circumstances have prevented me from doing so. be [*sic*] assured nothing but this affliction and trouble would have kept me from answering your letter. It is impossible my Brother to tell you how much I feel for my Dear Dolly to be afflicted twice in so short a time after being bless'd with such fine Infants,[53] however it is as [from] her God, and like a good Christian she has calmly and patiently submitted to his will she is really a pattern of affliction, which gives me much satisfaction indeed to see her so resigned to the dispensations of providence. I sincerely hope you with Eliza and little boys participate in the enjoyment of health a blessing I ardently hope you may long be in possession of we are all tolerably well myself excepted. I cannot say that I have felt well one day for some time just tho' am able to go about and endeavor to discharge the duties that devolve upon me. My beloved Husband left us on Monday last for Columbia in tolerable health but quite thin. I have not heard from him since, I trust he is well and will shortly return to his family, who feels his absence more severely than ever. It is impossible my Dear William that any occurrence in life can for one moment cause the least change in my affection for you. I have too long my Brother indulged that Sisterly affection for you to suffer any thing to make an alteration in my bosom. I often with much pleasure reflect on the many happy days you have spent at this place with us, and altho it has been long since we have been bless'd with your society, I flatter myself that we shall spend some time together this winter. Our dear William has been extremely sick this summer, he has quite recover'd and grows very fast, he attends School very constant[.] I have endeavor'd to pursuade [*sic*] him to write to you, he says he will when he can write good enough; he begs his love to you his Aunt and Cousins but particularly James who he is very desirous of seeing the Girls beg their love to you and Eliza and the little boys kiss them both for me, and remember me affectionately to Eliza adieu my Dear William and believe me ever Your truly fond Sister,

Ann C. Richardson

53 Genealogical records indicate that Dorothy and William Boone Mitchell had only one child, a son, WBM II, born in 1814; WBM died that same year.

[Addressed to]
Ja[me]s. Ville 10
19th Sept.
Mr. William Sinkler
Mail Charleston

CHARLES RICHARDSON[54] TO WILLIAM SINKLER, ESQ[UIRE, AT SPRING FIELD]
ELMSWOOD 27TH MARCH 1819

My Dear Friend,

Yours by your servant came to hand the last evening[.] I am happy to hear that yourself and Family are in the enjoyment of good health, receive my thanks for the letter you sent me from my daughters, & for your friendly attentions to them, letters from them tho' very desirable always produce sensations that it is impossible at this day to express when I receive them[.] I am alarmed & when I do not I am miserable. I trust and hope my friend you may never experience the same, but I know you have been deprived of children & so have I many, but that of my Beloved Harriet[55] was a deprivation. It is impossible for me to ever recover, she was my companion, Friend, nay she was every thing to me, I am thank God Blessed with other children that are dutiful & affectionate, but the mind of my lamented daughter soared far beyond her age—but why should I trouble you with my feelings on a subject that is past recovery, when I am with my friends I exert my self to suppress those sensations, & why trouble them when absent, I trust you will excuse the feelings of an afflicted Father. I have delivered the case containing the marble to your servant with strict injunctions to Him. I should not have known what it was but having expected one up for the grave of my daughter, & wanting resolution to put it up untill a short time before I went to Charleston it remained in the Barn—but on opening it I found the mistake, mine had been taken up to my Brother which I never knew until finding the mistake I made enquiry about it, I should have sent it down in the Boat but as the Boat sunk the last trip I was afraid she might have some axident [*sic*] again. Cicero[56] has just returned home from delivering Financier at his stand, as soon as he refits himself I will send him to you, it is unneccessary for you to send a hand in his place you are quite welcome to his services as also that of Lewis—and knowing the state of y[ou]r horse—It would be impossible for me to give such

54 Charles Richardson, born on November 20, 1774, was the younger brother of James Burchell Richardson.

55 Charles's daughter, Harriet, was born on August 24, 1803, and died on April 27, 1818.

56 "Financier" was evidently Charles Richardson's horse, and Cicero his groom or trainer.

advice as would be serviceable in his training he must have good sharp exercise & if not sweated yet, two or three sweats however y[ou]r Best chance is to depend on your own Judgement & whatever Cicero may possess—

our best wishes to your family & remembrance to My aunt[57]

I remain y[ou]r Sincere Friend,

Charles Richardson

P.S. I would send the horse cloths with pleasure but the only one I had, has gone wi[th] Financier—I am afraid you have not seen aunt since y[ou]r arrival at home, for I think she would have delivered my message at least, & consequently [you] would have relieved me of mention [word missing] [avail]abilaty [*sic*] of any Black seed—

[Addressed to]
William Sinkler Esq
Spring Field
By his Servant

∼

ANN C. RICHARDSON TO MR. WILLIAM SINKLER AT SPRINGFIELD
APRIL 4. 1819

My Dear William,

I have sent the Horse Clothes they are not done as well as I could wish. Your servant soil'd the cloth very much in bringing it up. They were done all but the binding the day after they came up, and I could have done them better if I had of had [*sic*] more time to put the binding on. You must however take the will for the deed and make every allowance not having so well done as they may have been. Mr. Richardson says he is so disposed to oblige you, he has sent you a suit of old Clothes—he sent you some cordial balls[58] enough for 4 balls—I am glad to hear you are well and your little [one] will so soon be with his Parents no doubt he is rejoiced at his return. Mr. R. says if you had seed to spare he thinks he would have as great pretentions to it as any one else he has understood you had engaged all you had, previous to his speaking to you—but for a Friend he would have reserved a few bushels, he does not think much of it he has got a plenty now. Our Love to Eliza and kiss the little boys tell my dear howdye for me[.]

Your affectionate Sister,

Ann C. Richardson

57 "Aunt" probably referred to William Sinkler's mother, Margaret.
58 Cordial balls contained numerous herbs and spices; the balls were added to liquids and were believed to cure numerous ailments in horses.

This jockey suit—
originally red, but
now faded—may not
have been the one Ann
Richardson made, but it
would have been quite
similar. Courtesy of the
Sinkler family.

[Addressed to]
Mr. William Sinkler
Spring Field
By his Servant

[Also attached (likely in error, as it is dated 1 July 1819)]
Subpoena to appear before the Court of Common Pleas in Orangeburgh on
November 8 to testify in a dispute between JBR, Plaintiff, and John L. Thomson
& wife, Defendants.

James B. Richardson to William Sinkler, Esq[uire, at Belvidere]
James Ville, 5th Dec[embe]r 1821

Dear William,
    How sincerely do I condole with you on the melancholy event of the death
of your dear Mother;[59] I trust & hope, & that is strengthen'd beyond measure,
that her change is a happy & blessed one, & that her vital spark, that spirit has
soar'd to the regions of Immortal bliss, mingling with its kindred spirits in joy &

---

59 Margaret Cantey Sinkler was WS's mother and Ann Richardson's stepmother; she
was James B. Richardson's aunt, mother-in-law, and close friend. She died on December 4,
1821; although records do not indicate the cause of death, she was only fifty-eight, so could
have been expected to live beyond that age.

wellcome, & in praise & adoration to that God Almighty, & Immortal creator, who through his blessed spirit, has by our Saviour Jesus, open'd to us the means of Immortallity; disdaining from thence, the insignificant cares & engagements of this world, to which while life is extended, frail beings, we are, too warmly to cling to them, as tho', there was any intrinsic value in them; if like us they were not subject to decay; or if all, could further us in our transportation to Eternity. It is wonderfull my Dear William to reflect on the frail state of our Mortallity, & how we cling to the world, & the things of the world, when we are even hovering over the verge, from time to Eternity. But perhaps it is Gods holy ordination, that the Body may cling to its own composition and nature, & the spirit to its own; that being component parts, each are steadfastly adhering to its nature. I trust & hope you will support the heavy affliction, and the great privation you will sustain, in that becoming manner, of a true Christian, believing in the promises of live [*sic*] everlasting; & that as creatures, we are disposable at the will of our Creator. I wish indeed that I was at this moment with you, that I might offer the solace from the heart of the truest & most disinterested friendship that ever warm'd the Bosom; but alas! I am deprived of the kind & friendly office. I would indeed have made an effort this day to have been with you in time to have accompanied you down, (for I spent a sleepless night indeed) but from the arrangement mentioned in Eliza's letter to Anna, I was deterred from the attempt; tho' I felt assured my friendship and aid would have been serviceable; and in the discharge of the last kind office to my dear & valuable friend I had allways enjoined upon myself to see performed, if ever I survived her; and if the delay of her interment had been longer, nothing short of the impossibility would have prevented: Hence it was that I req[ueste]d at the time of my departure, that if any change should take place more unfavorable, that I might be inform'd thereof. I would that I had remained longer with you, for it is the only sick friend that ever I did visit & find so low, that ever I left, untill I did see the last of them; but I hoped the event would not have been so sudden, altho' my judgement told me it was certain with that sickness, & that she could not recover, yet I could not stay, & will say more when I see you. Your distresses are shared by me, & tell your Sister[60] I tenderly sympathise with her in the loss of a warmly affectionate mother. You are a flock composed of few now from that Paternal line, let not the severing of that gordian knot, which hath been your point of union, & bound you more firmly in the ties of affection, & affectious kind offices, now make you stray from those duties [en]-joined from consanguinity, but rather let it draw you all more closely together, that you [may] in affection florish united. Adieu my Dear William, I write you in much hurry, but I could not find it in my heart, on so melancholy an event,

---

60 James B. Richardson's wife, Ann, was evidently with Margaret Sinkler near the time of her death.

in which my heart is so deeply concerned, not to have written you at all. May God bless us, & preserve us in his mercifull kindness, & may each day we live, in passing through this world be better & better prepar'd for that which is eternal.

    Believe me sincerely,

    Your affectionate & distress'd friend

    James B. Richardson

[Addressed to]
William Sinkler Esq.
Belvidere

ANN C. RICHARDSON TO MR. WILLIAM SINKLER AT SPRING FIELD
[DEC.] 1821[61]

My Dear William,

    I received your affectionate letter by Post on Monday I regret extremely to find you suffer the loss of our Dear departed Mother to dwell so much upon your mind the affliction is indeed great and weighty almost beyond compare, but think from whom you received the blow and for one moment reflect how long a time you had to prepare yourself for this truly distressing and awful separation. How kind and merciful in [sic] our heavenly Father, to give you so long a period to prepare for it. I[t] does not lessen the weight of sorrow in which it must necessarily involve us; and of this I am very sensible, but the shock was not so great; and often too you must have reflected upon the event that would sooner or later have taken place. Had it been sudden, nothing my Brother but that Almighty hand could have supported and preserved under this oppressive affliction with him, all things are possible, and I am, well convinced from experience of his mercy and goodness that he will succour and help those whom he thinks proper to afflict, if they will seek his mercy. Rouse and exert yourself my Dear Brother look to him for aid and he will comfort and support you, under this severe affliction. You have many blessings and comforts around you, be not unmindful of them; and bow with humble submission to his will who has deprived you of so dear and valued a Friend and the best of Mothers. To think we shall never behold her more. The thought is almost insupportable in destraction. Nothing scarcely can equal it. But I entreat you to erase from your mind as much as possible those reflections and do not grieve as one without hope, you have certainly great comfort in believing she was prepared for the event, and every hope of her being forever happy. Oh my

---

61 James B. Richardson wrote to William on December 5, noting that Ann had written to Anna (Thomson), her half-sister. It is likely that Ann's letter to William was written at about the same time or shortly thereafter.

William what a consolation to your afflicted heart is that blessed hope. Think not hard I pray you of your friend his heart and Soul was with you and nothing short of the very rainy day and the difficulty in getting across the swamp would have kept him from you, it was his determination to do so early in the morning but he could not travel on horse such a a [*sic*] day; and he could not get over the Swamp be assured we felt most truly for your situation we well knew the task you had to you had to [*sic*] perform it was indeed a severe and distressing one, and nothing but the causes mentioned kept him from you.[62] It is impossible to express to you what I feel for my dear Sister. Oh what a friend what an irreparable loss is hers. Great indeed I humbly pray my God to be with her and support her under this affliction and every other she may have to encounter with. My Dear William time is so short or he would certainly have been with you a day or two probably he will be down shortly he will then certainly go and see you, he desired his love to you and his Aunt and Cousins. I wish you could have sent James up to see us we would have been very glad to see him[.] My Richardson and the Girls beg their affectionate love to you and your good Eliza. Believe me my Dear Brother

Your fond and very affectionate Sister

Ann C. Richardson

Mr. Richardson begs you will prepare the Stalls for his Nags they will be with you about 10 days

[Addressed to]

Mr. William Sinkler

Spring Field

By Servant

---

62 The normal route from the Sandhills to Eutaw Springs crossed the Santee River at Nelson's Ferry and involved crossing extensive swamp.

Rutledge College, built in 1805, housed the early South Carolina College (later the University of South Carolina). Note on the photograph reads "Rutledge College, Right side, Brick, center building used as Chapel wings as dormitories." James B. Richardson's son, William Henry Burchell Richardson, was a student from 1824 until he graduated in 1826. Although there were at least two more buildings by this time, it is likely that he would have lived in this building. Courtesy of the University of South Carolina Archives, Columbia, SC.

Chapter 4

Mentoring Another William

William H. B. Richardson

William Henry Burchell Richardson (1804–1879) was the seventh of twelve children born to James B. and Ann S. Richardson. He was the third of five sons and the first of only two to survive. This undoubtedly contributed to JBR's close attention to every move of his son, on whom he pinned his hopes for greatness. In a letter of August 1807, he noted that "my sweet little William" and two daughters were extremely sick. He went on to express hope that the "mercies of my good God . . . will help my Son, my darling boy, with length of days and noble mental qualities."

Not much is known about his early education, but there are letters written to the seventeen-year-old William at Woodville Academy from April through October 1822. In one of these early letters, JBR chided his son for contemplating taking a break from school. While JBR did not come right out and say, "No," he enumerated the reasons why his son should not consider this vacation. It is hard to believe that WHBR would have persisted in the face of such reasoned opposition.

Woodville Academy was located about seven miles northeast of Stateburg, in western Sumter County, and according to some records, operated from 1816 to at least 1821.[1] There were several other academies in the area, most of which operated for a short time, so it is quite possible that WHBR had attended one or more of these before he was sent to board at Woodville.

---

1 Gregorie, *History of Sumter County,* 178.

By November 1824 he was at South Carolina College, from which he graduated in 1826, likely with honors. Reflective of college students across history, a
letter of April 14, 1825, notes that William had been complaining of the food. The
letter goes on to note that nonperishable food was being sent along with the letter.
In the same letter, JBR noted that he was sending "your horse" along with a slave
for a day or two for "the recreation you contemplate." In an undated letter—undoubtedly a short time later—there is allusion to an accident, to the slave, Jim,
having become ill and to a second slave being sent to look after Jim and retrieve
the horse. There is reference to WHBR having felt some responsibility in causing
the accident, which his father attempted to allay. Money was included with the
letter, and William was instructed to obtain "the best medical assistance & other
attendants & whatever may be wanted" for Jim and in the process not to neglect
his studies.

A letter from his uncle, Charles Richardson, on June 26, 1825, gives a glimpse
of how WHBR was to spend his summer. The entire letter brims with very specific directions for managing one of his plantations. It includes instructions for dis-
tributing corn, picking cotton and peas, and preparing the ground for other crops.

James B. Richardson wrote to his son in February 1826, commending him for
having been "steadfast," saying that "if you have not gain'd the Summa . . . you
have moor'd your Bark amidst the best . . . and the multitude will always hail
you with their kindest greeting." He may have studied law in Columbia, as some
reports suggest, but a March 28, 1827, letter was directed to him in Charleston. In
it, his father referred to WHBR's "Scientific pursuit" without specifying just what
this may have been; earlier letters indicate that he had been studying literature at
South Carolina College. The March 1827 letter admonishes William to "let the
object be effectually obtain'd, that you may hold up to the world a Success burning with a light of most brilliant lustre, not only to illumine the portals of your
own house, but of all connected with it, or that may come within its vortex."

The next letter—just a few days later—refers to his preparing to address the
Courts of Equity and Pleas, so perhaps he did study law. This same letter advises
William H. B. Richardson that his house had been framed and "the Sashes &
Doors & Window frames" would be ready shortly. Two and a half years later, on
November 5, 1829, he married his first cousin Dorothea/Dorothy Ann Richard-
son, with whom he had nine children. Census records all list him as a planter or
farmer.

~

[ALL LETTERS IN THIS CHAPTER FROM DU, JAMES BURCHELL
RICHARDSON PAPERS]
JAMES B. RICHARDSON TO WILLIAM H. B. RICHARDSON, IN
WOOD VILLE, S. CAROLINA
JAMES VILLE, 8 APR 1822

My Dear William,

I received your affectionate letter's [*sic*] by Len & that by the boy that went up
with James, who I expected would have call'd on me, which observe to him that
he ought to have done when I would have sent up your keys, that you were neglectfull in leaving, & but for the occasion of sending up for Mark Anthony that
took sick with you on your way up, it might have been long before you would
perhaps have received them. I have written Mr. J[oh]n Moore & thank'd him for
his goodness in lending you the horse to proceed on your journey, as it would
have been dangerous for you to have remained there a night on account of the
measles, & also for his taking care of your sick horse; I trust you also expressed
your thanks to him for his kindness. I did intend to have written you much more
fully than it will be in my power from the repeated interruptions which occurs, &
this moment your Aunt & Major Cantey & family have arrived on their way up;
& yesterday Mr. James Cantey & his Lady went up. I am truly glad to find you
are determined to pursue your studies with zeal & avidity & to look forward with
the reward & pleasures that are hereafter to result therefrom; there is nothing like
making yourself quite contented & happy in your situation, & think of nothing
but the object you have in view of attaining your Education, & such a one as
will rank you with the Literate of your Country. It is pleasing to see your Sister
Matilda's observations on the pleasures & enjoyments that attended those at the
wedding of your cousin, "they were fleeting & left no reality behind" while those
like her were pursuing instructions that would afford a lasting blessing." It is true
my D[ea]r William for it is only when we have attained the the [*sic*] one so primary, that we can properly enjoy the other; I trust you will hold the recollection
of this truth always in remembrance.

Your Sister Dorothy left us on Friday last to go down[.] She & Richardson &
Julia with her, they were all in good health then, & we are all here enjoying the
invaluable blessing, & I trust in my good God that you enjoy the same, & have
that perfect peace & content which will so affectually enable you to persevere
successfully in your Studies. All the family desire their love & best wishes to await
you, & Richard sends his love & says he will never forget you. God bless you my
Dear William & give you his most choice benedictions, as the fervent orison of
Your truly fond & affectionate Father

James B. Richardson
Master William H. B. Richardson
WoodVille

[Addressed to]
Master William H. B. Richardson
Wood Ville
Per Serv't Lenn on horse S. Carolina

JAMES B. RICHARDSON TO WILLIAM H. B. RICHARDSON, IN
    WOOD VILLE, S. CAROLINA
JAMES VILLE, APRIL 18. 1822

My Dear William,

Your dutiful and affectionate letter of the 12 ins[tan]t I duly received, & was very much gratified to find you so determined to persevere in your studies & to accomplish if possible the laudable ambition of attaining a distinguish'd Education, & what every mind ought to aspire to, if they possess the high feelings that attach to a mind that emulates to wisdom, & to preserve & inhance [sic] the dignity of their ancestry & whose opportunity & means will enable them to do so. But those whose Parents are blessed in having it in their power to hold out these advantages & do hold them forth, & when a kind Providence has endowed with capacity to obtain, that all important requisite of a distinguished Education, & fail to possess it, then it becomes unpardonable in them, because the delinquency is their own; they become faithless to themselves & blind to their true interest. How poignant in a situation like this, must the reflections be, that grow out of consequences of this nature to a sensitive reflecting mind; its recurrence to the thought must be an envenom'd dagger whenever it arises, that such a golden opportunity for acquiring a rich Treasure, durable as life (in all probability) has been lost or misspent by imprudence or negligently. I have never no fear [sic] that your conduct will give you cause to reprehend yourself with charges of this nature. You have too high a sense of the importance of the object, & of the obligations that rest on you to relax in your pursuit, or to be found wanting as far as it rests with you to obtain it, & may we not confidently hope that those zealous endeavors, a good God will not fail to crown with success. I really regret to hear of this vacation you speak of, you have already lost so much time this year that I am loath that you should loose another day; not but that I should be desirous to see you, for the pleasure is considerable to me, but I would forego it all for your future benefit; & the poignantcy [sic] of feeling at a separation, exceeds the pleasure of meeting; the latter renders but a sorry compensation for the uneasiness of the other. You write of forgetting home & pleasures, etc., but I discover you eagerly seize at the information of vacation, which indicates some lingering desire inhabits some corner of your bosom, which I suppose has not so fully renounced as the other parts. I have received a letter from your Preceptor & will either send it for your perusal, or reserve it for your inspection here. It will be gratifying & I trust will stimulate you in the Greek wherein he States your lost time has prevented you from your accustomed progress.

I have sent on the money for the accts. of the last quarters tuition which you enclosed to me. You will enquire of Mr. Furman if it is received by him, or I may enclose it in his letter & not yours.

We are all in the enjoyment of good health thank God & hope you enjoy the blessing, & wish you a long possession of it. Accept the tender of our best affection & good wishes for your success & prosperity, and believe me my Dear William

Your fond & affectionate Father

James B. Richardson

NB. I have just received intelligence that Mr. David Deas[2] had shot himself for Debt & expired immediately. What a dreadfull thing it is for a man to suffer himself to get so overwhelm'd in debt, as to drive him to such an extremity.

[Addressed to]
Master William H. B. Richardson
Wood Ville
Per Len on horse Sumter Dis[tric]t

[upside down]
I intended to send this letter on to you immediately, but having to send Len to Town prevented me.

ANN C. RICHARDSON TO WILLIAM H. B. RICHARDSON, IN
WOOD VILLE, S. CAROLINA
JUNE 4. 1822

My Dear William,

I received your affectionate letter yesterday, with the pleasing information of your enjoyment of health, and trust in the mercies of divine Providence you will continue to enjoy that greatest of all earthly blessings without which we are deprived of every comfort and pleasure in life. I humbly thank my God for his

---

2 David Deas, Jr., (b. 1771) was a younger brother to William Sinkler's mother-in-law, Mary Deas Broün. A lawyer and planter, he had served as intendant (mayor) of Charleston in 1802–03, before returning to the state house of representatives. Bailey, *Biographical Directory of the South Carolina House,* 4:149.

mercies in preserving you in health I hope my Dear Son you are not unmindful of the Blessing you receive from your Creator, that you never suffer neither morning or evening to pass without humbly thanking him for his unbounded goodness and imploring him to continue his kindness [*sic*] protection to you. I am truly glad to see my Dear William you have a just sense of the importance of a good Education and that you are striving to obtain so great a treasure exert yourself and apply with industry and diligence all your ability and trust in God he will bless your endeavors, and I hope will make a good a great a virtuous and Religious Man. It is what I daily offer up my prayer to that Throne of mercy for you. I am truly sorry Indeed to hear of the illness of our Thomas.[3] I hope he will be restored to health soon and will be enabled to return to his studies. Your Papa left us on Sunday last, he did not intend going further than your Sisters, and send Moses on to town for Matilda, it is late in the Season and I am glad he determined not [to] go to Town. I sent your letter on to him by Post yesterday. I entreat you my beloved William to apply yourself to your Studies and suffer nothing on your part to be wanting on your part to fit and prepare you for College you know what is required of you there. I pray be no[t] deficient in no one thing my love for you is such I wish to excel in every respect. Your Sisters beg their love affectionately to you and Richard sends you many kisses and says he will never forget you. Adieu my dear Boy and believe me

Your very affectionate Mother

Ann C. Richardson

I have sent you some Sauges ginger cake[4] And Sugar Biscuits

[Addressed to]
Master William HB Richardson
Wood Ville
By Len on horse

James B. Richardson to William H. B. Richardson, in
    Wood Ville, S. Carolina
James Ville, June 17. 1822

My Dear William,

I am allowed but a few moments to address you, stating that I had received your letter requesting me to get you the white Hat & shoes, they are procured for you, & if I can get Capt. Spann to carry the Hat for you I will send it by him. I

---

3 This is probably a friend or relative who was a classmate; there was no Thomas in the immediate family.

4 Sauges was a brand of ginger cake.

did not go on to Charleston, as I had my business all to arrange & inspect for the summer, I rec'd your letter while at New Belvedere [*sic*], and I was very glad to find that you were in good health, & fill'd with the determination of persevering to the utmost extent of all your efforts to acquire a distinguished education. You know what I have always told you, that if you ever become the able & accomplished man my fond heart would in reason wish you to be seen, that no behest in reason, within the gift of your earthly Father would be withheld from you. Surely then this ought to stimulate you to formidable exertions, in order, not only to attain a summit of public admiration, but to exult in the exquisite delight that must fill your bosom, at affording such a high gratification to your Father's bosom, & to that of a more than tender Mother & to kind & charming Sisters.

I am sorry to inform you that your Sister Dorothy & Richardson & Julia have all been very sick. Richardson[5] has been extremely ill, we did not think at one time that he would have lived, & could only get part of the way up with him the day we sett off, & had Dr. Cox & Boyd with him. They all are some better particularly your sisters, & Richardson we find some better also, but he is yet very low, but we hope for the best, as he has been now ten days sick, that holding out so long is much in his favor. The rest of us thank God are all in good health, & so soon as the sick ones can be removed, I shall move up to the Sand Hills, where I trust if nothing unforeseen prevents, I shall have the pleasure of seeing you for a few days the 4 July.

All desire their love to you, & offer their best wishes for your success in the laudable measures you are pursuing. I tell James the same, & to remember he bears my name & never to disgrace in no way. Adieu my Dear Son, may God bless you with wisdom & virtue, honor & bravery, & give you acute judgement to select wisely, & firmness to support it, are the devout orisons of

Your fond & affectionate Father
James B. Richardson
Master Wm. HB. Richardson
Wood Ville

NB. I have just rec'd acc[oun]ts by the papers that McDuffie was shot in the duel with Col. Cummings, but not mortal. His shot was premature I suppose from his nerves being weak_____ [6]

---

5 It is unclear who this is, but Ann Richardson referred to her husband as "Richardson," so this may have been JBR's nephew, also named James B. Richardson, whose father, John Peter, had died in 1811. JBR had assumed a guardianship role. Dorothy (b. 1791) and Julia (b. 1813) were JBR's daughters.

6 What started as a political debate between George McDuffie (later a U.S. representative and South Carolina governor) and Colonel William Cumming, a Georgia planter,

[Addressed to]
Master William HB Richardson
Wood Ville
Sumter Dis[tric]t
To the care of Capt. J[oh]n R. Spann[7]

James B. Richardson to William H. B. Richardson, in
    Wood Ville, S. Carolina
Sand Hills, 4 o'clock P. M., Aug[us]t 3d. 1822

My Dear William,

I have just received your affectionate letter of this day by Mr. Potts servant & in compliance with your request have delivered to him the Dog puppy that he made choice of for your young friend. I hope he may be successfull with it, if well train'd, I have little doubt but it will prove excellent the stock is so genuine & fine.

I am truly happy to learn that you are in the enjoyment of good health, & fill'd with the determination to persevere in your studies to acquire the Summit that I hold in view for you; I pray God to help you with the former & crown you with the latter. The Convalescents of the family are progressing in health & I hope may soon be thoroughly restored to their pristine State, & the rest continue in the possession of that blessing.

The accounts that Mr. Furman gave you to enclose, I wish you would observe to him always to rec[eip]t when he sends them down, which would save the returning them to be receipted; I will however send them for that purpose & the money by draft [to] Rob[er]t Dow, & you will get the rec[eip]ts & return them by the boy that goes up with him, as this serv[an]t stays so short a time that I cannot affect the change, & indeed I have barely time to address you these hurried lines. All the family unite in the tender of their love & best wishes to you, & hope confidently in your success of being qualified to enter college by next November, in which I cordially adjoin them, & subscribe myself.

My Dear William
Your fond & affectionate Father

---

boiled over into a series of three duels. This was the first, which lodged a bullet in McDuffie's back. J. Grahame Long, *Dueling in Charleston* (Charleston, S.C.: History Press, 2012), 84.

7 John Spann was a family friend and fellow horse racer; he married James B. Richardson's daughter, Margaret, about 1825.

James B. Richardson
Mast[e]r William HB. Richardson.
Wood Ville

[Addressed to]
Master William HB Richardson
Wood Ville
Per Serv[an]t of Mr. Potts

JAMES B. RICHARDSON TO WILLIAM H. B. RICHARDSON, IN
  WOOD VILLE, S. CAROLINA
SAND HILLS, AUG[US]T 18. 1822

My Dear William,

When I wrote you last by Mr. Potts['s] serv[an]t, I mentioned therein, that I should do myself that pleasure in a few days again by the return of Master Rob[er]t Dow whose mother had promis'd me that she would advise me of the time of his returning but who fail'd to do so; & that, by that conveyance I would send the money for the payment of Mr. Furman's acc[oun]t which you forwarded to me: I desire you to say to him, that I seriously regret the disappointment, as the money may have been wanted; & that no opportunity has since offered, I would otherwise have forward'd it, but that I send now particularly on that account & hope the money will be in due time to answer the purposes desired.

I have also sent the two acc[oun]ts receipted at the time I expect'd to send them by Robert Dow, you will get Mr. Furman to sign them & return them enclosed in your letter by the return of the bearer hereof, & pay Mr. Furman the Forty Dollars enclosed herein being the amount of the two accounts.

I was extremely glad my Dear Son to find by your letter that you continued to enjoy good health, & you were pursuing your studies with full determination of a completion of the object you have in view, & that which I have mark'd out for you: I trust my good God will bless you with health & strength of mind & body & a fullness of spirit for the consummation of this laudable attainment of which every possession has a just right to be proud of, as it is from the minds exertions under Gods blessing that it is obtained, & my orisons are daily offered to his Throne divine, for wisdom & virtue to be pour'd in upon you, & that you may be bless'd with a mind that can wisely & elegantly [blurred] indite & with speech fluently & eloquently to give utterance, that you may be admired wise among the very wisest of your contemporaries. I think it cannot but be a circumstance of pleasure to Mr. Furman to have the sole preparation of you & your cousins for College, & ought to be a cause for stimulating him to exercise his best exertions that you should distinguish yourself in entering, & afterwards to arrive at the point of honor & distinction, that you may be a lasting credit to him hereafter in learning & literature. Let these sentiments be known to him not only as my own, but of other persons of learning who have expres'd the gratification of his having an opportunity to manifest his abilities in rearing youths for College.

The family are all well with the exception of Matilda who has not yet entirely recovered her health, but she is up, & improving & has a very good appetite. Poor Capt. Springs died on Thursday last & was interred on Fri. 16 Ins[tan]t he has left a helpless family. I was at the funeral and it delayed my sending to you on that day instead of this. Your Mother has sent you up several [li]ttle necessaries, & I will, if you improve fast in [blotted] learning, particularly in your writing & orthography [blotted] I may have them to judge of, send up a boy to you every two or three weeks regularly to enquire after your health.

The wishes & expectations of all the family are alive for your wellfare [*sic*] & prosperity, & all desire their love to you & Richard & Richardson begs that you will not forget them.

Adieu my D[ea]r Son my devout orisons are offered in your behalf that God will pour his blessings & let them abide with you always. My Dear William

Your fond & affectionate Father

James B. Richardson

[Addressed to]
Master William HB Richardson
Wood Ville
Per Serv[an]t Abram with articles. S. Carolina

Ann C. Richardson to William H. B. Richardson, in Wood Ville
September 6. 1822.

My Dear my beloved William,

It is with much pleasure I inform you of the health of our family except my Matilda and our Richardson who has very often a return of fever but not violent or lasting, how thankful ought we to be to that good and merciful God who has been so kind to us, his <u>unworthy Servants</u> altho we have been visited with sickness in some of our family we are all preserved. I sincerely hope my Dear Son yourself and Cousin are in the enjoyment of that inestimable blessing health and trust it will please my merciful Father to preserve and grant you long continuation of the greatest of all earthly blessings. I flatter myself my William you [are] pursuing your studies with every possible diligence and your best exertions are used to obtain that important treasure a good Education. I am very sorry to inform you that John[,] Charles and Henry Brown are all very ill John and Charles particularly also Powell Mc[Crae] your Papa with your Sisters have been backwards and forwards for ten days or a fortnight up with your Aunt where your Papa and Mag now are they went up the day before yesterday and have not returned. You[r] Dear Papa mentioned he would send up to you, but I expect those Boys are so ill he cannot leave your Aunt[.] Poor old Lady she is in much trouble indeed. Mrs. Dow was kind enough to let me know she was going to send up she is indeed very good, and I embrace the opportunity with pleasure[.] I am truly anxious to hear from you, it is very sickly in Manchester and around it. Dolly Sarah Hermione Julie and the Boys beg their affectionate love to you[.] Matilda is now writing, adieu my beloved Son I pray my God to be with you, is the devout orisons of Your very fond Mother

Ann C. Richardson

I have sent you some Potatoe Pone and some Sugar biscuits hope you will receive them safe

[Addressed to]
Master William HB. Richardson
Wood Ville
By Mrs. Dow['s] Servant.

ANN C. RICHARDSON TO WILLIAM H. B. RICHARDSON, IN WOOD VILLE
SAND HILLS, SEPTEMBER 19. 1822

My Dear William,

I received your very affectionate letter by the return of Mrs. Dow's Servant with the pleasing information of your enjoyment of health and that of your Cousins[8] long very long my Dear Son may you continue to partake of that greatest of all earthly blessings without it we are quite incapacitated for any thing in life. I am much gratifyed [*sic*] to hear you are pursuing your studies with so much zeal and that you know so well the importance of a good Education continue in the noble pursuit my Son and while you have it in your power embrace the opportunity and lay that treasure for yourself nothing earthly can divest you of. I hope my William you are never unmindful of your Creator for the many comforts and blessings you daily receive from him let [it] be the first thing in the morning and the last at night thank him for his bountiful goodness to you and implore him to you under his care and protection. With much concern I'm in for[med] [*sic*] of the death little Arabella McCra[e] she died on Friday morning last after a very short illness the distress and affliction of her poor Mother is beyond description.

8 One cousin might have been John P. Richardson's son, James Burchell, who was two years younger than William H. B. Richardson.

I feel for her most truly, I mentioned to [you] in my last letter that the three Browns and Powell McCra[e] were extremely ill they are much better now. Arabella was then in blooming health but Alas! she is now no more, how wonderful are the works of divine Providence.

I am glad to inform you we all continue quite well[.] Matilda and Richardson still a return of the fever but it is not so severe, and does not last so long[.] I hope they will shortly be perfectly relieved from it. Your Papa says he has sent for the Book you requested and it will be up by Thursday Post, he has sent you a pamphlet to read and you must take particular care of it and when you come down bring it with you. You will receive by the bearer a few articles which I have noted at bottom if there is any thing you particularly want let me know by the return of the Boy and I will endeavor to have them ready to go up by October Court. Your Papa desires his love to you and says he will write to you[.] Dolly Sarah Matilda Julia and the Boys beg their affectionate love to you[.] Margaret is with your Aunt Singleton they are truly distressed and troubled. Give my love to your Cousins and believe me my much loved William[.]

3 pr of thick Pantaloons
1 pr of Drawers
3 pr of woolen Socks.
1 bottle of preserved plumbs [*sic*]
    Rolla Cake and Potato Pone.

Your truly fond and very affectionate
Mother
Ann C. Richardson

[Addressed to]
Master William HB. Richardson
Wood Ville
By Mrs. Dow['s] Servant.

Ann C. Richardson to William H. B. Richardson, in Wood Ville
September 25 . 1822.

My Dear William,
    Your Papa has sent up expressly to send you the Books you wrote for which only came by the last Mail, he has sent them up that you may loose no time for the want of them and begs you will suffer not one moment of time to pass you with using your best exertions to improve yourself in every branch of your Education every moment is indeed very precious to you my Dear Son and I flatter you

are sensible of it and will with every possible diligence apply yourself and study with great attention. I am truly thankful to my God for the blessing of health you enjoy[.] I trust you will continue so we are all quite well the Shoes which your Aunt sent for the Boys were forgotten they are now sent, also some little Cake for you, your Papa and Sisters beg their love to you believe me my Dear Son you must write to your Papa[.] Your very affectionate Mother

Ann C. Richardson

Abr[ah]am must start early your Papa wants him.

[Addressed to]
Master William HB Richardson
Wood Ville
By Abraham. With Sundries.

Ann C. Richardson to William H. B. Richardson, in Wood Ville
October 2. 1822.

My Dear William,

I have but a few moments notice to write you which I gladly embrace to enquire after your health and sincerely hope you are in the enjoyment of that greatest of all earthly blessings, and am glad to inform you we are all quite well.

You will receive this by your Aunt's Servant who is going up for your Cousins your papa desires me to say to you suffer nothing of the kind to effect you and look to noone but yourself and continue diligent and attentive to your studies and exert yourself as much as you possibly can and learn fast he hopes to see you soon and I hope my Son he will be much pleased with your improvements. I expect you will be with him a good deal the next week, keep up your spirits and think of your studies more than any thing else, your Papa got a letter from your Uncle William on Monday he mentions there was a most dreadful Tornado on Friday the 27 Sept. and a great deal of mischief done in Town several lives lost, how fortunate were we all to have none of it comparatively speaking there was a great Rain and severe wind here but no injury done at all.[9] Your Papa and Sisters beg their affectionate love to you and the Boys send many kisses for you God bless my beloved Son may every happiness await you is the ardent prayer of

Your very fond and very affectionate Mother

Ann C. Richardson

9 A hurricane on the South Carolina coast on September 27–28 spawned tornados. Rogers and Taylor, *South Carolina Chronology,* 77.

[Addressed to]
Master William HB. Richardson
Wood Ville
By Servant

Ann C. Richardson to William H. B. Richardson, in
    Columbia, So[uth] Carolina
Sand Hills, November 10. 1824.

My Dear William,

Your truly affectionate letter I received by Sammy and was truly happy to hear you were in the enjoyment of good health, long very long may you be partaken of this inestimable blessing. I humbly ask of my God which will enable you to pursue your studies and prevent your loosing [*sic*] any time, that you may accomplish in the time allotted to complete your Education, that you return to us and remain with us my dear Boy is my earnest and sincere prayer. You do not know my Son the heartfelt pleasure and gratification I experienced to hear from you, were already prepared for your examination; continue to conduct yourself my beloved Son as you have done let nothing lead you astray or tempt you to deviate from the path of virtue and rectitude.

I am truly happy to inform you your Father's health continues to mend and hope he is now in a fair way to recover his usual good health, I hope you feel perfectly satisfied of the perfect confidence your Papa and myself have in you and believe that nothing but occular demonstration would ever make him think you would do any thing wrong or improper; you must not suffer anything to make impressions on your mind, or for one moment to think that your Papa would believe any report he could hear of you for you have no doubt ere this heard of the death of your Aunt Charles Richardson [Elizabeth Eveliegh 1774–1824] her sufferings were beyond every thing I ever witness'd which she bore with Christian fortitude and the most exemplary patience I am glad to say your Uncle and his daughters bears [*sic*] with fortitude the heavy loss they have sustained, he is indeed a true Christian and bows with submission to the will of his Maker. Write as often as you can conveniently, let me know if you have received the basket sent by Mr. Spann's Cart; your Sisters all beg their affectionate love to you. Your Papa also sends his love to you and says he will be up to commencement[10] and hopes to see you all his fond hearts desires you to be. God bless and preserve you my beloved Son <u>may</u> every happiness await you prays

10 James B. Richardson would have been attending commencement as a trustee; William graduated in 1826.

Your fond and very affectionate Mother
Ann C. Richardson

[Addressed to]
Master William HB. Richardson
Mail Columbia
So[uth] Carolina

James B. Richardson to William H. B. Richardson, in
   Columbia, So[uth] Carolina
James Ville, Nov[embe]r 25. 1824.

My Dear William,
   I have just received your very affectionate letter of the 18 inst[ant] & was extremely happy to hear from the contents that you was [*sic*] still in the enjoyment
of good health, & pursuing your studies with zeal & avidity. May you my Son
long be endowed with that greatest of all blessings, health, & with industry &
determination to persevere in the course mark'd out for you, & that you may be
enabled to obtain the object of pursuit at its most exalted Summit, are the orisons
fervent & devout of that parental bosom that heaves with such fervour for you
& your future prosperity. My time will not admit of my writing to you as fully as
I should desire, but it would be unnecessary as I promise myself the pleasure of
seeing you about this day week in Columbia, and would not now have written,
as this is the day that the Post passes & this must be hurried to the office to be
in the mail in time, but that your last letter expresses such surprise at my silence.
It must be well known to you my Dear William how many engagements I have
to attend to, & more particularly at this Season of the year, & immediately too
after removing from our Sand Hills residence. I am more particularly concerned
that you should impute my silence to any displeasure of your conduct, not so my
Son, far from it, on the contrary, I should hasten to let you hear directly from me
if I had any cause of disapprobation to urge to you, & my silence you may, as I
have frequently repeated to you before, construe into entire approbation; indeed
your conduct hitherto has not only been highly approved by me, but has given
me great pleasure, more especially to see you maintain so high an estimation in
the affection of all your fellow students; it is indicative not only of a goodness of
heart, but a talent capable of engaging & controlling the affections of mankind,
which is a valuable quality to cherish through life. You have heard the melancholy
tidings of the death of poor M^rs. Richardson [see previous letter], it was a lamentable calamity & depress'd the fortitude of your Uncle exceedingly, & the manner
of it added more poignancy: I trust however his fortitude will regain its firmness. This event will prevent your Sisters from accompanying me to witness the

evening commencement. Your Uncle William [Sinkler] has also lost his youngest Son Archy, I truly sympathize with him for his misfortunes which seldom come alone, & too often tread on the heel of each other.

I find that the notification for the Executive Chair has produced with some persons great commotion, but let nothing of this transpire, I will communicate more to you when I see you on that subject. I hope to see you soon & have the pleasure of greeting you in good health: mine too is much improv'd thank God, & I hope may continue to thorough restoration of health & strength once again: which blessing your Mother & all here do exuberantly participate; your Sister Dorothy, Julia & Richardson having gone down on Monday last & I hope are also well. Adieu My Dear William, all here unite in the tender of their love & best wishes to you, & little Richard particularly. Adieu again my dear son, & believe me very Sincerely,

> Your fond & affectionate Father
> James B. Richardson
> NB. Remember all our loves to James affectionately [*sic*].

[Addressed to]
May [?] 10
M^r. William HB. Richardson
Mail Columbia
S^o. Carolina

James B. Richardson to William H. B. Richardson, in Columbia,
   So[uth] Carolina
James Ville, March 14, 1825.

My Dear William,
Your very affectionate letter directed to the care of Mr. James G. Holmes of the 5 ins[tan]t I did not receive untill the 10th ins[tan]t not being at Court at the commencement of it, & the letter was forwarded on to me, or if it had been received in time, you may be assured I would have promptly complied with your request & sent on to you, but I trust you have experienced no inconvenience from it. Going on to Charleston & the family also, & then having to hasten up to attend the court at Sumter Ville, prevented me from attending at Camden or Columbia with the young ladies to witness the visit & reception of the National Guest[11] there, to which I was particularly invited by several of my friends at both places, & by letter from the Governor covering invitations for your Sisters, & to

---

11 The Marquis de Lafayette made several stops in South Carolina on his tour through the South. William H. B. Richardson attended his appearance in Columbia.

which I should have attended had they been rec'd in time, but the letter was not deliver'd me untill the 12th ins[tan]t too late to make any efforts to embrace it. I have no doubt but great exertions were made at both places mentioned, but I had no curiosity to gratify & assure you at such pageantry to a human being like ourselves, it is almost carrying things to too great lengths, & resembles the deifying a mortal; & I have little doubt but it is burthensome to the Visitor himself, a plain & wellcome reception would have been more congenial with his feelings. I should have went [*sic*] on account of the young Ladies seeing the General, hearing the address to greet his arrival, & to participate in the enjoyment of the Ball, which to them would have been more desirable than all, but I was prevented by the circumstances above stated, so we could not be at every place; I am however glad that you was [*sic*] there to witness that at Columbia. It afforded me great happiness to find by your letter that you continue to enjoy good health, & that you are persevering in your Studies; God grant you a continuation of both, and give you in the sequel a rich reward, for all your labors & perseverance, & crown you with his greatest blessings through life. He will not fail to regard with his most choice gifts the persevering exertions of the virtuous & the dutifull, & as such, I trust you have strong claims to his mercy. Continue then my Dear Son in the steady course you have hitherto gone, & you have every thing reasonably to expect from God & man, & but little to fear in this, & in the world to come. These Sentiments must give you great gratulation [*sic*], to reflect on the goodness of God to have kept you in the correct way, & to cause you to offer your humble homage for his mercies, & to supplicate the continuance of his care & guidance; I must stimulate you to persevere in the correct course, & to resist all temptation to swerve therefrom.

You will observe that I address you from this habitation, I am alone here, & as you may suppose solitary indeed, but I am but little in the house, & I shall hasten so soon as I can to Belvedere [*sic*] where I left your Mother & the family on Wednesday last, all in good health; & your Sisters spoke of returning to Town with your Uncle William to be present at the arrival of the General [Lafayette] there. Your Sister Margaret & the Captain[12] came up with me, & went up on Thursday the day I went to Court, & return'd on Saturday finding I had no business that would be done that week, & came by & saw them. I may have to return this week for which I left directions to inform me should it be necessary; if I should, it will prevent me from going down as soon as I contemplated, which I shall regret, tho' I am desirous to get through all my business there.

My health has continued to improve, & I hope may be so far restored as to enable me to stay the Summer with security at that pleasant Summer retreat, when I look forward with peculiar pleasure for the enjoyment of your endearing Society, when we all gather together from our present divided situation. I shall

12 Captain John Spann was Margaret's fiancé or husband; they married in 1825.

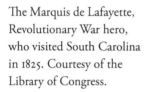

The Marquis de Lafayette, Revolutionary War hero, who visited South Carolina in 1825. Courtesy of the Library of Congress.

not make a long stay below when I go down for your Mother, & as soon as we return I will send a boy up to you, with your Summer Clothes, & other articles that may be to send. Your Suit of Clothes I got in Town I will retain untill you give directions respecting them. You must never ascribe to my Silence any thing like neglect to you, or your giving any cause of offence; you may [be] assured that I shall write you whenever I can, if only a few lines, & if the latter was the case, I have stated a thousand times to you, that you should hear promptly from me; & why presume that I should intentionally neglect you, from any offence, when conscious you had given no cause? Indeed my Son it is a great source of pleasure to me to say that your conduct in every instance merits my approval, & you must not therefore produce an exception, by constraining without a cause, my Silence into neglect towards you, or as offence for your conduct, which I have so often & in such general terms approved.

Adieu my Dear my beloved William, may my mercifull God bless you with health & happiness, & pour in upon you his most choice benediction, & fill you with wisdom, virtue & understanding, & the ample means of disseminating that treasure to the world. [faded/torn] the daily devout orisons to the Throne of Grace & Power from my Dear Son,

Your truly fond & affectionate Father.

James B. Richardson

NB. Give my love & best wishes to James & tell him the gay world has made him forget the friends of <u>youth & infancy</u>.

[Separate note]

You need not be apprehensive, I am not at all discouraged by the [torn] in Charleston, a combination of circumstances conspired the last [torn] does not lessen the reputation of Bertrand; more has been won than will cover the unlucky purchase which Graves is asham'd he was the cause of, & the nags were in the way of ours, & one good for nothing Cherokee. Seagul stands high, & the Sorrel has rais'd Virginia's reputation from $10 to $50. the Season, in order to keep the applications off.[13]

[Addressed to]

Fulton SC 10

18 March

M^r. William HB. Richardson

Mail Columbia

So[uth] Carolina

James B. Richardson to William H. B. Richardson, in Columbia,
    So[uth] Carolina
James Ville, 14th April 1825.

My Dear William,

I have not done myself the pleasure to address you a few lines, since mine to you from this place, in which yours of the 22 Ult[imo] the receipt of it is acknowledged. I am truly happy to find by that letter that you are in good health & pursuing your studies with zeal & avidity, & that you were gratified with the feeling I express'd therein. I hope in the mercies of my good God that you may continue to be bless'd with good health, & to be strengthen'd to persevere in the commendable course you have hitherto gone, & long very long, to merit the commendation of your Parents, & society wherever you are known.

Being so long from home & not having an opportunity of send[in]g to the post office, I got yours of the 1 & 15 ult[imo] at the same time, all of which announced your good health at which I rejoice; the one directed to Nelson's Ferry I got at this place no office being there. I did not return from St. Johns with my

13 Horse racing matters.

family untill Monday 4 ins[tan]t I made a longer stay after I went down, than I intended when I wrote you, but I was engaged in my business there, & we were comfortably situated. I found as usual on my return here my business in the planting interest backward, but I am using every effort to advance it, and trust soon to get it comfortable. Altho' I have not written you so frequently as I otherwise should have done, it was principally as I knew you would often receive letters from some one of the family that would inform you of the state of our health. In compliance with my promise of sending up to you after my return home, I now do so, & shall direct the boy to be with you on Friday evening that you may have the benefit of using the horse as you express'd a wish, & as you wanted a good one sent I have sent your horse as he is in fine order, and have directed the Serv[an]t to deliver him so, & you can detain him a day or so, but do not consume too much of your time to reply to all the letters herewith sent you, as it may prevent you from the recreation you contemplate while the horse remains with you. I [am] truly sorry my Dear Son that your fare in Commons is so bad, I know you are one that can support rough fare, & it must be ordinary indeed when you complain of it: I certainly think that the Faculty of the College ought promptly to attend to it, & have it immediately remidied [*sic*], & to report the Steward to the Trustees & have him dismiss'd, or give security for his better fulfillment of his covenant. Your Mother will send you as much as the boy can carry of such things as will be best calculated to go sound, independently of your Summer clothes, which has not been wanted yet from the coolness of the Spring, as there has been but very little warm weather yet, & even now I write it is sufficiently cool to make it comfortable by a fire; but you know I am one that delights in this cool weather, but in consideration of the crops; the corn all up & some cotton. I wish indeed that we were so contiguous to you that we could furnish you with many good things that would be very acceptable to you, but these privations tend to heighten pleasures when we meet them, & it is to the support of them with resignation & patience that makes the merit so great in accomplishing the objects of our pursuit in this life. I notice in one of your letters your intention of forwarding me your oration for my perusal, & that too by mail, by no means do so my William never hazard it by mail for the risk would be too great, independent of the expense for the letter you put under cover, the direction of which was sufficiently good enough they charged thirty cents; besides I hope to see you sufficient time this summer before you will have a call for it; & it will be your own, & I trust I may have the delightfull feelings of the Father of Patrick Henry at his debut in speaking the first time in public. Your letter to one of your Sisters of more recent date than that to me, mentions the Death of Richard's little Daughter; I sympathize with her parents the loss; she was an engaging child. I sincerely hope my Dear William that you will not neglect the opportunity now afforded you to acquire that treasure which will in its consummation enrich you through life, & that you will not be neglectfull in due gratitude to a kind Providence for furnishing you with the means & opportunity of pursuing it, & of the resolution & determination to persevere in the pursuit. The opportunity is so good [torn] that I cannot think of sending you a small addition to your funds as stated below, not that I think that you need it, but it may not be unacceptable. You must put down every sum you receive & learn my Son to economise, & to keep a little by you in case of emergency, & never to be entirely run out. I should have done the same to James[14] but I have not heard a sentence from him, & being surrounded by his connexions, & friends his necessities may be more amply supplied than yours, you need not say any thing respecting it. Adieu my Dear William all unite in love & best wishes to you, several of whom will write you, but [Julia (torn)] & your dear little Richard particularly. Adieu again, D[ea]r Son, & believe me with the most unfeigned affection [blurred]

 Your Sincerely fond & [affectionate]
 Father.
 James B. Richardson

NB. Enclosed I send you herein Twenty Dollars for your use.

[Addressed to]
Mr. William HB. Richardson
Columbia
So[uth] Carolina
Per Serv[van]t Jim on horse with Sundries.

James B. Richardson to William H. B. Richardson, in
 Columbia, So[uth] Carolina
[Probably late April or early May 1825, as there are
 references to events in April.]

[top of first page missing several lines]
the sentiments which I dictated to her, in order to quiet any inquietude that had, or might pervade your bosom, as touching your imputing to yourself the being instrumental in any way to the occurrence; which she did in a letter by mail dated on the 24th ins[tan]t But as soon as I this Evening received your letter of the 20th ins[tan]t informing of the still precarious state of Jim's health and of

14 This is probably John Peter Richardson's son (b. 1806), two years younger than William. In an earlier letter, James B. Richardson mentioned being "a second parent" shortly after the death of his brother in 1811.

the uneasiness within your mind from the groundless impression of your being the cause measurably, by urging that a messenger should be sent to you, which accidently happen'd to be him; I did not hesitate but a few moments, to determine that I would forthwith send up Moses to you, who as well as conveying my communications to you, could satisfy you in many respects verbally, that I had directed him to Say to you; & may tend in addition to what this letter may inform, to calm an uneasiness that you have no cause, imputable to yourself, to suffer for a moment to impress your mind.

It is to be sure unfortunate that Jim should be taken so extremely sick at the particular juncture; at a time when he was intended to gratify his warmest inclination; & at his particular entreaty; & to afford you a partial gratification from his voluminous & entertaining communications. But from all this it does not follow that you or any person whatever could be correctly
[top torn—missing several lines]
but Jim was so exceedingly desirous to go, & plead [*sic*] hard for the indulgence, & enlisted a warm advocate in his behalf, that I felt measurably compel'd to privilege him, & to place Lenn in his stead tho' less expert & usefull at the then occupation than he was. No blame or charge therefore can attach to any. Why then My Son give yourself such uneasiness, more than what would naturally result from feeling for a fellow creature, a valuable Servant, & one extremely fond of you, & warmly attach'd to you & all that you are interested in? but never for a moment suffer uneasiness under the impression that you are in the smallest degree the cause of it. You know very well that I had promised I would send up to you, the time was not identified particularly, & sooner or later I was resolved to do so, for I never violate my promise, if in the event of things I can possibly perform; only give me time, (which I require I must have) & I will do all I can. This event then (or may be worse) may have occurred to any one that I should have sent; consequently give yourself my Dear William not a moments unnecessary anxiety that things are as they are, let Jim want not for the best medical assistance & other attendants & whatever may be wanted; but by no means let it occasion you to neglect your Studies; It is all that can be done, & we can only hope in the mercies of our good God that he may be once again restored, but should it not be his will to indulge us, we must quietly submit; He gave & to him belongs the right to take away. On Moses arrival with you no doubt but the fate of Jim will be decided; if he should be no more, Moses will bring your horse down. I shall enclose some money to defray his keeping; & if Jim should be so that he can come with Moses you will send him; but if he should be better, but yet not able to travel, you may send both horses on with Moses & let Jim remain until he gets able to travel slowly on foot, & from time to time you can [blurred and torn] should [blurred] he should set out. I never distrust the mercies of Providence, his manifestations of kindness have been too abundant for me ever to let go his

comforting Rod & Staff whereby I trust he will strengthen me steadfastly to hold but yet in adverse fortunes I know I must not be exempt & therefore pray his mercy to sustain me under it. This my D[ea]r Son a lesson you must never forget, cherish & inculcate your mind to this discipline, & let it grow with your growth & strengthen with your strength.

I am happy indeed, my Dear William to hear that you [torn] times [torn] &, I pray God to bless you long with that [torn] your [torn] to persevere in the object of your purs[uit] (torn)] the most consummate attainment, & that I may [torn] that I may lift up my hands & heart in thankful [torn] good God that he has vouchsafe[d] to grant the [torn]plications of an Earthly Parent in behalf of the [torn] he hath bless'd him.

It is late at night [torn] the world are hush'd to rest, wrapt in the [torn]nes, to whom ambrosial sweets are indulged by [torn] Mother alone awaits & while I write, the [torn] Adieu my Dear William let not your effort be wanting to meet my expectation, My God I trust will fill your mind with Wisdom, Virtue & understanding, & enable you engagingly to pourtray [sic] it. All unite in love to you, they are well & my health improved. God bless you my D[ea]r Son, give love to James, & believe me very truly Your truly fond & affectionate Father.

James B. Richardson

NB. I enclose you Ten Dollars [torn] physicians bill you must let me kn[ow] [torn] send the money.

[Addressed to]
Mr. William HB. Richardson
Columbia
Per Serv[an]t Moses So[uth] Carolina

CHARLES RICHARDSON TO WILLIAM H. B. RICHARDSON,
  IN SAND HILLS
[WORD ILLEGIBLE] QUARTER—26TH JUNE 1825

Dear William,

It was my intention to request you as you w[oul]d have much time to Ride to my Lotchway plantation as frequently as convenient & overlook my plantation there—

Mr. Ellis has instructions to attend to whatever orders you give him, & give him directions to have shucked & let Dr. Boyd have as much as 50 Bushels of corn, as soon as the crop will admit of it let him turn his attention to clearing up the new ground, I wish to take up the whole of the new ground, but this need only be done when there is no cotton to pick & when it will not interfere with any other Business, I Believe you will readily do this, it will save your father trouble on whom I should otherwise have to impose it—advise with him. My ginn [*sic*] there is in such bad order—that it is my wish not to give any time until my return so that there will be no hindrance in picking Cotton & Peas, let the Peas not interfere with the Cotton—I have informed Dr. Boyd to apply to you for the corn when ever he wants it—I suppose he will wish to have it in the Ear—in that case measure a Barrel well packed & then Shell the Barrel and ascertain what they will contain, you will have to Borrow a Seal half Bushel from some Neighbor— Believe Me

> My Dear William you have My Sincere affection & affc to Uncle
> Charles Richardson

[Addressed to]
Mr. William H. B. Richardson
Sand Hills—
By Ser[van]t John

~

James B. Richardson to William H. B. Richardson,
   in Columbia, So[uth] Carolina
James Ville, Feb[ruar]y 18th. 1826

My Dear William,

How extremely happy was I made by the rec[eip]t of your affectionate letters, the last of which was the 31 ult[imo] by Capt. Spann,[15] in hearing of your continued good health, & of your persevering, & continuing to persevere in the pursuit of your Education, to the entire consummation of it, in both of which, I trust that my good God may bless & strengthen you to the end, & in the acquirement you may have your measure fill'd to overflowing. My devout supplications are daily offered to the throne of divine grace for the benediction on you of its most choice blessings, & that wisdom, virtue, & understanding of the highest order may be pour'd forth on you, & that I may be spared to witness you in the enjoyment of that rich reward for your efforts & perseverance, & disseminating its light & influence to an admiring world; that I may lift up my hands & heart in humble homage to my God that he has vouchsafed to hear & grant the supplication of an earthly Parent in behalf of the offspring wherewith he hath bless'd him. Be assured my Dear Son I look forward to that period with most exquisite delight, & trust my kind Creator will not disappoint those pleasing, & I trust not unreasonable expectations. Not that the calculations & hopes are founded

---

15 Captain John R. Spann was the husband of JBR's daughter, Margaret.

in your transcendent superiority of your contemporaries; that seldom falls to the portion of any one, & ought not to be expected; & I should be ungratefull & unreasonable to look forward to it, but as <u>one</u> is to excell, it may be so, & why not? may be ask'd, Should it not be you; but it is gratification sufficient that you have faithfully perform'd your duty, that you are allways found at your post, like a faithfull Sentinel, persevering & pursuing the course mark'd out for you, & with every possible effort your talents will admit, striving to land in that haven of excellence, that you have held steadfastly in view; & if you have not gain'd the Summit (only indulged to a few, very few) you have moor'd your Bark amidst the best, & with the throng, & the multitude will always hail you with their kindest greeting. It was my intention my Dear William to have written you earlier than this, but after receiving your letter by Jim, I entertained some intentions of sending up to you, & that measurably stayed one from writing; & really one occurrence or other, so repeatedly intruded on me, that I have delayed so long from executing my intention of sending to you, so that between the two causes you have been thus long prevented from receiving a letter from me; Indeed I have been more harrass'd & perplex'd in having so much of my time consumed by the almost daily application of persons either to sell me property or borrow money; some of whom you would little expect; it does in point of perplexity appear to differ but little in having some money that you might loan, & the country around in want; & that of wanting it yourself. One may have no money & yet be in no immediate want of it, having quieted all demands for the time: But depend upon it to want, & to have no way to procure it, presents a bitter torture in this life. I have allways implored my good God to bless my humble efforts & crown them with success, and to enable me to shape my wants & expenditures to my means, & forever to preserve me in this world, (& hereafter if Man has any scope to reign) from the grip[p]ing oppression of [word unclear] hand, more terrific to me than the roaring Lion of the forest. You may be assured that money is indeed a very scarce article here in our district, & he that is known to have it, has but little peace from their overpressing solicitations. I shall leave this my <u>Home, Sweet Home</u> in a few hours for New Belvedere [*sic*] on my way to Charleston. I have thus long been delay'd by unavoidable preventives, as I ought to have gone a few days earlier, to examine my business in St. John's, where your Mother & the boys at School there, will remain to await my return; & your Sisters Hermione & Matilda, with my dear little Julia (to be place[d] with Miss Dolly) are to accompany me on to Ch[arle]ston, & from there you will here [*sic*] from me. [T]his letter I shall send you from Belvedere [*sic*] by a messenger conveying you some Supplies that I trust may not be unacceptable. I have thought it could not be uninteresting to you to know our excursion & the arrangements of it; that in imagination you may paint the pleasing enjoyment of another annual visit by the goodness & permission of my God, when you will be with us to adorn our society, the pride & glory of admiring Parents, beholding & adoring you as the brightest Gem in the constellation which our group shall constitute.

I have had the misfortune to have my mills burnt down with all their contents, not a Single article saved out of them, & by the carelessness of my Miller (who I have not yet touch'd) he made fire in the cellar of the Grist Mill, & when he came to the house in the morn[in]g he left it there; & between 10 & 11 o['] clock a.m. on the 31stJan'y it was discovered from the House here, before he got back, to be in a blaze of fire. I hasten'd there [with] all my force of hands but not the least thing could be Saved; my loss I estimate about 3000 Dollars, yet I thank my God it was nothing more vital. I shall be soon at rebuilding them again by this workman Mellett.

I could not rest satisfied without writing you [prior] to my leaving home, & not resting well, I have arisen to [torn] all around (& perhaps the world who are not distress'd) are wrap[ped in] the arms of Somnus overpowered with his drowsy potion, while I alone am awake devoting my sleepless moments to sweet communication with my Dear William, who doubtless too is reposing Sweetly, & perchance, kind Morpheus may in goodness be pouring in Some delightfull dreams from his abundant treasure—to please the wing'd imagination, & bring a Father to his view employed for him in some kind & pleasing office for his Dear Boy. Adieu my Dear William the clock has just announc'd to me that [it] is 5 o['] clock a.m. & the joyous sound of the Drivers Bugle is resounding to summon the workmen to their labor; to rouse the drown[ed], & stimulate the industrious. All the family offer you their love & best wishes. Remember me often, & hold the regard of all good measures for yourself, & you will not fail. God bless my Son, & believe me with the most unfeigned affection.

Your Sincerely fond Father

James B. Richardson.

NB. I send enclosed Twenty Dollars it may be acceptable to you, tho' I know you econom[ize] well.

[Addressed to]
Mr. William H. B. Richardson
Columbia
So[uth] Carolina
Per Serv[an]tLen on horse with sundries.

~

James B. Richardson to William H. B. Richardson,
  in Columbia, So[uth] Carolina
Col. J^N. R. Spann's, Sun[day] n[igh]t 12 Mar 1826

My Dear William,

On my way to this place today going on to Sumter Court, I was informed by
John P. Richardson who I met at Church which I took on my way up, that he
was going to Columbia on Tomorrow or Tuesday & would convey to you any
commands that I might have to convey to you: So direct an opportunity I could
not suffer to escape unattended to, & particularly to acknowledge the rec[eip]t
of your affectionate letter rec[eive]d by Me yesterday, & which I forwarded on to
your good Mother, who I left on Thursday last with the family at New Belvedere
[*sic*] all in good health, & who I know would be anxious to hear from you. In
your letter by Mr. J[oh]n I. Moore[16] you requested me when in Charleston to get
you a Six key'd Flute (yellow)[.] So moderate a request from So dutiful & affectionate Son you could not but believe I would comply with & with the utmost
gratification; consequently I got your young friend Mr. Mortimer to select it for
you, & he made choice of the one herewith sent at $25. & assures me that he
thinks it an excellent tone'd one, & that he is of opinion it will please you; I wish
it may be so. You mentioned slightly that you had received my letter addressed
you from Charleston, I assure you it was address'd you in great hurry, & as too
much the case with me in that place, almost always hurried & perplex'd, I wrote
you very unsatisfactory to myself, but in my letter from Belvedere [*sic*] by Peter,
I promis'd to write you the result of our Races, I felt myself under obligation to
do so, however imperfect. I suppose you have seen the detail'd acc[oun]ts of the
sports of the Turf in Charleston through the Papers; they were indeed splendid,
Such through the whole as perhaps have never before been manifested on that
or any other ground, & may never happen again, or for twenty years to come. I
send you herewith two papers containing the acc[oun]ts of Friday & Saturday's
racing that of Sea Gull & Bertrand the most interesting, & in which both have
evinced their superior excellence, & have more than fullfill'd the high expectations entertained of them; particularly Bertrand[17] who came out this Winter in
such miserable condition as to induce the best judges to predict him unable with
every care to make more than one saving race. Strange to tell how much betting
was going on the Turf, altho' the scarcity of money was never more evidently seen
& felt than at the present time, & never was property selling lower than while I
was in Charleston, great sacrifices of property were making, & greater still I am

---

16 John Isham Moore was married to JBR's daughter Hermione.
17 Bertrand was a horse owned by JBR's son-in-law John Spann.

confident must be made as cotton of the short staple was selling so low, & no prospect of doing better; the Sea Island sells freely & well some has sold as high as 92/100 great indeed, & the Santee's Roll'd + 30/100 to 40/100 which is well, & the short only at 10/100 to 12/100. I have not yet sold a Bale, & my long I have roll'd out, So that I am in hopes I may bear up yet with the times yet, but I have made one pretty considerable purchase in Charleston, & am in treaty for one or two more, but truly I am cautious, for you may be assured my Dear William that it beho[o]ves every one that has a little money at this time, to economize it with the utmost frugality, for the distress around us here & in Charleston I do not recollect to have ever seen greater, & the scarcity of provision is equal to that of the scarcity of money. It is unnecessary to descend to particulars, the thing is general.

I hope my Dear Son that you continue to enjoy good health, & feel the firmest determination to persevere in your laudable pursuit of literature, in which I trust my good God will bless you & enable you to effect to your honor, & the high gratification of your affectionate Father. I have before me much to do in the present year if it pleases my good & mercifull God to preserve my health & enable me to effect it, & which is not improper I should forward to, & trust in him for its accomplishment. I write you late at night, & shall be off by Seven O['] Cl[oc]k in the morn[in]g. it is now half past 12 O[']Cl[oc]k. I was requested by my At[tor]n[e]ys to be very early at Court tomorrow.

Adieu my Dear William you cannot desire more to see me than I long to see you, but all our privation, my God I trust, will make redound hereafter to our tenfold gratifications in the rich results from your labors, attention, & perseverance. Adieu again my Son, God bless you abundantly with his most choice benedictions, are the devout orisons of your truly fond & affectionate Father.

James B. Richardson.

My hurry warrants me to offer you no further apology for the incoherence of the Scribe. Remember me affectionately to James & Thomas.

[Addressed to]
Mr. William H. B. Richardson
Columbia
S°. Carolina

[Addressed to]
Mr. William H. B. Richardson
Columbia
So[uth] Carolina
Post care of Capt. Richardson with a mule bundle

~

James B. Richardson to William H. B. Richardson,
in Charleston, So[uth] Carolina
St. John's, Belvedere [*sic*], March 28:th 1827

My Dear William,

I did myself the pleasure to write you yesterday to the care of Mrs. Flud which
I calculated you would receive before this could possibly reach you; but contrary
to my expectation she will not leave this before tomorrow, as they were committed to her care, I will not retract it & no doubt will be sent you so soon as she
arrives in Town. This opportunity however occurring so direct I cannot omit to
embrace it in addressing you a few lines, expressing my hope that it may find you
& my little Julia in good health, which I sincerely hope my good God may long
continue to bless you both with, & to enable you both with zeal & avidity to
persevere in your Studies, you in particular my Dear Son whose time is so much
more important from a variety of causes, & as such that your engagements may
be pursued with redoubled Solicitude, that you may as early as possible attain
the achme [*sic*] of your Scientific pursuit; that you may return to your family
& abode, a treasure fill'd with richest fruits, to deseminate [*sic*] for the benefit
of all which falls within its influence, to the admiration & astonishment of an
admiring and marveling world. To be bles'd in the indulgence of living to witness
all these fond anticipations reallized [*sic*] would indeed my Dear William be to
me an intellectual banquet rich & va[l]uable almost beyond comparing, & but
for that promised enjoyment, that high & inestimable treasure both to you &
me, would I have willingly foregone all the privations I have in the enjoyment of
your Society, and the aid in your Services. I flatter myself with your unremitting
exertions that you may be enabled to accomplish the object of your pursuit in the
time that we contemplated, could it be so effected it would be beyond measure
gratifying, & suffer me to impress upon your mind the necessity of holding constantly in view the attainment of that object; but should the period be shorter or
longer let the object be affectually obtain'd, that you may hold up to the world
a Success burning with a with a [*sic*] light of most brilliant lustre, not only to
illumine the portals of your own house, but of all connected with it, or that may
come within its vortex.

In your next mention if you have met with Mr. Rob[er]t James, & how he
seems dispos'd to you, & if you deem his pursuit in any Study calculated to
redound to his importance or advantage: you will no doubt cultivate friendly intercourse with him as you have hitherto done at College; coming from the same
neighborhood, & where it is likely you may have future intercourse in life, it
would be well to do so. Some little time hence I may give Mr. Andrew McDowall
an order on you for the payment of his acc[oun]t which I neglected to pay when

in Charleston of ab[ou]t $81. but of the order from Mr. J[oh]n Frierson, but this will depend on circumstances. I am sure my D[ea]r William I need not urge you to care & economy in your pecuniary matters, your own Judgment will dictate to you the difficulty of the times, & the necessity of care & good management of finances. Did you leave a little acc[oun]t & Note with Isaac Lyons of Columbia, if you did let me know & I will have it immediately adjusted. I trust you will never be unmindfull in thanks, & adoration to a kind Creator for all his mercies to you & particularly of the present opportunity he affords you of acquirement, & to supplicate devoutly the continuance of his blessings; no pressure of business ou[gh]t to interfere to prevent you from it; a little earlier rising, or a proper economy of time will always afford you the opportunity. I expect to be down in town this Spring, & I should rather it be about the time of your coming up, that I may have the company of you & Julia than before, if I can possibly make it suit me, but that will much depend how I get on with my Domestic business which at this time is considerable from the various sorts & avocations. Give my love to my dear little Julia & tell her to be dutifull & learn fast, that she may be a blessing to us all, in which your good Mother & all adjoins me, & in the same to you, & our best respects & remembrance to Mr. & Mrs. Phelon.[18] Adieu my Dear my beloved William, my my [*sic*] good God of his infinite mercy [sh]ower on you his most choice benedictions, and give you peace & con[ten]t, Wisdom virtue & understanding, & firmness & perseverance through this life, and supplications most devoutly offered for you. God bless you my dear William and believe me Sincerely

Your fond & very affectionate Father.

James B. Richardson.

NB. The Bedstead you got for your Sister Dorothy is not mahogany, & the price high, enquire of the man if he would take it back, & give a mahogany in lieu at the difference of price. Your Uncle Charles has sent Cicero down, but as he has not written to me I know not for what he has sent. Adieu again my Son.

Mr. William H. B. Richardson

Charleston

[Addressed to]
Mr. William H. B. Richardson
Charleston
So[uth] Carolina
Per Serv[an]t Cicero

18 William H. B. and Julia (b. 1813) may have been boarding with the Phelons.

James B. Richardson to William H. B. Richardson,
    in Charleston, So[uth] Carolina
St. John's, New Belvedere [*sic*], 2 Ap[ri]l 1827

My Dear William,

I have duly received your very affectionate letter of the 31 Ult[imo] by Cicero
in reply to mine by him & was truly happy to find that you & your Sister Julia
was [*sic*] in the enjoyment of good health which being the object of first importance, always engages my attention first; and which always have my best &
daily orisons, that my good & merciful God will long continue the inestimable
blessing to you, that you may not only be enabled to pursue your Studies to
advantage but to enjoy the blessings of life. I assure you my Dear Son I have experienced exceeding concern at that paragraph of your letter that conveys to me
your fears & regret to find, that I have any fears inhabiting my Bosom respecting
your prudence & propriety of conduct in any respect; I defy you to point out
any thing in my letters to you, or any thing that I maybe ever said to you that
evinces any thing like my want of the most entire trust & confidence in you; in
not only one, but every respect. On the contrary, I have both in my personal dec-
larations & my writings to you, express'd it to you in the most full & unequivocal
terms, why therefore you should harrow my mind with the reiteration of your
groundless fears, is to me most astonishing? I feel well aware that you cannot feel
the least gratification in adding one Scruples weight of uneasiness or inquietude
to my mind; indeed, I know you would delight in the kind office to relieve it of
any burthen that would oppress it; and yet my Son, you know not how much
such expressions of groundless fears, disturbs my quiet. If it were express'd to me
when with you, or near to you, when I could give a prompt refutation to it, then
it might not be to me a matter of such magnitude; but when a distance divides
us, & no immediate conveyance existing whereby your mind, as well as my own
could be relieved directly, it makes me unhappy to think you had misconceived
any thing said, not intended by me in a general caution given you of prudence &
propriety &c, & I feel that you would experience anxiety, hastily to relieve one
in what you may have intended as an assurance of your due observance of these
valuable qualities; by charging me with entertaining any distrust distrust [*sic*]
of your duly & properly appreciating them. I shall therefore console myself my
Dear William with the hope that you could never have intended to give me any
uneasiness by the representation of your "fear & regret" and pray you once for
all, never to question my entire confidence in your good conduct, your prudence,
economy & care in the most general acceptation [*sic*] of the terms, for I feel well
assured, that if ever a Father has given testimony of it to a Son, I have given proof
of it to you my Son; & you rightfully have no cause to charge me (a Father of

whom uniform kindness you can vouch for) with any expression of the want of confidence in you, & I trust you will never urge to me any more, the belief of impressions on my mind, that I do not expressly convey to you; for you have just cause to indulge in your vanity if such you term'd it, that you do stand preeminently high in my estimation, & that you have always given me cause to have the highest confidence in you, & to love you, the more if possible for it. I will therefore desist from dwelling longer on a subject, which is uncomfortable, & which has already occupied too large a portion of my paper & time; I trust will not arise again; for as your confidence is great in me (which I hope) so always regard mine to reciprocate in the same with you; I feel that conscious rectitude of having never done any thing to forfeit it, and you must feel always secure in the full possession of it. Your letter I received at Belvedere [*sic*] where I have been detained longer than I calculated; & the bad weather detain'd me when I was ready to depart; but my Visit there is always some relaxation from that over pressure of care that I have at home; that when my business there will permit, I do sometimes indulge myself in a little longer Stay; & I therefore devote a part of this day in writing you as the day is so wet & prevented me from going up as I fully intended. I shall go the first day that is good, & will Send this letter next day to the Post Office that you may receive it as early as possible, if no safe opportunity occurs from here. Your enquiries about your House in a former letter, I did not from my then hurry to reply to, but it goes on very well; it is all framed and I intend to raise it immediately as I go up, by which time the Sashes & Doors & Window frames, & the material to enclose it in, will be all ready I expect as I left the workmen all at that, & they mentioned to me by letter, all is going on well. So Soon as I get up I will expedite every thing with all efforts, & you may be well assured that every thing shall be done to forward it, & by the time you address [the] Courts of Equity & Pleas, it may I hope be ready to greet your friends in. Your Horses too shall be carefully attended to. God I hope will grant us health my Son, & in his mercy permit us to live to enjoy the realization of all the blessings we share & hold by anticipation; which health I humbly thank my Creator my Dear family here participated, & myself in tolerable enjoyment of it, & I trust soon to be better & to enjoy more of it.

Adieu my Dear William may peace & happiness by yours; you [torn] believe it most sincere. You may not now see with all the [torn]cuity you may hereafter see; but the time may come when [torn] see & feel, that him who you now call as Father, you will [torn] to honour with the appellation as the most distinguished & exemplary of Fathers. Adieu again my Dear William; God bless you & my Julia; remember us with tenderest affection;

And believe me my beloved Son,

Your very fond & devoted Father.

James B. Richardson.

Home.

Friday Morn[in]g 6th March[19] 1827

This will inform my D[ea]r William that I have with my family arrived safe last night at our D[ea]r Home & in our usual good health, & I hasten this to the office that you may get as early tidings of us as possible; for no mail going by Nelson's ferry, there is no opportunity from thence, but by private conveyance, to there from here, or from there to Town. Your Sister Dorothy would remain, tho' alone & goes Monday next to see Mrs. Waring. I trust you will write us occasionally as your time will admit, at least once a week, to mention yours & Julia's health, & you will hear from us, some or other every week. Our united love to you & My little Julia & best regards to the Col. & Mrs. Phelon, & believe my D[ea]r Wm.

I am Y[ou]r Sincerely affectionate Father

James B. Richardson

NB. I hope to receive a letter from you on the return of the boy from the office.

[Addressed to]

Fulton S°Car 12 1/2

9 April

Mr. William H. B. Richardson

Charleston

So[uth] Carolina

Mail

JAMES B. RICHARDSON TO WILLIAM H. B. RICHARDSON, IN CHARLESTON
ST. JOHN'S, APR[IL] 9 1828

My Dear William,

I just received your truly affectionate letter of the 1st ins[stan]t by Mail on Saturday last, at the moment of my leaving Home for this place; too late for me to acknowledge the rec[eip]t by the succeeding mail, or it would have delayed my departure to such a protracted period as to have made my travel down very late at night; as it was, having so much to do at all times just at the eve of starting, that my arrival here was late, & I traveled with the greatest rapidity. I am happy indeed my Dear Son to hear of the good health of yourself & my dear little children, & of the contentment they manifest with their situation, & the readiness to pursue their little studies; I trust that they (the Boys) have commenced with

19 Apparently, he meant April. A perpetual calendar indicates that Friday was April 6.

lattin [*sic*], if not, I must get you to use your influence with their Teacher to put them immediately at it, that when they come up for the Summer they may have some of the principles laid down, which will enable them to pursue it. I have the gratification to state that I found your Dear Mother & Sisters & all well at my return here, after an absence longer than usual on my annual visit up to my lovely Home, & thank God I have returned to them in better health than I left them; & truly my Son it is to be marvell'd at, somewhat; when I assure you of the innumerable calls & variegated cares that continually assail'd me, & the perplexities I encountered with numerous visitors, many intrusive, & but a few desirable, there was not a day but this was the case. I live in the sweet hope that the blessings of a kind Providence will await us respectively in our divided situation, & bless us in our several pursuits, & bring us all together in health & happiness at our appointed time, and afford us that enjoyment which we anticipate from each other, at our joyfull interchange of wellcome greeting. While I was up I rais'd the Grist Mill House, & had the satisfaction of seeing the saw mill work very well, tho She has not near a Sufficient head of water, as I was afraid to let them venture the Dam too much yet, but it cut all the frame & plank for the Grist mill house, & it was at work long before I went up; I think I will derive some of its benefit when I go up. I found Mr. Shiver had done the Scroll to the Stair case, after the manner I suggested to him, & confess'd he never had made one before, & but for the idea given, he does not believe he would have affected it; He has gone up to the first flight, & put the balisters [*sic*] & brackets to it very handsomely; He was rejoiced to see me, & see me approving it, & all the <u>little</u> <u>occurrences</u> previous to leaving home were buried in oblivion, without ever an expression of it having ever occurred; & owing much to an event which when I see you I may relate, that took place the very evening of my arrival at home. The busy time of plant[in]g with me, above prevented the giving any additional work to the Mill Dam, or I could have tested the performance of the saw, however I was not very desirous to try it, as time is sufficient when done. This exceeding cold weather has destroyed all my Cotton that was up down here, which was planted on the 28 ult[imo] the day I began down here & continued on; I must have lost 300 acres, & yesterday finished planting that much over. Above I was rather more backward in planting Cotton that there was none up; the Corn was all beautifully up but the Frost laid it level to the earth, but I trust the roots are not destroyed, & if not it will revive & come good again. I am glad my Dear William to find that you afford me assurances of your perseverance in your studies, God of his mercy bless you with Wisdom virtue & understanding, & enable you to accomplish the object of your pursuit, [torn] you with me, sharing in the duties that devolves up [torn] now regarded with the Eye of admiration by all [torn] expectations are entertained of you, very far beyo[nd] [torn] God of his infinite mercy grant the realization [torn] full extent, & that I may be permitted to live to [torn] my Dear

William be tenderly kind to my little ones [torn] youngest & most need care, he is the Joseph of my [torn] but feel beyond the power of expression. Tell R[torn] & good to him, & for him & Richard to be brother [torn] other, & both to try & excel in their goodness & [torn] Julia. Adieu my beloved Son, make my [torn] to Mrs. & Col. Phelon & my love & a fond embr[ace] [torn] [chil]dren, & two for my dear Richard. Adieu again [torn] bless you all, & believe me very sincerely [torn]

Your fond & affe[ctionate] [torn]
James B. [Richardson]

NB. The Boat has arrived safe here on this day week; I have taken out what is to remain here, & will send her on in [torn] box of lamps is safe, & the marble mantle's. Mr. Ki[torn] his Harness is not come, in mine or Mr. Moores Boat [torn] by first opp[ortunit]y. I am glad you did not exchange [torn]ence was great; I have got in trade a good Saddle & [torn] could not well accept [torn] Your Mother & S[isters] [torn] & best wishes to you & the little ones, & a fond kiss for them. You forgot my Dear William to send me up by Jim the Phials of Quirk spence of tyre[20] for which I gave you the $5. bill; you may however send it up here after by some very safe opp[ortunit]y. Soon as I hear that all my cotton is sold, I will trip down for a few days & see you all. I trust the long Rollered will bring 20/100 & the long saw'd 13 at 14 Cts & the short 11 at 12 Cts per lb.

[Addressed to]
Vances Ferry
William H. B. Richardson Esq.
Charleston
So[uth] Carolina
Mail.

20 "Phials" is obviously a variant spelling of vials or small containers. "Quirk" is likely a brand, and "spence of tyre" probably a medication. James B. Richardson had numerous health issues in later life.

Belvidere house, believed to have been built about 1800. Photo by Edwin Green. Courtesy of the South Caroliniana Library, University of South Carolina, Columbia, SC.

Belvidere: view of the front yard from the porch. Photo by Edwin Green. Courtesy of the South Caroliniana Library, University of South Carolina, Columbia, SC.

Chapter 5

The Twilight Years

Throughout his adult life, James Burchell Richardson seems to have dealt with periodic health issues ranging from toothache to blindness. This was especially so from the 1820s and frequently required his wife, Ann, to write his letters. Considering the volume of his correspondence, and the customary length of many of his letters, this was no small undertaking, and his less-frequent letters recognize this. In an August 1824 letter to her brother, William Sinkler, Ann described her husband's "extreme debility," noting that he was "a day or two better," then "scarcely walk[ed] out," and "at times he [could not] sit up." In a letter JBR wrote in 1833 to his daughter-in-law, Margaret, thanking her for a vest she had made for him, he referred to his "seclusion from the World."

This vacillation is evident in his July 1834 decision to decline William Sinkler's invitation to accompany him to White Sulphur Springs, Virginia. Later, in May 1835, he wrote WS that his "prospects [were] so precarious ever to live to see you again." Then, in August he said, "Death would be infinitely preferable to such a state of existence [total blindness]." In the same letter, he professed to "meddle but little in my Domestic affairs," yet claimed that "but for my impaired sight, I could fish, Hunt & fowl it <u>almost</u> as well as ever I did."

Despite this, James B. Richardson seems to have retained his interest in horses: a note added to a June 1826 letter mentions breeding details, and in one of his last letters, in 1835, he claimed to be still interested in horse racing. His enthusiasm for politics also appears to have remained strong, as a July 1830 letter states that he was "adversed [sic] to disunion or nullification."

In a letter of April 22, 1823, Ann Richardson thanked her brother for visiting "my Dear Dolly" every day. This obviously refers to their oldest daughter, Dorothy Mitchell, who had been widowed since 1814. She appears to have been living at Belvidere Plantation, just across Eutaw Creek from her uncle William Sinkler.

ACSR expressed concern about her adjustment to living alone after having been among a large family.

Letters of this period include one to WS from his younger sister, Anna, describing the difficulty of a trip home (near Ft. Motte), probably returning from a visit to Eutaw. Another, from John Peter Richardson's daughter, Camilla, invites him and Eliza to dinner at her parents' home. An 1824 letter from JBR's daughter, Margaret, invites her uncle William to her private wedding to Captain John Spann. It is unclear why it was a small home wedding, but she was quite urgent in wanting WS in attendance.

William Sinkler's wife, Eliza, died on June 3, 1824. His sister, Ann, wrote him a long letter commiserating with him over his loss, stating that "such a Wife and such a Mother is rare to be found" but urging him to put his trust in God to provide him strength to endure.

Eliza's mother, Mary Deas Broün (1762–1857), lived in Charleston, and appears to have made a major contribution toward raising the five children, the oldest of whom was thirteen when their mother died. Mary wrote William a beautiful letter on January 12, 1825, expressing concern that he was not sufficiently careful of his own health, especially as his "five little Children depend on you for advice & protection." While expressing her own "humble resignation" to the loss of her daughter, she begged her son-in-law to consider that Eliza would probably have wished him "to lament her but not to grieve immoderately."

This same letter mentions the "landing" of William's oldest son, James, who appears to have been away at school. A letter to WS from Charles Richardson on December 27, 1825, describes his having visited James at his school, evidently in Middletown, Connecticut. After some difficulty establishing his family connection, CR received a report describing James as having "conducted himself in every respect attentively to his avocations & his deportment was honorable & gentlemanly."

Many of James B. Richardson's letters include instructions for his oldest son, William H. B., which suggest that he was assuming duties of managing the property. Letters to William Sinkler in 1826 and 1829 include requests regarding the purchase and exchange of carriages. The 1826 letter includes JBR's thanks to WS for having written a letter to his youngest son, Richard, who was ten, noting that it was the first letter that Richard had ever received.

James B. Richardson died on April 28, 1836. A letter that Eliza Sinkler, fourteen, wrote to her brother Seaman Deas Sinkler says that their father (WS) was with him when he died. A brief listing appeared in the *Charleston Observer* in the June 11 issue: "Died on the 28th April, at his residence in Clarendon, Col. James B. Richardson, formerly Governor of this state."[1]

1 Brent H. Holcomb, *Marriage and Death Notices from the Charleston Observer, 1827–1845* (Greenville, S.C.: A Press, 1980), 112.

James B. Richardson
portrait. Copy courtesy
of the South Carolina
Department of Archives
and History.

CAMILLA F. RICHARDSON[2] TO MR. WILLIAM SINKLER AT [PROBABLY EUTAW]
CLARENDON, 19TH MARCH—1822

Dear Cousin

Mama requests the pleasure of your, & Cousin Eliza's Company on Tuesday
evening the 26th also with that of your family. We request you will not deny us,
the gratification of your presence for the pleasure of seeing yourself & family
here, we have long fondly Anticipated—Mama had desired me to say, that she
has taken the liberty of enclosing to your care, a letter for Mrs. Thomson, which
she begs of you, as a favour, to forward to her, as soon as you can conveniently.
Mama & family joins me in love to yourself & Cousin Eliza, A kiss from me for
the little Belle, and my remembrance to Miss Brown. Accept the assurance of
affectionate regard,

2 Camilla (1798–1866) was the daughter of John Peter and Floride Peyre Richardson.
Mrs. Thomson would have been WS's younger sister, Margaret Anna, who married John
Linton Thomson.

And love, from your Cousin—
Camilla F. Richardson

[Addressed to]
Mr. William Sinkler
Springfield
P. Servant St. Johns

MARGARET ANNA THOMSON TO WILLIAM SINKLER [PROBABLY AT EUTAW]
[PROBABLY BELLEVILLE, NEAR FT. MOTTE,] MARCH 27, 1822

My Dear Brother

I received your affectionate [letter] By Colidore and was happy to find that You were all well. I cannot say our Ride up was very pleasant finding The Road very bad, and what made [it] worst when We got at the Creek near our house found it so high that We had to walk over the Mill Dam and send the carriage around[;] the Boat never arrived untill late Saturday Evening and unfortunately lost a little Meigro[3] on the way.

We had not heard of Betsey going To be Married previous to your letter: but cannot say I was much astonished[.] Mr. Thomson begs to be remember'd and

Margaret Anna Sinkler Thomson and her daughter, Anna Linton Thomson. After Margaret's death in 1829, Anna was raised by her uncle, William Sinkler. Courtesy of the South Caroliniana Library, University of South Carolina, Columbia, SC.

3 This is clearly the spelling in the letter, but she undoubtedly meant "Negro."

Says he is indeed very busy but expects To be Down the 10 of April on his way To Town, my love to Eliza and kiss the Children For me. And believe me Dear Brother your Fond and affectionate Sister. M A T

I must beg you to excuse my detaining Colidore a couple of Days but really the Things from the Boat was so completely Wet and had been in that stat[e] so long that it required a great many to unpa[ck] in order to save them. Again adieu and Believe me your fond

Sister Anna Thomson

[Addressed to]
Mr. William Sinkler
St. Johns

ANN C. RICHARDSON TO MR. WILLIAM SINKLER AT SPRINGFIELD
APRIL 22, 1823

My Dear William,

I have only time to write you a few hurried lines to let you know we are all quite well and sincerely hope yourself my Dear Eliza[,] Miss Broün[4] and Dear Children are in the enjoyment of the same blessing[.] You cannot think my Brother how much I miss your society and your kind attention with that of my Dear Eliza will ever be remember'd by me with gratitude I often reflect with much pleasure of yours and my Dear Eliza's goodness and unremitted kindness and attention to me and mine, what a blessing to have such Freinds [*sic*] I hope my Dear Brother you will not delay too long in performing your promise in coming to see us. I did fondly hope I should have had the pleasure of seein[g] Eliza Miss B and your Dear Children at this habitation for a few days this Spring which would give me much happiness indeed. I trust in my God that we shall all meet in the winter in health and happiness when I shall then hope to see you all here. I thank you most truly for your attention to my Dear Dolly[5] in visiting her every day how kind it is in you my Brother she must pass a lonesome time of it more so after having so large a family with her I know she has great resolution

4 Miss Broün probably refers to one of (WS's wife) Eliza's two younger sisters, Mary Deas or Harriet Broün.

5 Family records and the tombstone transcription indicate that James B. and Ann Richardson's oldest daughter, Dorothy Sinkler Richardson (Mitchell), died in 1820 and had only one son. It should be noted, however, that "0" and "8" can easily be confused, especially on worn tombstones. However, JBR's 1826 will leaves to her Belvidere plantation, "where she now resides containing Two hundred acres more or less, & for which I have given her a Deed of Gift." She was not named in her mother's 1845 will, which suggests that

and she amuses herself much with her domestic concerns, but she feels her lonely situation I well know, it is impossible to tell what I feel for her. I pray my God to be with her[.] My beloved Husband and the Girls beg their affectionate love to you and Eliza, to whom I beg you will say all an affectionate heart can dictate[.] Kiss all your Dear Children for me my William and Miss Sinkler give many adieu me [*sic*] Dear Brother believe me always

    your Affectionate Sister

    Ann C Richardson

    Your friend has sent you two hams two gammons[6] and [scratched out] when you eat them think of him the old hams are only for you to see how good they keep[.] Tell Eliza I have sent a few preserved Peachs [*sic*] Cherris [*sic*] and a few Mangoes[7] I don't know if they are good.

[Addressed to]
Mr. William Sinkler
Spring Field
By Boat

[SCHS 73-VI-19]
ANN C. RICHARDSON TO MR. WILLIAM SINKLER [IN CHARLESTON]
FULTON, SC, AUGUST 26, 1824

My Dear Brother,

    I have just now sat down to acknowledge the receipt of your very affectionate letter of the 15th and to return you my grateful thanks for your goodness in sending the articles up for me, indeed you are very kind to me my Dear William I received them safe and they arrived in good time. I have just this moment I [*sic*] received your letter of the 24 and am truly sorry to hear your children has [*sic*] that dreadful disease the Hooping [*sic*] Cough it is dreadful indeed when you have so many to take it, but I trust through the mercies of divine Providence they will all have it favorable and soon be over it. I have indeed been very anxious to hear from you feeling much uneasiness about the yellow fever and thank you kindly for writing to me, for I have not deserved it. Indeed my Dear Brother I

---

she had probably died prior to that. James Sinkler's 1798 will had left Belvidere to William Sinkler when he became twenty-one, and Margaret Sinkler's will, proved January 16, 1822, left Belvidere to William Sinkler's oldest son, James.

    6 Gammon is a special cut of ham.

    7 It seems doubtful that they would have grown mangoes; this name was sometimes used for what are now known as bell peppers, which seems more likely.

feel very much for you I know the loss you have met with[8] and I do most truly sympathize with you, but you must recollect from whom you received the blow and as much as mortal can bow with submission, and endeavor to support with Christian fortitude the will of your Creator. He alone can support you in your heavy affliction it is him alone can strengthen you in your trouble such a Child such a Wife and such a Mother is rare to be found, but my Dear William you must indeed exert yourself and be resigned to your fate you have many claims that demand your exertions, and I trust and hope will do so, would to God you were with us I really long to see you that I might use my feeble efforts to comfort and console you. I am thankful to my God you are with such friends who I know are kind and attentive to you and I hope and trust time the elleviater [*sic*] of all troubles will calm and compose you and give you peace and comfort which I do ardently offer up my feeble prayer to the Throne of mercy for you. It is with much [blurred] my Brother I inform you my beloved Husband is still extremely poorly. Indeed my fears are greatly awaken'd about him he is more reduced than I have ever seen him, he is a day or two better and then he is so weak and overcome at times he cannot sit up not much fever but extreme debility and no appetite and his spirits very low[;] he has never been to the Plantation but once and scarcely walks out he rides out morning and evening which I think is of much service to him but he does not recover or gain strength. I am wretched about him, my William but I endeavor as much as possible to conceal it from him. I never leave him one moment if I can avoid it, I really do not know what to think of the extreme debility, he has taken several tonics but none seems to benefit him long. I recollect when Doctor McBride attended him in 1809 he gave him some drops which he said was the tincture of Iron they were of infinite service to him there is no one here can prepare such I think they would do him good now he desires me to say to you he would have long since written to you but he is really so poorly he cannot, he begs his affectionate love to you and says so [*sic*] soon as he possibly can he will write to you. Dorothy the girls and William send their love to you also my Julia Richardson and Richard who beg their love to all their cousins do give my love to Marg and Deas I thank them for their remembrance of me. Kiss your Dear Children for me do not let them forget me. I hope and trust they will soon be over that dredful [*sic*] Hooping Cough, adieu my beloved Brother believe me always.

Your fond and affectionate Sister

Ann C. Richardson

8 William's wife, Eliza, died on June 3, 1824, at age forty. The mention by ACSR of WS's "uneasiness" regarding yellow fever suggests the possibility that this was the cause of her death.

We are obliged to send our letters to the office now. If you have heard from my Sister do let me know how she and her family are and give my affectionate love to her when you write her.

[Addressed to]
Fulton S.C⁹ 12½
26 Aug.
Mr. William Sinkler.
Charleston.
Mail.

Margaret Cantey Richardson[10] to William Sinkler in Charleston
Calm Delight, December 5th. 1824

If no unforeseen accident intervenes—My Dear Uncle—your Niece, will change her situation—and as you possess a great share of my affection—I fervently wish to have the pleasure of your company on the 21st of December. The celebration of my Nuptials will be very private none but my most particular friends—and as such My Uncle—I have ever viewed you—and believe you warmly interested, in my welfare and happiness, it is a satisfaction to have those we love with us at al-times [*sic*]—particularly at that period—the most important of my life. You must not doubt my affection for you. I have always look[ed] upon you—in the light of a Brother, I have been much with you in the early part of my life and affections form'd then are not easily eradicated—this salutation you cannot Dear Uncle, deny—if you have any regard for your ever warm and very affectionate Niece
    Margaret C. Richardson

    PS. kiss My Dear little Cousins for me—I long to see them—and My Uncle, too

[Addressed to]
Mr. William Sinkler
By Mail Charleston

9 Louise Simons Richardson's 1938 "History of Pinewood, South Carolina" notes that before Pinewood was established, mail was handled by the Fulton Post Office, initially once a week, then twice a week. Fulton, about three miles west of Pinewood, no longer exists.
10 Margaret (1794–1845) was James B. and Ann Richardson's second oldest daughter. She married Colonel John Spann, as noted in the letter.

⌇

[SCHS 73-VI-19]
MARY DEAS BROÜN[11] TO WILLIAM SINKLER
[PROBABLY IN CHARLESTON,][12] JANUARY 12, 1825

My Dear Son accept my warmest thanks for your truly affectionate letter which I received this fornoon you say nothing of your health & I much fear from our Dear James's account that it is any thing but good I sh[ould] be truly happy to see you[.] I hope you will arrange it so as to make some way to enable you to take a Physicians advice & also his prescription. recollect my Dear Son how much you [have] to answer for[:] five little Children depend on you for advice & protection[.] Do not give way but endeavor to bear up for their sakes the advice does not proceed from one that has never felt you know my heart has & does bleed at every pore it is our duty to do our best to submit with humble resignation to the will of our God who certainly knows what is best the stroke has been most heavy but I humbly trust our loss has been her gain[.] Oh may her spirit hover over you & yours I am certain could you have her sentiment it would be to lament her but not to grieve immoderately once more let me entreat of you to look at your Children & think how great there [*sic*] loss & how much more it would be if they were to lose you[.] Great God spare me that additional misery—Our Dear James[13] got here safe once landing & resumed his studies yesterday. You may depend that I will watch over him with a Mothers Eye & do my best to prevent any thing wrong as yet he has been all that we could wish or expect & I have no doubt will grow up to be a comfort to you & an example to his Brothers. But Dear Little Priss is well[;] she is a complete pet in the House & among one of my greatest comforts she speaks of you every hour of the day also of the Dear <u>Bozo</u> I long to see them & you & shall anxiously expect you.[14] I heard from our Dear friends at No[rth] Santee yesterday by the Bozo who came down to school they were all well but have made no mention of when they would return—James & family arrived from Santee about one o Clock all in good health. Priss has just kiss'd the paper & desires I will send that & that she wants to see you too much

11 Mary Deas Broün (1762–1857) was the mother of William's wife, Eliza, who had died on June 3, 1824.

12 Charleston city directories, 1822–25, show Mary Deas Broün living at 97 Boundary Street, the eastern end of what is now Calhoun Street.

13 James, William Sinkler's oldest son, was fourteen and probably in boarding school.

14 "Priss" was undoubtedly Elizabeth Allen (1821–1908), WS's only daughter, who married Richard Irvine Manning in 1845. It is unclear who "the Dear Bozo" was, but it was probably a family member.

all day long. These are her own words. Mary my two sons[15] & Charles with the young folks write with me in tenderest Love to you & the Children & believe me my Dear Son as I truly am Your affect[ionate] Mother

Mary Broün

Sand Hills, So[uth] Carolina, 25 July 1825

My Dear William,

I was not solicited by you to write you; I therefore calculated that I should hear from you at the first stage you should make to refresh yourself & your cavalry, & then I should have received from you something like a request that I would let you hear from me, when my time would conveniently admit of it; but as yet I have not heard a sentence from you; transient information gave me some tidings of you at Mr. Cantey's, but nothing since, & a month has elapsed since you left this airy sweet habitation, (& may I not be permitted to add without the charge of ostentation.) & its engaging society; & you have not vouchsafed to make one solitary inquiry after us; to express one regret at leaving us; or to give us an intimation where you are; that our communications, solicitous for the knowledge of your wellfare, might seek you out. What a field this has afforded me for supposition & conjecture; can I be permitted to indulge in the belief that the old adage is verified by you: "that no sooner out of sight than out of mind," or in that which is more reasonable & comports better with my feelings, (for it is too insupportable to believe myself forgotten by a friend & that too in so short an absence,) that you have more interesting correspondents to attend to than I could possibly be; with whom you have more lively engagements; & as many as your time will enable you to preserve the intercourse of; but be that as it may, I cannot find it in my heart wilfully to perpetrate a dereliction of duty, upon the supposition of its being an intrusion on your time & pleasurable engagements, untill [*sic*] I have sounded for the result in discharging my duty; when measures will be clearly pointed out, how in future I should proceed & whether I should or should not trespass further on your time. I trust by this time you have safely arrived to the place of your first destination & that you are enjoying good health. It affords me great pleasure to inform you that health, rosy health, is still the inmate of my family, & I trust in the mercies of my good God that the blessing may be extended to us throughout this dreary season of Summer, & that we may all be

---

15 Mary (1789–1847) was a daughter—also named Mary Deas Broün—and the sons mentioned would have been John Deas Broün (b. 1793) and Archibald Broün, Jr. (1795–1863).

landed safely on the borders of Winter, & be well & happy there to greet the return of our friends, that are now distant, with hearts overwhelm'd with gratitude to that God of mercies, who tho' we have abided here, & not sought for health in distant climes, has us nevertheless secure beneath the protecting Shadow of his wings. Health is not however generally predominant, several are sick around us, & more remotely from this high & dry situation, disease & sickness is infinitely more prevalent; it makes me rather more cautious in my movements than I have hitherto been accustomed to be, & may, therefore prove serviceable. Mr. Johnson poor man has fallen a victim, perhaps to his obstinacy, in not removing to the Sand Hills, he repeated it sincerely in his last moments, & reproach'd himself for it. Mr. James Cantey has lost his little daughter, they are now down here. The Gov.[16] & his family are down but they came too late to derive any benefit from the salubrity of the place, his two youngest sons are very sick, one very ill indeed, & both may be regarded to be in danger. Maj[or] Cantey has just gone up & his second Son very unwell, & I should not be surprised if they, more or less, get sick from changing situations so late. It was my intention earlier to have detail'd to you the happy result in the celebration of the anniversary of that memorable day the 4 July, & I expect my delay of it is long, augers with your unfavorable impressions, more particularly as I would calculate on the interest you would take in your young friend William[17] who had been call'd by unanimous voice at the preceeding one, to deliver the oration. I should have rejoiced sincerely if you had been present to have witness'd the event. I think I know the good wishes of your heart towards him, in that it would have joined heartily in the exultations fervently manifested by his friends in particular & by a most numerous audience collected around, & from Stateburgh & Sumterville, & from the other side of the River. Our expectations appeared alive, calculating on hearing something good, but when the torrents bursted forth from him, so far beyond expectations even the most sanguine expectations were astounded to find all so far surpass their calculations. I cannot but hope that tho' divided from us, & continually within the sound of the commemorations of that auspicious day, your heart would sometimes revert to us, & a kind wish would fall from you for the success of my William, in the discharge of his duty that day. I think I may say that you would have been gratified in the extreme; you may then judge of the gratefull sensations of the fond Parents, witnesses on that occasion. No expectations you may have entertained of him or his efforts, but what I hazard nothing in saying would in the reality have been far surpass'd, both in composition, Style & delivery. Public

16 In office from 1824 to 1826, Governor Richard Irvine Manning was James B. Richardson's first cousin once removed and was married to JBR's niece, Elizabeth Peyre Richardson, known in the family as Betsey.

17 James B. Richardson's son William Henry Burchell Richardson, born on December 19, 1804, was a student at South Carolina College in Columbia.

acclamation has given him much, more than I would v[en]ture here to recount, or even that it would be proper I should [torn] that he left to some less interested few; fame in [spite] of every [comp]osition will fly, tho' on leaden wings; tis not like [torn] "on Ea[gles' wings] immortal Scandal flies"[18] for fame will, must be told tho' too often told reluctantly. It is only to you & those I regard as his best friends, that I would say so much to of his distinguished performance. I find that I have gone already to such a length that I have scarcely any space for mentioning a word about domestic concerns. I must here only briefly observe that the accounts received from below (of which I have had two or three) that my prospects of crops are extremely flattering; & the boy says yours is so, but I have directed my overseers in their weekly acc[oun]ts to report of yours particularly, & of all in their reach, that I may know how others go out as well as myself. There has been an abundance of Rain since you left here & still continues. My Prospects up here have been greatly improved by the Seasons, I promise myself an abundant harvest, if no [torn] or unforeseen accident intervenes: I think infinitely better than the past years. I must desist & hold something in reservation for my [torn], if I find you desirous to draw it forth. Adieu my D[ea]r friend[.] Your Sister & all the family desire their love to you & with me wish your health & a safe return to us. God bless us & give us a happy meeting is the devout orison of my Dear William. Your friend and sincerely affectionate

James B. Richardson

NB. Edw[ard] Richardson spent a week here, said that Anna & children were well[.] Tell my Brother if with you, that I have written him on the 18. inst[ant].

[Addressed to]
[different hand] Futton [Fulton?] 25
26 July
William Sinkler Esquire
White Sulphur Springs
Or
Sweet Springs
Virginia

CHARLES RICHARDSON TO WILLIAM SINKLER [PROBABLY AT EUTAW]
ELMSWOOD, 27TH DEC[EMBE]R 1825

My Dear Friend—

It gave us pleasure to hear by my good Sister[19] that you were in the enjoyment of good health & that you had the happiness of finding your children in the

---

18 "On eagles' wings immortal scandles fly" is from Harvey's translation of Juvenal's *Satires IX.*

19 He probably meant his sister-in-law Ann Cantey Sinkler Richardson.

enjoyment of good health also on your return. Be assured that your happiness always adds to my own. But a line from yourself to this effect would have been more welcome than the intelligence derived in this way, but I suppose you thought me indebted a letter at least & that was as much as I was entitled to, as I understand from my Sister you had not rec[eive]d my letter from Middletown nor from Philadelphia from both of which places I wrote you. I regret extremely you have not rec[eive]d the former of these letters [because] I flatter myself you w[oul]d have been pleased & gratified by it. I hope it will still get to you but if it should not whenever we meet it shall be my first communication or as much of the subject as will convince to you, that I was steady & not unmindful of my promise to you, that if I went to the north I would see your Son.[20] I did so & found him a youth of fine reflection & manly determinations capable of much reflection & the higher sense of honor & propriety, on presenting him your letter (I did so alone) I told him to read it deliberately & alone, & to think while he read it that you were looking on him and observing his most inward sensations & to remember that it was completely in his power to give lasting pleasure or pain to one who had no interest but his own at heart, that he should treasure that letter and frequently look it over. I know it won't be serviceable to him to do so, for I know all that was in it, as you had done me the honor of reading it to me—he pressed my hand his Eye filled with the tear of affection he put it in his pocket & supped with us & spent two or three cheerful hours with [us] & then marched to quarters. We spent five days there most of which time he was with me that is his time that could be shared from business. I got introduced to Capt[ain] P[artridge] and after getting acquainted with him & he understanding my connection with the young men, & my interest in them I made every enquiry respecting them, his report to me respecting your son, was this[:] he had during the whole time he had been with conducted himself in every respect attentively to his avocations & his deportment was honorable & gentlemanly. In short he had no fault to find with him, & otherwise got as much into the deportment of our young friend as possible & I had frequent opportunities of doing so. John Brown supports a fine standing with the Captain & among all the youn[g] men, they call him old rock—let me assure you my friend I think you have very little to fear for your son [torn] that anxiety & interest natural to a parent. I wish I could say so for others that are a [torn] the north. I hope I shall soon have the pleasure of seeing you, I did not go on to Boston as I intended owing to two causes the one was my spending so much time at Middletown[21] & my not being able to get

20 William Sinkler's oldest son, James (b. 1810).

21 Later known as the American Literary, Scientific, and Military Academy, it was established 1820 in Norwich, Vermont, by Captain Alden Partridge, former superintendent of West Point. In 1825 it moved to Middletown, Connecticut, and later became Norwich

permition [*sic*] for James to be absent long enough to go with me. I thought such an excurtion [*sic*] w[oul]d be serviceable to him, & not contrary to your wishes[.] I have taken all my paper & not said half to you I wished. I did not get the gun because I could not find one[.] I got y[ou]r letter the very day I set out & had no opportunity of looking out. My daughters unite in affectionate good wishes to you. Believe me Dear Sinkler

Y[ou]r Sincere f[rie]nd & affect[ionate] Cousin
Charles Richardson
(Excuse haste which by the By should be no excuse)

[Addressed to]
William Sinkler Esq.
Springfield
By Tom

JAMES B. RICHARDSON TO WILLIAM SINKLER, ESQ[UIRE, AT SPRINGFIELD]
JAMES VILLE, 2 FEB[RUAR]Y 1826

Dear William,

I received your affectionate letter by the Postman with the little bundle to your Sister & the little letter to my d[ear son] Richard[22] which was the first he ever had written to him, & which he is exceedingly proud of, I thank you ten thousand times [for having] noticed him; the little fellow is now alone in School having no little companions to accompany him, & goes with the greatest willingness; & says he will write you, & if he knew of this opportunity would be restless untill he could embrace it. I am happy to hear that you have safely returned to your Home & in good health; I trust you may very long enjoy the blessing; I have no doubt but that you find it very lonesome without the society of your Children which I observe you have left in Charleston, the privation must be very great indeed to you, & to one at my time of life would be almost, if not entirely insupportable. It would afford us the greatest pleasure if you could divide your time with us, & the distance is not so much but you might; I trust however that you give my Dorothy[23] as much of your society as you possibly can, & find her

University. Porcher listed James Sinkler as one of about fifty South Carolina cadets among about three hundred total. F. A. Porcher, "South Carolinians at The Partridge Military Academy, 1826," *South Carolina Historical Magazine* 44, no. 3 (1943), quoted in *SCHM* 61, no. 1 (1960): 11–12.

22 Richard was born on December 28, 1815, so would have been only ten years old.

23 Probably Richardson's daughter, Dorothy Sinkler Richardson (Mitchell). See note on letter of April 22, 1823. She would have been living just across Eutaw Creek from William Sinkler.

more important to you from her contiguity, than you ever could have believed would be; I wish very sincerely that we were all more contiguously situate than we are, it would much to our comfort & happiness add, & perhaps to our mutual advantage; I know it would to mine, for I am getting more & more a recluse every day, & becoming more & more attach'd to it, & consequently needing aid, & the exhilirating society of my few friends, whose society I delight to associate in, & which afford me great gratification.

I regret very much that it is not in my power at this time to spare you my Bricklayers I am busily engaged in resilling my corn house & have immediately to do the foundation under that, & two other considerable buildings which [they] are to do also; which I was hurrying to effect, that I might be ready to go at my William's building; but does seem as if perp[l]exities were never to end now, untill he himself ends, for while looking forward to the accomplishment of these objects; new employments seem to rise continually; on Tuesday last I unfortunately had my mills burnt down, by the carelessness I have no doubt of my Miller, leaving fire in the cellar when he left the Mill in the morn[in]g & every thing was consumed therein, not a vestige was saved; if I could have saved the Mill Stones two most excellent pair, I should have been truly glad, for they are difficult to replace, even in rebuilding again if I ever should; & with them & all the materials & workmanship, I could not have lost less than three thousand dollars, & the privation exclusively being so unexpectedly & unprovided. Thank God my family are all in good health, & that of my own much improved; & with this blessing, others are only secondary; & much can be surmounted that makes rugged our pathway in this life.

I expected that the Gig was done & the workman would not care how soon I had it, so that he had the money, but I shall have no opportunity of getting it before I go down, & I wish sincerely wish that I had got you when you went down to get instead of that a fashionable Gig for my William as he appeared to desire one, & my Gig will serve me very well yet: Could you think you get him to dispose of that, & build such a one as that, which you had before described? that would be large enough to carry me in the need of requiring it. You would oblige me if you would write him on the subject with your usual pe[r]suasive stile, & let me hear the result. I think it may possibly be effected, for I think the top to those little vehicles are more burdensome than useful, at least the one is not an equivalent for the other.

I have detained the boy to write you this, he is anxious to depart, I must therefore desist. Your Sister who is busy now will reply to your letter first opp[ortunit]y presents you with her tenderest & warm love, & so does the family. Give my love to my Dear Dorothy as I have not time to write her, & my dear little children with her, who expected to be down to see before this, but unavoidably prevented for a while. Adieu my Dear William

Believe me sincerely
Your friend & very affectionate
James B. Richardson

[Addressed to]
William Sinkler Esq.
Springfield

JAMES B. RICHARDSON TO WILLIAM SINKLER, ESQ[UIRE, AT
ST. JOHN's, BERKELEY]
JAMES VILLE, 9TH JUNE 1826 [POSTSCRIPT 10 JUNE]

My Dear William,

Your letter of the 9 ins[tan]t I have received & it has cast a damp over my spirits, it conveys intelligence that you are soon to leave us & to go far away; how enviable will be the spot that you locate yourself, but how much more enviable will
be the coterie, that is to partake of your valued society, your cheering & engaging
converse that dispenses pleasure & gratification wherever your voice resounds, &
constitutes within yourself that rich phalanks, that bids defiance to the encroach-
ment of intruding vapors or Hipo's,[24] that prey on the weak & effeminate mind.
But wherefore my friend may I presume to ask do you thus fly your country &
your friends, nay' your more than friends, those whose interests & happiness are
identified & interwoven with your own? Do you go to show how deeply you can
sadden their hearts by your absence, after the promise of their enjoying a portion
of it? Or do you fly to seek [she]lter & shade, dreading an influence you regard
as hostile [to] the peace & repose of your heart, & whose ascendency you fe[el]
without even daring to acknowledging a wisper of [torn] to yourself; that in that
retirement you sigh, & mutter a word, a [words missing] suspicion, & deliberate
upon the future course necessary to pursue, & return on the borders of Winter
with invigorated firmness to storm the citadel or perish on its environs. You must
always hold in remembrance my friend the old adage "that a faint heart never
woos a fair Lady" & remember too that within yourself you are [word illegible],
(so your friend that sees with impartial eyes regards you) & remember also that
you have in your friend a host (so the world ascribes[)], & with all this about you
& surrounding [y]ou, pray what is it that you have to dismay you? I would fondly
add my solicitations to the many that I know would be wished if they were not
openly offer'd for your detention among us, if they knew of your determination to
go, or at least "one sweet look before you go" that you may carry even far [a]way

24 The website *Vocabulary.com* defines hipo (usually plural) as "reflex spasms of the
diaphragm . . . producing an audible sound"—commonly called hiccoughs today.

the recollection of what we were when you left us; that in imagination we will go with you whithersoever you go, tarry with you where you tarry, & return with you, enlivening the expectation with ten thousand blisses to greet you at our happy meeting. I am serious when I assure you, that when you left me for Charleston I knew I should read your destination for summer, & altho' your letter carries allusions to the contrary, I cannot change that opinion of Charleston being your abode for the summer; & altho' far from my wishes to divert your intentions if I could, yet I would fondly wish one interview, before the veil was cast to sever us for the summer; long dreary period, that forg[torn] to divide friends by its insufferable barrier, that none can safely surmount. I hear of the tidings of gloomy times in the commercial & agricultural concerns with serious regret, but I fear the worst has not yet reach'd its ach[torn] & in [torn] benignant influence I live, & hope for more prosperous times. My Dear William arrived here on Monday from Columbia, & in good health but very thin, he requests his tenderest regard & affection to you & wishes very much he could have the pleasure of seeing you if only for one day & says that he will write you so soon as he knows of your location. We suffer here much for Rain, tho' on Tuesday last bless'd with a good one, the only drop since the first day of May last, & we were at the last gasp of vegetable existence. Adieu my Dear William you must be tired of me now, for indeed I am so of myself. All the family desire their love & best wishes to you; & if I see you not before you go, my assurances of affection await you always, & keep one kind thought occasional of your friend & very affectionate

James B. Richardson

NB. I thank you for your goodness in delivering my message to Dr. Burgoyne[.] I shall reprimand him for his indifference, or inattention. I send you enclosed the money for the Bottle sent of Swaim's Panacea[25] & my obligation for your goodness. Your mare insists peremtorily [*sic*], in preserving her distance from Seagull, but I hope you will be fortunate. Great tidings from Virginia in the sporting way, them fellows tho' dead, they are alive & risen again when sporting is in question. We were bless'd with a fine Rain last night, this will increase the bloom of my Cotton, which was discoverable on Thurs. 8 June, & yesterday 9th June 5 full blooms were brought to me, the earliest I have ever seen a blossom; at the Rocks[26] a blossom was on the 4th so says [torn]. But wherefore all this a [blurred] the bloom, excep [words missing] unimportant, except we need once in

---

25 Swaim's Panacea was a popular patent medicine.

26 This is not to be confused with Peter Gaillard's 1804 plantation near present-day Eutawville. Richardson's will referred to the Rocks as having been "bought of Richard Singleton containing one thousand eight hundred & Seventeen acres, more or le[s]s." There is no evidence of its having a home on it.

a [words missing] it may aid the cause if [words missing] Adieu my Friend I think this will do [words missing]cript. 10. June.

[Addressed to]
William Sinkler Esq.
Springfield
St. Johns Berkley [*sic*]
Per his [fell]ow
Hercules [word illegible]²⁷
Mare & [torn]

[DU, James Burchell Richardson papers]
James B. Richardson to Ann C. S. Richardson, in Fulton Post Office
Charleston, 9 [O'clock] p.m. 22 May 1829

My Dear my beloved Wife. I arrived at this place half past 1 Oclock p.m. & found my Brother²⁸ as ill as he could be, to be alive, & on my approaching him he endeavored to raise his hand to me, which I caught & assisted, & ask'd him if he knew me, & his answer was "yes perfectly." It is better to be conceived by you, that it is possible for language to convey the idea, the emotions that thrill'd through the whole system at the scene that presented. I found him surrounded by those of his few friends, & his immediate family awaiting his hourly dissolution, without a solitary ray of hope in a single individual; one which they could loos[e] one glimmering prospect of his surviving, but from hour to hour; so much so, that they ventured not to give one particle of nourishment, which was stated to naeuseate [*sic*] his stomach, which proceeded even from Ice water, all that was administered. I however urg'd the Doctor to try the nourishment at intervals, & altho' without a hope my Anna of anything being beneficial, yet it would not do to let a Being live without some effort, upon which nature can exist; he has therefore received the nourishment, but were you to see him you would coincide with me, that there is no earthly chance of his surviving of more than a day or so, & perhaps not beyond this night. As the mail does not close before tomorrow 2 oclock, I will retain this letter to the latest period of the mail's departure, & advise you of what may occur between this & then. I have not yet been to my lodging, finding them all in waiting for his dissolution; but I have seen our little children & they are in perfect health. Julia has been complaining, but looks as well as I have seen her, & Richard & Richardson never look'd better. I encountered immense Rains on my

27 Hercules was William Sinkler's horse trainer, who became quite famous in racing history.
28 Charles Richardson, James's youngest brother, died on May 22, 1829.

way down, they were before me & behind, & on each side of me, but I was more than fortunate to experience so small a portion of it considering the very great inundation of the country from Belvedere [*sic*] to within ten miles of Charleston, where seasons have been good but moderate. I was repeatedly stopp'd on my way by Rain, & at Mr. Geno's the day I left home for two hours at least; where I was glad to hear it extended to our Home; it so retarded me on my progress as to prevent my arrival here last night as I had fully determin'd. But thank God that I am in time to see my Brother alive, and that he promptly recognized me. How long he may survive God only knows; but I expect to send the Boys up Sunday & I shall review the issue with him; which I do not expect will be protracted but a little time longer; my Julia will await to go with me. I hope in God my Dear Anna that yourself my William & Matilda continues to enjoy good health & that the blessing may be extended to you all, & that we may have a happy meeting in health & thankfulness. I have not been well yesterday nor today entirely, but I feel some better this evening, & I hope my God in his mercy may return me to you in health. Tell my D[ea]r William, to urge the Drivers to the faithfull [*sic*] performance of their duties, or to persevere in his endeavors & have everything fulfill'd to the regulations established. Cotton well come up all in St. John's & from thence all the way down here; But we must not despair up there, tho' later. I hope that all the Peas are planted at the Sand Hills, let them have sufficient to do it; & plant the Brick yard in Cow Peas in the furrows run between the corn tell my William. You see I cannot forget things with you, tho' in the House of Sorrow & Suffering, for indeed my Wife such it is with my poor Brother, who lies like the Suffering Lamb about to be immolated on the alter [*sic*].

I write you hurriedly at detached intervals, & have not yet been to see where I shall recline my head, at such moments as I may snatch for repose, to refresh weary nature. Adieu my Dear Wife, God bless you all, & preserve you in peace & happiness, and the devout orisons of your truly fond and affectionate Husband in the greatest haste.

James B. Richardson

Mrs. James B. Richardson

Saturday morn[in]g. 3. O['c]lock A.M. the scene has closed; my poor Brother departed this life last night twenty minutes after 11 o[c]lock P.M. So little time after I had closed the foregoing to you, without the least struggle or motion; & I have not [torn] made a happy exchange. He scarcely ever spoke & I am told of the things of this World, & never once [of] ever [return]ing to his Home. We are mak[in]g preparations to [torn] with the Corpse today & will be up Monday early in the day as possible. Adieu my Wife my love to you all & believe me yours truly & affectionately.

J.B.R.

9 [o'clock] A.M.

[Addressed to]
Mrs. James B. Richardson
Fulton Post Office
So[uth] Carolina
Mail

[DU, James Burchell Richardson papers]
Ann C. Richardson to William H. B. Richardson,
    at Fulton Post Office, South Carolina
August 26, 1829

My Dear William

Your Papa begs you will take out of the Meat house a Barrel of Fish one of those that is on the Side for Ned to bring up tomorrow with two Shotes he must start very early. Tell Elsey she must send up three of the young geese by Ned. Your Papa begs you will get out of the Box in his Store Room 3 whip Saw Files and see how many more there is if there are a good many you may bring him 6. do my Son charge Henry—about the garden, tell Elsey to send me all the Bags that had dozen Peaches. I want them, don't stay my dear William begs your fond Mother
    Ann C. Richar[dson]

One version of what was called a whip saw, this 64-inch long saw required two men to make boards from logs. Some versions were used on a high frame or over a pit, in which case it was called a pit saw. Courtesy of the Sinkler family.

[DU, James Burchell Richardson papers]
William Sinkler to William H. B. Richardson
Cannons Boro[ugh, Charleston], 14 Sept. 1829

My Dear William,

Your much esteemed letter of the 1st Inst[ant] I received on friday [*sic*] evening last and the next day wrote on to Weaver for the Carriage—I observed your directions and added to <u>them</u> such as if <u>attended</u> to and no doubt will, will enable him to furnish, such a vehicle, as you require—you did not say what kind of a carriage and as it would be too late, to wait for further instructions—I ordered a Chariotter—I have limited Weaver, both as it respects price and time—the cost of the carriage is not to exceed $460—and it must be finished, and sent out 'ere the navigation is impeded by ice— The colour, ordered is a dark green—or any other <u>fashionable</u> colour—should you be particular—and wish anything further added, either as it respects, colour or any thing else, write immediately—that I may communicate with Weaver—he will let me know whether he can furnish a Chariotter for the price I have specified—in the event of his asking more shall I direct him to proceed—a few dollars, ought not to be an object, in procuring an article that is to <u>last</u> so <u>long</u>—and which may be the means of its being <u>higher</u> <u>finished</u>—and of <u>course</u> more to your satisfaction . . . . . . Make no apology in calling on me to be of any service to my friends—is always the source of gratification. I only request you will let me know, if the directions given, meet your approbation . . .

I am extremely sorry to hear of your fathers indisposition—at his time of life, sickness, in its smallest shape, becomes serious. I sincerely hope he may 'ere this be much better, and may very soon be restored—I know he has all that, good care, and good and tender nursing can give—my best wishes await him—God grant him long life and happiness—I feel anxious and have therefore concluded to send a servant up that I may hear particularly—I beg you will give my love to him, your dear Mother and all the family—and with the warmest wishes for your and theirs—believe me Dear William.

Your sincere friend
and affectionate Uncle
W Sinkler

I sent immediately to Goodman—he informs me he has forwarded your bundle—Say to your Sister Dorothy, Mrs. Waring has been apprised of this opportunity—adieu. I have much to do today—

James B. Richardson to William [Sinkler]
Sand Hills, July 28. 1830

My Dear William.

I received your affectionate letter of the 23 ins[tan]ton yesterday by your man Hercules, with the enclosure of the Six hundred Dollars perfectly safe; I do assure you that I am very sorry that you should have taken the trouble to send up expressly to convey it to me, as I should have been well satisfied in the security of sending it by the mail; I am however the more obliged to you for the trouble you have taken in get[t]ing it to me.

It gives me pleasure to hear that yourself & Dear children enjoy good health, that greatest of all earthly blessings; it is the happy situation of my little family (which is indeed few in number now) except that of my Dorothy, & I really think she is considerably better; but intends to travel & will leave us on Monday next. I do not feel well myself, & have been indisposed for several days past, & indeed tho' I write you I feel so much so, to disqualify me from writing you satisfactory. I am truly sorry to learn from you the imprudent & outrageous conduct of my fellow Charles on one of your fellows, he is reprehensible for it in the extreme, & it is to be hoped that the prosecution will make a legal example of him; but I shall write Mr. King & direct him to investigate the matter strictly & to inform me on the subject, when every proper measure will be pursued, & the proceedings of the prosecution will be over. I do assure you that I have always endeavored to inculcate into the minds of my negroes feelings of kindness towards yours, & to direct them to live in habits of kindness towards yours as tho' they belonged to one man and were living on the same plantation, & when my negroes would repeatedly tell me that they had been severely corrected by your Overseer for being on your premises within your enclosures; & that he stated to them that he could not help it, for that it was by your order; I have always contradicted it & said that it was not so, or that the overseer had discovered that they were at some improper conduct, or lurking about perhaps for that purpose, & by that precaution warded it off. A case of that kind occurred when I was last in St. John's, & I then told them if [they] had been forbid going on your plantation they would be served right to be corrected for trespassing when they had been prohibited; but as it respects myself I do assure you that I have never had any objection to your negroes having intercourse on my plantation, nor never instructed my Overseer or Drivers[29] to inhibit it; so far from it I have the rather encouraged it, so far as you would permit it; for they have always appeared very friendly to me & every thing that concerns me. Nor indeed have I ever interdicted the indulgence to the neighbors negroes around there, that would have permits from Owners or Overseers. I regret very much to learn that the reverse of this conduct in mine towards you have ever been manifested, & particularly from the time you date it; the contiguity of that Belvedere [*sic*] plantation of Dorothy's[30] to you I was aware of at my settling, & though inhabited by Friends & near relatives after She got

29 The driver was a slave who supervised other slaves; he worked under the overseer, who was white.

30 Dorothy was obviously living at Belvidere at this time; see the comment in the last paragraph of the February 2, 1826, letter.

it, to prevent collision of interests, which tho' the most consiously [*sic*] guarded against may sometimes occur, was the inducement to me to enlarge the territory in the purchase at so high a price of that land from you, and I do assure you my friend that whatever you deem right & proper in the business shall be done.

It seems hardly worth our while to confer on the prospect of crops while our political horizon seems so convulsed by contending aspirants to power, by advocating the rights as they say of the People. You know my sentiments on the two offensive measures of the general Government, but I am aversed [*sic*] to disunion or nullification which amounts to it; or as Mr. Drayton[31] said (whose address I highly approve) what is worse, civil war. My trust & hope is in the cool and dispasionate wisdom of the people under the guidance of a mercifull God, that all the portentous evils that threaten our State may be averted. I was really gratified at hearing by your former letter that you would be a candidate for Senator for St. John's Berk[e]ley; I had received no previous intimation of it; I sincerely wish you success, for at a crisis like this, it becomes the duty of every friend to our States best interest, that can render her service to advance it; Our Country never required more than at this time, all the collected Wisdom talent & prudence in her Legislature.

The prospects of our crops are still very promising, & the Rains have been sufficient to make the Corn Crop fine for me, & I believe is so below. I trust we may experience a rich harvest; & [all] the political tempest may blow over, & we may have a quiet & good market. I have written you longer than [I ex]pected. Adieu my Friend may health & happiness awa[it] the Summer & give us a happy meeting on the borders of Winter is my ardent orison. Our united love to your Dear little ones, & our kind remembrances to Mrs. & Miss Broün,[32] & believe me truly

Your friend & very affectionate
James B. Richardson.

NB. You will not I trust forget the arrears due on Tom's Debt & get it for me as early as you can.____

31 William Drayton (1776–1846) was a Charleston lawyer who served in Congress from 1825 to 1833. He gave a speech on July 1 in Charleston that JBR apparently attended; after the nullification crisis, Drayton moved to Philadelphia.

32 Mary Deas Broün (1762–1857) was the mother of William's deceased wife Eliza; Miss Broün probably refers to her daughter, also named Mary Deas (1789–1847).

[DU, James Burchell Richardson papers]
James B. Richardson to Dorothy R. Richardson[33]
Home, 15 Dec[ember] 1833

Dear Dorothy,

I received last evening your present of a very superior Vest, & tender you my cordial thanks for it, & the remembrance of me; it is too good for me to wear, bearing about with me all my infirmities of Body, under this season of my affliction, & period of heavy trial; & where it will not be seen to any advantage in my close retirement, & seclusion from the World, during this weighty visitation, which I feel it my duty to do.

I shall nevertheless wear it for your sake, & while I do so, I shall not be unmindfull [*sic*] of you, & the affectionate motives that prompted you. Receive assurances of my best wishes for your being happy here, & for that of your very kind Husband & children,[34] & that

I am your very affectionate
James B. Richardson
 Home. 15 Dec. 1833
 Mrs. Dorothy A Richardson

[Addressed to]
Mrs. Dorothy A Richardson

[DU, James Burchell Richardson Papers]
James B. Richardson to William H. B. Richardson
22 July 1834

My Dear William

I paid Mr. Sims in Jan[uar]y last Nine Doll[ar]s 60/100 for yo[u] which was exactly the amm[oun]t I owed Ja[me]s B. Rich[ar]d[son] for y[ou]r 4 Bushels of Wheat at $2.40/100 per Bushel. Y[ou]r Bushel at the same time I p[aid] him for my toll wheat on 12th Jan[uar]y 1834. Does Capt[ain] Sims forget the paym[en]t to him? I am much as I was yesterday, the family are well.

Your af[fec]t[ionate] Father
James B. Richardson

---

33 Niece/daughter-in-law (Charles Richardson's daughter, who married JBR's son William Henry Burchell Richardson).

34 The Singleton family genealogy shows children of William H. B. and Dorothy Richardson born later than this date.

[Addressed to]
W. H. B. Richardson Esq[uire]

[DU, James Burchell Richardson Papers]
William Sinkler to William H. B. Richardson at
    Fulton Post Office, So. Carolina
Charleston, 25 July, 1834

Dear William,

Your very affectionate letter of the 19th I received on Wednesday. Your attention is very gratifying—and the prompting you manifested, in complying with my request merits my warmest thanks. Acts speak for themselves—I am quite glad to hear you are all well, but sorry to find, my friend, your father, has declined, going to Virginia—God grant he may do well—I hope he will but in my mind, the journey to the mountains, the salubrious air, of that region—would have had a powerful affect on his system generally—this warm weather, which we have experienced, so well calculated to debilitate, at the Springs of Virginia—would only have been felt in the day—the nights cool always places the system in a situation, to contend with the evils of the warmth of the day. Say to my good friend Dorothy [WHBR's wife] my best and warmest wishes await her that it will afford me pleasure to comply with her & your request—a request highly

Entrance and Springhouse of White Sulphur Springs, VA, where WS frequently visited. Courtesy of the Library of Congress.

flattering—I am now making preparation for tomorrow a day, which to many were to be one of joy—will be to be [*sic*] me a day of gloom—to leave my children, at this perilous season, is a trial, that is very chilling to the feelings. I trust in the mercies of a good God, and hope all things will eventuate well. A great many persons have gone from this place to the Virginia Springs—it takes not more than a week to perform the journey—and by far the most economical—however I would have preferred to have gone by land, nothing prevented me from doing so—but sickness in the first instance, and the necessity of going to Philadelphia with my niece[35]—I regret that I have been prevented going by land, particularly as I may have been instrumental in prevailing on your father to accompany me. Remember me affectionately to Dorothy, your children, to your father Mother & all friends—adieu dear William, and always believe me sincerely.

Your affectionate Uncle

& friend

W Sinkler

I will write to your father and if possible to my dear Sister. God bless you all, goodby—a happy summer I sincerely wish you

[Addressed to]

William H. B. Richardson Esq.

Fulton Post Office

Mail So[uth] Carolina

James B. Richardson to William Sinkler, in St. John's Home, May 24. 1835

My Dear William.

I received your favor of the 23 inst[ant] & in conformity with your request I have written to Mr. C [name unclear] relative to my young friends mare & desired his particular attention to the admission of her to Muckle John, & sincerely hope he may be successful in having a colt, & I would recommend you to send her as often as appearances may prove she requires it, however inconvenient it may be; for independently of y[ou]r advantage of having a foal, the accountability will be with me for the amount thereof, and I should much regret indeed that my friend Seaman should be disappointed in getting a colt. With respect to the services of Jesse beyond the time I allotted him with you, what can I say? but to acquiesce in your request to have him the time you mention, for I have ever been

35 William Sinkler was raising Anna Linton Thomson (b. 1823), the daughter of his sister, Margaret Anna, who had died in 1829. Comments suggest that they were probably sailing from Charleston to Philadelphia.

disposed to serve my friends whenever I can do so, with-out making a sacrifice too insurmountable, in which case candor would allways induce me to avow; his services are now wanted to prepare my new Building at the Sand Hills to be measurably tenanted during this summer. I regret most exceedingly that during my visit to St. John's, I did not Dine once with you; nor even go into your house; a thing I believe never occurred before, & becomes the more lamentable to me, because my prospects are so precarious ever to live to see you again there, so (I truly fear); but I must endeavor to submit to these privations, severe & oppressive as they are, with all the fortitude that I can control; and my God knows I humbly & devoutly pray to him to strengthen & support me in my best endeavour for resignation & submission to his holy ordination in all things appertaining to me, & may I not hope for the endowment to me in his own good time. I cannot express to you sufficiently important the burthen of my regret at not spending one day with you while down, & partaking with my kind companion (my better part,) at your hospitable Board, such provision as I have always enjoyed with gratification. A long & dreary summer lies before us, all the mysterious events that are awaiting it are obscured behind the veil that no human imagination can penetrate. I live under the kind influence of sweet hope, & pray that God will extend his blessings to us, & to me also, poor, weak & debilitated as I am at the present time. I am very desirous to write to my Dorothy, but I cannot write her now, this confinem[en]t fatigues me too much to prolong it, you must therefore express it for me, & tender her & all with her my sincere affection & earnest wishes for their health & prosperity. Adieu my Friend, we all unite in love to you & your Sister particularly, & believe me my Dear William your sincere Friend & very affectionate. James B. Richardson.

P.S. My boat will not go to Town again this season, & only to Belvedere [*sic*] to remove my Dorothy's things up; or she should be made serviceable to you in conveying your articles down. Adieu again.

[Addressed to]
William Sinkler Esq.
St. John's

⁓

James B. Richardson to William Sinkler, Esquire, in Charleston
Sand Hills. 19 Aug. 1835

My Dear William.

It is very evident that Procrastination is [the] ravisher of time, & makes us truant to our duty be that what it may; Wherefore then so long withhold from thy friend your kind communication you know to be so endeared to him from sincere declaration made to you. I cannot [account?] for the cause of your long delay, & the reason your offer in your letter for it, is by by [*sic*] no means justifiable in my opinion; for being in possession of all the faculties to write your friends, why deny the indulgence so long. I should have written to you 'ere I received your favor of the 1st inst[ant] but in truth my Friend that my Eye Sight is so extremely impaired that I write with the utmost difficulty, as I am aware you will readily percieve [*sic*] , and feelingly commiserate with a poor afflicted Being; for all tho' my bodily [*sic*] is greatly improved, beyond any thing I ever did expect, yet I tremble to think from the decline of my vision, that I may ultimately become entirely blind. Death would be infinitely preferable to such a state of existence, & may my good God Almighty of his infinite & unlimited mercy rescue me from by his boundless power. It would indeed soften the feeling of your kind heart to behold in me the blessing of improved bodily health, & the gradual decline of that inestimable treasure of Sight: Jesus my Saviour in whom I steadfastly trust, & hope will save me form [*sic*] so bitter a calamity. I meddle but little with my Domestic affairs, but as much so as my Situation will possibly admit of, & but for my impaired sight, I could fish, Hunt & fowl it <u>almost</u> as well as ever I did; and strange to remark, with all my health & strength in their pristine state, & in the full vigor of body & mind, I have never no year for the last ten or fifteen, been so successfull as the present year in my Agricultural pursuit, no never than the present year, and that on each of my Plantations (not but one excepted) I have not a better crop of corn, cotton & Potatoes & peas than Crops I have the present year; & if no unforeseen event shall occur from this time to the Harvest Season, I shall have my Garner full, press'd down & to running over, & my cup full, full & to overflowing; that my friends when they visit me say with joy & glee "share what the time may afford, & then spread the board for tomorrow."

The Domestics of our State, & unquieted situation of the free & coloured population of the Southern country, is indeed a subject of deep regret; to all well wishers of our peace, happiness & prosperity; & that sooner or later there will be severe wrestling & vital conflict; but my infirmities & my Age lead me to view it at a distance beyond the approach of me, & it must be left in hands of others in State & Council, than I could in my best period ever have been; & I must be content at the issue. I did expect you would have went [*sic*] on to the North this Summer, & met with my very Dear Richard who has determined to go as his time will indulge him, & to see I know all that can by him be ascertained; the last intelligence received, he was at Saratoga, & was to see the falls of Niagara; & all from his return through New York again and Philadelphia & to the watering places in Virginia, & perhaps some of the Sports in that, & the Seat of U. States Government; he will then bend his direction for the Westward, see the canals go down the Ohio & Mississippi & see New Orleans, & from thence via Charleston to his Home by the last of December to meet the welcome greetings of his

Parentage & friends. I would that you could have been with Son on his travel, or at least occasionally w[i]th him, & feel that it would have made him happy, you could have been his instructor, his Guardian & Guide. But I have been highly gratified on the perusal of his letters, which he addresses from every important place, descriptive of it, & of every thing worthy appertaining to it, which observation or tradition can grasp; & does very much appear from all that can be the trail by observation, to be perfectly himself in all situations, & under all circumstances; a Host 'tis said (apparently) within himself, a prototype of the original stock from which he sprang. God grant in mind & manner the true emblem of my Honored Father after who he is called[.]

Adieu my Dear William, I am tired myself & trust have wearied you with the banquet I furnish, poor in material, & still more indifferently served up; the will kindly [word unclear] for the Deed; I believe that nothing would afford me more pleasure than to see you here in this improved Spot, with every individual of my family (but my more than beloved Richard) now here. God bless you my D[ea]r friend, your Sister & the family unite with me in tenderest affection & best wishes for you and each individual of your family, & kindest remembrance to Miss & the Mrs. Broün[s][36] and I am my Dear William very truly,

Your Sincere friend & very affectionate.

James B. Richardson.

[Addressed to]
William Sinkler Esq.
Charleston.
S. Carolina

P.S I truly condole with you in the loss of your fine mare Carolina particularly as she was in foal By Muckle John who has brought $1000. late as he went, her loss is considerable to you I am well ass[ure]d for that crop would have been excellent. My Stock, is at this time is very ample & very flourishing; & I have [now] in train a very fine Stable of 4. tho' I never mean to run another in my own name. I wish you were here with us; indeed I do. Manning. R.I. & his clan has just sail'd yesterday (by land) for the White Sulphur, report says he is low indeed not expected to _____ .[37] Tho[ma]s Richardson poor fellow, with a complication of disorders, from the Throttle to the [word unclear]: and litttle [*sic*] Johnny with the <u>high Strikes</u> & apparition visits. Adieu, you have it all now.

---

36 William Sinkler's mother-in law and sister-in-law, both named Mary Deas Broün.
37 Probably "live." Richard Irving Manning died May 1, 1836. William Sinkler's daughter, Eliza, was married to RIM's son.

James B. Richardson tombstone in the Richardson family graveyard, near Rimini. Courtesy of the Clarendon County Archives, Manning, SC.

No published obituary seems to have survived, but if the facts had been gathered and it had been written in the style of that era, it might have looked like this:

OBITUARY

DIED, on Thursday, 28th instant, at Momus Hall, his residence in Clarendon District, Col. James Burchell Richardson, Esq., aged 65 years. The son of Gen. Richard Richardson and Dorothea Sinkler Richardson, he was born at Big Home, and was a life-long resident of the area, as well as a founder and vestryman of St. Mark's Church. At age 20, he married Ann Cantey Sinkler, with whom he had twelve children, eight of whom survive him. Family was of considerable importance to James Richardson, who took great pride in his children and throughout his life derived great pleasure from being part of a large extended family. At various times, he also mentored his younger cousin and nephews, after the deaths of their fathers. Considering public service as a duty, he enthusiastically pursued politics, first being elected to the South Carolina House of Representatives in 1792. That body selected him to serve as Governor from 1802 to 1804, and he served in both the House and the

Senate until 1817, always being engaged on numerous committees. At the same time, he was actively involved in Clarendon District projects, especially those for improving roads and establishing schools. Even after declining health made it too difficult for him to hold office, he continued his participation in politics by sharing his opinions with his friends. The Richardsons enjoyed an active social life which included music and dancing. Col. Richardson will be remembered for having organized a group of slave boys who eventually came to be known as the Liliputian Band, who entertained locally and also toured the state. Col. Richardson was not only a successful planter and landowner, but also a breeder of fine racehorses and was active in the South Carolina Turf for most of his adult life. His name appeared on the winners' list at the Washington Race Course in Charleston as early as 1793, and in 1833 he was one of only three men to have taken all the South Carolina Jockey Club Purses at one meeting. He was also active at the local racecourse at Manchester, which he founded, and frequently participated at Pineville, Augusta and elsewhere. James Burchell Richardson will be sorely missed by a great number of friends and family.

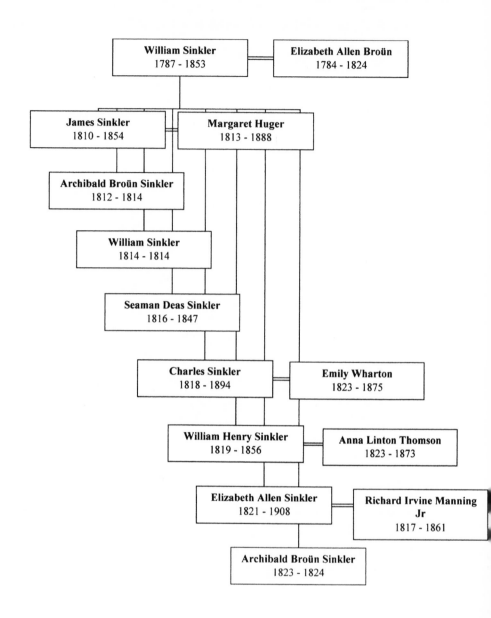

Chapter 6

Everybody Loves Seaman

In the fourteen years they were married, William and Eliza Sinkler had eight children, only one of whom was a girl. Although only five children lived to adulthood, it is a reminder of a family story. Eliza's grandfather, John Deas (1735–1790), who came from Scotland, when asked how many children he had, liked to reply, "I have nine fine sons, and each son has a sister."[1] The startled questioner usually assumed that he had eighteen children. Actually, some records indicate that they had eleven—not ten—children.

1773 John Deas miniature by John Smart. Courtesy of the Gibbes Museum of Art/Carolina Art Association, Charleston, SC.

1 Sinkler, "History of the Sinkler Family."

Seaman Deas Sinkler (1816–1847) was the second oldest surviving son of William and Eliza Sinkler. Not much is known about his early education, other than from a program of a November 27, 1829, titled "Exhibition of Charleston College" (see appendix C). It lists twenty-nine orations presented by students, including Seaman's "Extract from Mr. Clinton's Discourse at Schenectady" and his younger brother William Henry's "Cœur de Lion at the bier of his father, (Mrs. Hemans)." SDS would have been thirteen and WHS ten years old.

Records of the Medical Society of South Carolina reveal that SDS received his M.D. from the University of Pennsylvania in 1837 before spending another two and a half years in continued study in Paris.[2] These letters cover the period from September 1835 to January 1837, when he was making decisions about whether to stay in Philadelphia or return to South Carolina. It was also a period of frequent disease and illness, and letters reflect this. Two of WS's letters refer to "sickly" Pineville, and one from Seaman's friend, Robert Press Smith, who had family in the Pineville area, described it as "most horrid PineVille it proves a Buryal Ground to all Children." This same letter, referring to Charleston, says, "This City has had, and still has many cases of Cholera, many more than you see reported in the daily papers."

Seaman appears to have been loved by everybody. His maternal aunt Mary Deas Broün seems to have been a regular correspondent, soliciting advice and including family news about younger siblings, moves to and from Charleston, travels, and illnesses—even the occasional gossip. Her letters refer to having seen his friends, some of whom mention having written or received letters from him. It is also from her letters that one learns how William Sinkler had managed to raise his children after the death of his wife, Eliza, in 1824. Her widowed mother, Mary, and Eliza's younger sisters, Mary Deas and Harriet, had obviously taken them into their home on Archdale Street in Charleston; letters suggest that at times the women also stayed at Eutaw Plantation with the children.

Mother Mary Broün had had plenty of experience with raising young children alone, as her husband, Archibald Broün (1752–1797), had died when the youngest of their seven children was only two years old. Letters attest to the delight that the Broün family felt in being close to the two young children of William's oldest son, James.

Two of the younger Mary's letters in 1836 and 1837 are written from Eutaw, and an April 28, 1836, letter describes her pleasure in visiting there, where, she said, "many of my happiest days have been spent." She also mentioned missing

---

2 *Medical Society of South Carolina Minutes: February 7th 1847,* 207 ff., Lowcountry Digital Library, http://lcdl.library.cofc.edu/lcdl/catalog/lcdl:42987 (accessed May 20, 2015).

her nephew's presence for an hourly walk through the garden each evening.[3] In the same letter, she admitted to dreading the departure of her fifteen-year-old niece, Eliza, for school in Philadelphia, claiming that she had been "my nightly compan[io]n since she was three years old."

The young Eliza (1821–1908), had other concerns: her letters express misgivings about her father's decision to send her to Philadelphia to school. Although her first cousin Anna (1823–1873), who was being raised by William Sinkler, was already there, it is clear that she would have preferred to stay closer to home. Her letters to Seaman—sometimes quite lengthy—express her longing for the company of her brother.

While letters are replete with advice and suggestions for Seaman, it is abundantly clear that William was leaving many of the decisions to his son, much as had been done for him. An August 26, 1836, letter contains extensive but balanced advice about dealing with strangers. This was precipitated by Seaman's friendship with a young man referred to only as "Richard" or "the Frenchman," from whom Seaman was having difficulty collecting money that had been loaned to him. It is also equally plain that William trusted his son's judgment on many other matters and seems to have confided in him more as a contemporary than as a parent.

This is especially evident in his concerns about his next-younger son, Charles (1818–1894). A June 30, 1836, letter laments "how dreadful it is, to see a youth well blessed . . . spend his time in idleness." On August 16, 1836, WS referred to him as "a smart, fine looking youth" but expressed concerns about what was evidently an alliance with a woman not considered acceptable. In a subsequent letter, he expressed relief at having received a letter from his son indicating that he was trying to remove himself from the situation. Interestingly, at least two of William Sinkler's letters contain requests for letters to be burned. A letter of January 17, 1837, acknowledges how helpful Alfred Huger had been in getting information for getting Charles into the navy. Besides being a first cousin to WS's wife, Eliza, Alfred was also the brother to James Sinkler's father-in-law, John Huger.

William's letters from White Sulphur Springs,[4] especially one of August 19, 1836, provide detailed descriptions of the amenities of the resort, where he sought

---

3 The daughter of Charles Sinkler, she described the garden as "large . . . with a high, white fence, outside of which" were various trees. Over the gate was an arbor of pink and white multiflora roses. The garden walk was bordered by crape myrtle and strawberry beds. Elizabeth Allen Coxe, *Memories of a South Carolina Plantation During the War* (Privately printed, 1912), 91.

4 Later known as the Greenbrier, this resort of nearly seven thousand acres, where patrons consumed and bathed in the mineral water, was on the border of Virginia and what became West Virginia. It was quite popular with southern visitors, some of whom built cottages for their annual visits. Robert S. Conte. *The History of the Greenbrier: America's Resort* (Charleston, W.V.: Pictorial Histories Publishing, 1989), 43.

relief from what were evidently gastrointestinal issues. Frequently, he had one or more sons there with him, especially his oldest, James, who appears to have also had some health problems. These letters refer to meeting friends there, suggesting that there was considerable socializing and networking. It is also interesting that travel between home and Virginia appears to have been primarily by carriage—frequently several traveling together, as letters describe making side trips to Philadelphia and New York and stopping in Fredericksburg, Virginia, and Greenville, South Carolina. A letter of July 25, 1834, refers to the trip taking "not more than a week." A later letter, of September 17, 1850, mentions "the cars," suggesting that by then, there was rail travel between Richmond and Charleston.

Another letter from White Sulphur Springs, on August 22, 1836, contains great detail for some dress clothes WS wanted his son to order from a local (Philadelphia) tailor. The same letter has instructions for ordering "a keg of about 60, or 70 lbs. of the best—butter—I wish you would procure one—and a half keg of good tongues (beef)," suggesting that Seaman might enlist the help of his landlady with this last order.

In a January 19, 1837 letter, William Sinkler said, "It is now to my children, I must look for happiness—every thing depends on them—this, they ought to keep in mind and act accordingly—" Ten years to the day later, Seaman Deas Sinkler died after what the Medical Society called a "short illness." A family letter of January 21, 1847,[5] indicates that he died of consumption and that he had been planning a trip to Cuba in search of a cure. He was buried in the family cemetery at Old Santee, southeast of St. Stephen, and his tombstone was later relocated to St. Stephen's churchyard. The inscription reads as follows:

UNDER THIS STONE

REPOSE THE MORTAL REMAINS OF

SEAMAN DEAS SINKLER

DOCTOR OF MEDICINE

A BELOVED AND CHERISHED SON OF

WILLIAM SINKLER

TO A VIGOROUS INTELLECT

DILIGENTLY CULTURED

HE UNITED HIGH MORAL

CHARACTERISTICS AND

ENDEARING SOCIAL QUALITIES

HAVING MASTERED THE

DIFFICULTIES WHICH BESET

THE THRESHOLD OF PROFESSIONAL LIFE

5 Emily Wharton Sinkler, Seaman's sister-in-law, in a letter to her brother, Henry Wharton. SCL, Sinkler, Coxe, Fishburne, Roosevelt & Wharton family papers.

A BRIGHT CAREER OF DISTINCTION
AND USEFULNESS OPENED BEFORE HIM.
DIED 19TH. JAN. 1847
AGED 30 YEARS[6]

At the February 7, 1847, meeting of the Medical Society of South Carolina, Dr. P. C. Gaillard offered a lengthy preamble and the following resolutions:

In expression of its regrets at this sad event, the Society therefore adopts the following Resolutions.

Resolved. That in the death of Dr. S. D. Sinkler, this Society has lost one of its most diligent and useful members; the medical profession, a highly informed, intelligent, zealous and dedicated physician, and Society at Large an amiable and accomplished member.

Resolved. That the members of the Society wear crape on the left arm for the space of thirty days.

Resolved. That a copy of the Preamble and Resolution be sent to the family of the deceased. On motion of Dr. Desaussure, it was further resolved that the above Preamble and Resolution be entered among the minutes of the Society and that they be published in one of the daily papers of the city.[7]

~

WILLIAM SINKLER TO SEAMAN DEAS SINKLER [IN PHILADELPHIA]
WHITE SULPHUR [SPRINGS, VIRGINIA,] 5 SEPTEMBER 1835

My Dear Seaman—

I received your letter of the 27th yesterday and hasten to reply. It would be very gratifying to have you near me next Winter, when I could sometimes see you, but, if you think it best, and have determined to remain in Philadelphia and your object in so determining, has been with the view, entirely to accomplish your studies, and to graduate creditably—and at an early period, I certainly can have no objection—and will endeavor to reconcile myself to the separation. I am now more than half inclined to return to Philadelphia, that I am [*sic*] might have the gratification of being two or three days with you and Charles. If I can make any satisfactory arrangement, for William[8] to get back I believe I may be

---

6 S. A. Graham, "Inscriptions on Tomb-stones, Private Burial Grounds, on the Santee River in Old St. Stephen's Parish S.C.," *South Carolina Historical Magazine*, no. 26 (1925), p. 117. This article lists the date as 1846, but other records of St. Stephen's Parish show 1847.

7 *Medical Society of South Carolina Minutes: February 7th 1847*.

8 Charles, seventeen, was younger than Seaman; William was sixteen.

tempted to pay you a visit—between this and tomorrow I will determine—If I come to Philadelphia—I will be there by the 19th or 20th. It would be best that you do not write again, until you hear from me. Col. Hampton will leave this place in a day or two for the North and I would not be surprised that Mr. Singleton[9] joined him. When once you have determined [positively on] remaining in Philadelphia—it would be <u>best</u>, to place yourself under the <u>direction</u> of a Physician to have the advantage of <u>his counsel and patronage</u>—, but more of <u>this</u> in my next or when <u>we meet</u>. I have this moment got a letter from Eliza—all are quite well and the City healthy. Pineville unfortunately is very sickly. Miss Julia Porcher, daughter of Mr. Isaac Porcher, has fallen a victim, to the disease of that place—The fate of Pineville is now fixed—it <u>must</u> be abandoned, this will be attended with great disadvantages to its inhabitants—Thomas Lesesne and Henry[10] have returned from their visit, to Buncombe[11]—the latter much benefitted from his short excursion. I presume, we will not soon hear something of Thomas—in the <u>matrimonial way</u>. If your brother, has not stopped in Greenville, he must be near home, or rather Charleston—had he remain'd he could have taken William on—and saved me these few days of suspense—for the mind is always laboring, disagreeably so—when it is a <u>state of doubt</u> or undetermined—I will write you positively, on Wednesday the 7th if I determine, to go on to Greenville with William. adieu, my dear Son

    Your affectionate father
    W Sinkler

I fear our crops at home will be short—this makes me anxious to get back, to regulate, and, arrange accordingly—I am uneasy about my negroes—the wheat and provision crops in Virginia, will be very deficient—this will be a a [*sic*] year of trial to this planter—economy is all that will save us.

[Postmarked WHITE SULXSPRS VA SEP 5]

[Addressed to]
Mr. Seaman Deas Sinkler
Philadelphia

---

9 Colonel Wade Hampton and Richard Singleton were friends from the Sand Hills who also bred racehorses.

10 First cousins of Seaman Deas Sinkler, their mothers being sisters.

11 Buncombe was a health resort near Asheville, North Carolina.

~

Mary Deas Broün to Seaman Deas Sinkler in Philadelphia
Eutaw, April 28th 1836

My Dear nephew—

This day week you embarked for Philadelphia and already did it appear an age to me since you bid me farewell painful wince to be thrice I'll now endeavour to turn my thoughts to the anxiously anticipated period of our meeting the Heaven grant us a happy one—I hope long ere this you have met your friend Mr. Stoney I am rejoiced you have a friend with you do my dear Seaman let me entreat you to be careful of your health run no unnecessary risk[.] I know you will laugh at your <u>old aunt</u> for this request—but you have not been anxious I am about you or you would not—Your Sister and myself left James's on friday [*sic*] & got here between two & three once your father arrived from Woodstock about an hour after we did he has suffered no inconvenience from his harried travelling to & from the City he says he was notified by Mrs. L that his presence would be required on the fifth of May[12] he has not at present the slightest Idea of being in town at that time by a letter from Deas, to Eliza too says James[,] Margaret & myself he hopes he will be in town by the fifth. I suppose of course we are to receive more particular invitations—<u>They say</u> he regrets very much that you could not remain & witness his happiness—your father left here yesterday morning to visit Mr.Richardson. I do not think there was much probability of his finding him alive on his arrival his Physician has left him for a week he says he can do nothing for him poor old man his sufferrings must be great indeed he is now so <u>low</u> that he cannot move & has had the hiccups for several days so there can be no hope. I expect to leave this Saturday or Sunday your father & William will start for Columbia & at the same time we will for Charleston[.] I always feel deprest [*sic*] when the time arrives for me to leave this place many of my happiest days have been spent here[.] I dread this summer your father appears determined to take Eliza on to the North[.] I shall miss her more than it is possible for my feeble pen to express[.] She has been my nightly companion since she was three years old but you know the old vulgar saying "what can't be cured must be endured"—The garden looks beautiful abounding with sweet flowers & the strawberry beds covered with delicious fruit what would I not give if you could be transported to us every evening for an hour to take a walk with us but this would be too much happiness for us frail mortals—your Brother & Sister speak of going down the beginning of next week I was sorry to see Margaret [JS's wife] still looking so delicate, Mrs. H wishes

12 Mrs. Lesesne was Mary Deas Broün's sister, Anna, whose son was to marry Harriette Petigru on that date.

her to visit the Hagan[13] & go down from there with her to town but James was too busy indeed I can see no good to result from her taking such an additional ride at this period of the yea[r] poor old Charles [one of Seaman's patients] still continues sick[;] your father has employed Doctor Flud he apprehended dropsy the negroes tell me he speaks with gratitude of your kindness and attention to him[.] Eliza & Charles are gone to call at Mr. J. Gaillard[']s[.] She dreads the going down—Mother has hired an Omni[14] in Trad[d] Street—this letter is sent without the postage I am a poor scribe but I am conscious you my Nephew will accep[t] the "Will of the Duce" when next I write I'll give you all the news of the wedding—I'll not lay aside my pen till your father's return. I give you the latest account of Mr. R—Hercules has just told us you are the owner of a remarkable fine colt—& Mag & your father returned on Saturday the scene is closed[;] Mr. Richardson has ceased to suffer in this world he died on Thursday at sunset his sufferings were very great—your father bids me give his aff[ectionate] Love your Sister desires hers & says she will write you as soon as she goes to town we start tomorrow—we all feel dull—I hope my dear Seaman I will soon hear from you believe me Your aff[ectionate] aunt & sincere friend MDB

[NOTE: This letter was evidently not finished on Apr 28, which was a Thursday.]
[Postmarked CHARLESTON MAY 5]

[Addressed to]
Mr. Seaman D. Sinkler
Philadelphia

[PART OF A LETTER TO SEAMAN DEAS SINKLER FROM HIS AUNT,
   MARY DEAS BROÜN.]
ELIZABETH ALLEN SINKLER TO SEAMAN DEAS SINKLER IN PHILADELPHIA
EUTAW APRIL 28TH. 1836

Do not, Dear Brother, think me negligent for not writing to you—believe me it is not that I do not think of you—I miss you terribly—we are just now on the eve of leaving home—my dear home—you know what I feel—as you were in the same situation but a little while ago—it is worse to me than ever when I think it may be two years before I see it again—and what may not happen in that time? At any rate—there is no prospect of my seeing Father or any of you as I would

13 The Hagan was a Huger plantation at the fork of the Cooper River, purchased in 1748 by Daniel Huger. Claude Henry Neuffer, *Names in South Carolina* (Spartanburg, S.C.: Reprint Company, 1983), 28:24–25.

14 Omni would have been an abbreviation for Omnibus, a type of housing in Charleston in the 1830s.

wish—for an immense time[.] Father cannot go down with us—and I feel very uneasy about his having to stay here late—Adieu—My dear Brother—and be assured that you can never be forgotten or neglected by Your Sister[.]

Elizabeth Allen Sinkler to Seaman Deas Sinkler in Philadelphia
Charleston, 7th May-Saturday [1836]

I have left my dear home and am now in town as you will see by the date of this, my dear Brother—I hope you do not think me negligent for not having written before, but indeed it has been unintentional—you know how few opportunities we have when in the country, and we came down only on Wednesday— Father did not accompany but was to leave home for Columbia on Wednesday with William. We met Brother James in town—he came, via the Hagan—he & Charles left yesterday—I do not know what Father intends doing with regard to a house[.] I hear of none—he has promised me not to stay longer than the 4th or 5th of June. I suspect he will have to come down and take rooms somewhere—I went to the Wedding[15] on Thursday night—it was a pretty large one—the groom appeared very happy, and not at all frightened—the bride really looked pretty— the bride maids were Miss Emma Huger—Caroline Petigru—Miss Patsey—Miss Robinson—C. Porcher—M Kinlock—Miss Eliza Pringle & Cousin Anna[;] the grooms men—his brother—Mr. Rutledge & Mr. R. Parker—Mr. Roper and four others who I do not recollect—Mrs. Petigru behaved like a crazy person—that is the only excuse that can be made for her—Dr. Nott[16] & party arrived here Wednesday afternoon. I saw cousin Sally & Margaret—they both looked well— they came from New York. Dr. Nott & Cousin Margaret have gone to Columbia for two days—the rest will meet them at Augusta and go thence to Alabama—We are now moving to a house in Tradd Street and I am surrounded by confusion. Dr. Frost is going to his own house in June & Cousin Henry & his lady spend the summer with them—Brother James is perfectly disgusted with Mrs. Petigru— Sister did not go—neither did Charles—he intended going—& dressed himself & went to the door but thought it was too late—I suppose you have heard of Uncle Richardson[']s death—Father was with him—He died early at the last = two days before I left home I went to see your patients—old Charles—I am afraid for the last time—he seems to breathe with great difficulty Dr. Flud who is now attending him has no hope—Did you find your friend immediately and how are you pleased—I long to hear from you—two letters have gone up to Father it was very tempting to me—you cannot know, Dear Brother how dredfully [*sic*] your

15 Henry Deas Lesesne, son of Mary Deas Broün's sister, Anna Caroline, married Harriet Louise Petigru.

16 The husband of Mary Deas Broün's cousin, Sarah Deas.

society was missed—I used to wish for you every evening—to take a walk with us—and refresh yourself after study—we had a great many strawberries before we left—and home, that looks sweet at all times, was doubly so = I feel lonely here without any of you—I felt worse at leaving home this time than ever for I know not how long it will be ere I see it again—and till I do I cannot expect to be much with Father—if I felt so lonely and dull at parting, just to co[me] here—I cannot bear to think of my sensations when Father leaves me next summer at Philadelphia—I expect to see you in July—now that you know what it is to go, My dear Brother, you will not think it strange in me—your being there will be a great comfort to me—though I dare say you will not be able to see much of me— Do you go to see Anna often? Cousin Nancy is going back soon when she & Cousin Deas—go I will miss them dreadfully the house will be dull and nobody to be like very intimate with—for the rest are differen[t] [long line scratched out] Aunt Mary though kind—and they will be much out—except Aunt Mary—has written to you—she is up stairs but I know will send her love to you—Adieu My dear Brother—they are calling to me. I cannot fix the sentence on the other page to express what I mean I am in such confusion = Adieu, write me soon if ever so short and never doubt the sincerity of Your affectionate Sister EAS

[Postmarked CHARLESTON SC MAY 7]

[Addressed to]
Seaman D. Sinkler
Philadelphia
Pennsylvania

MARY DEAS BROÜN TO SEAMAN DEAS SINKLER IN PHILADELPHIA
[CHARLESTON,] MAY 20TH. 1836

My Dear nephew—
    Your truly welcome & affectionate letter of the sixth I received a few days since & now take my pen to thank you for it—which I assure you I do most sincerely[.] I really am glad to hear you say you are pleased with Philadelphia[.] I am not all fearful of your becoming indifferent to your home as the <u>friends</u> you have left are of the sincerest & most affectionate you must ever class me—you say I must write you often & fully cheerfully will I comply with your desire but I am afraid you will find my letters very barren of news—I suppose ere' this you have received Eliza's letter giving you all the particular's [*sic*] of the Beah's[17] wedding[.]

17 It is unclear to whom this name refers, but it is undoubtedly the Lesesne-Petigru wedding.

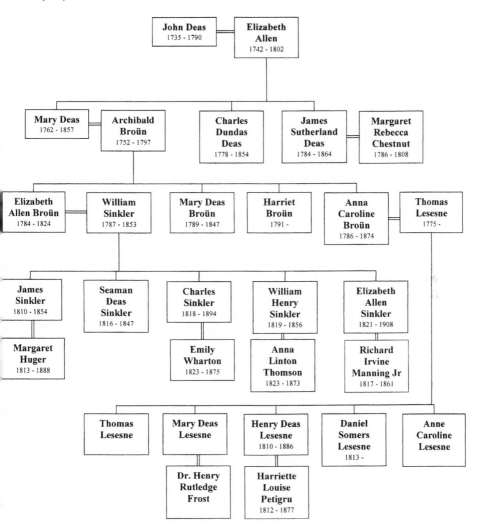

I found it quite a flat party so much so that I retired before the supper[.] James & Eliza were the only ones of the name that were there[.] I could not persuade Charles to go he did not think he was properly invited but I very much fear there was <u>an attraction here</u> where he spent that evening[.] I wish he would turn his mind to study & give up this boyish liking—I believe I wrote you that Mother has moved to a very uncomfortable house in Tradd St. notwithstanding which Mrs. L— gave a Tea party last evening it really was <u>an attempt</u> I wished often during the evening for you there were several of your young friends & it is probable you would have enjoyed yourself—Miss Emma Huger "a bride maid" came in at ten oclock hanging on <u>Chapman</u>'s arm[;] the remainder about half an hour

& their entrance with her usual ease and grace—Miss Petigru[,] Miss Kinloch[,] & Miss Porcher came in between ten & eleven remained about fifteen minutes & then took leave they were in the house just sufficient time to take an Ice cream[;] it was very evident that they considered & were considered by the other guests the <u>Exclusive</u> of the party—your friend Pringle was here but I had not an opportunity of speaking to him—R Smith[18] told me he had written you a long letter before he received yours[.] I wrote you before I left the Eutaw—John Bran is in the City on his way to Alabama. I expect my friend Mrs M—this evening she wrote me by John requesting me to go on with her to the North[.] I wish it suited me in all respects it would afford me an opportunity of seeing you my dear Seaman[;] your Father still speaks of taking your Sister on to Philadelphia I do not like to anticipate trouble but I do indeed dread her leaving me[;] without <u>her society</u> I know not what I would do in this house the Dr. & Deas & Henry & his bride dine here without ceremony[;] it is no longer thought wrong to have persons dine here on Sunday how people change their opinions when it suits them the two pair are to spend this summer together. Deas has lost her good looks completely she begins to look like an old Lady quite suitable for the Dr[.] Margaret was invited here last evening but excused herself saying she had a cold. William & Anna[19] are quiet[;] she is trying to learn to speak but she can only say Kate[;] they are two sweet little creatures. James is yet at St. Stephens I feel uneasy about him he has not yet <u>commenced</u> building in the pine land & I know him to be very imprudent the [torn] him on Tuesday he was well—if [torn] ere this you have heard that William has entered Columbia College[20] it was a great relief to me when I heard it for I feared he felt a little uneasy—I heard from your father a few days since he was well & ere' this is in the pineland[;][21] I hear Mr. Richardson has divide[d] his property very unequally[;] his Sons he has provided much more amply for than his Daughters this was to be expected—I have seen Paris he says he has your measure for a coat if you wish any thing you better get your father to take it in for you—I already [long] for the winter as I hope it will bring us all together again—Adieu My dear Nephew write me as often as you can. Yours truly
    MDB—

[Margin notes:]
    Nancy Broün is still here & I do not see how she will get to Alabama in the disturbed state in which the country is at present—Dr. Nott & Sally left this Tuesday since I feel quite uneasy about them[;] you have heard I suppose that

---

18 Probably Seaman's friend, Robert Press Smith.
19 James and Margaret Sinkler's young children, ages two and one.
20 South Carolina College in Columbia.
21 Pineland refers to the homes where families retreated in the warm months.

poor Gough Simons has has [*sic*] been killed in a Duel.[22] His antoginist['s] name was Pillings[—]perhaps you knew him—I forgot to tell you I he[a]r Miss Hanckle is engaged to a Mr. Means of Beaufort.

[Includes notes on margins, etc. written by sister EAS; transcribed separately]

[Postmarked CHARLESTON S. C. MAY 21]

[Addressed to]
Mr. Seaman Deas Sinkler
Philadelphia
Pennsylvania

[Notes on back, probably made by SDS]
Cost of Books & Where bought

Dungleson Physiology)	$7.00
Eberles Practice) Charleston	5.00
Dicksons Syllabus)	1.50
Tusons Desection)	1.25
Dewees Med ?)	1.30
Bryants Examiner) Philad	.40
McIntosh)	1.25
Smith & Merias)	4.00
Bee on Nerves)	2.00
Byrons Works)	2.00
	$ 25.70

ELIZA ALLEN SINKLER TO SEAMAN DEAS SINKLER IN PHILADELPHIA
[CHARLESTON 20 MAY 1836]

[NOTE: This was written by Eliza Allen Sinkler on the margins of a letter written by Mary Deas Broün.]

I do not think, Dear Brother that I will be able to write you this week so I will add a postscript to Aunt Mary's—I wrote you last Saturday—I suppose Aunt M has told you all the news of the party that was here last night—B. Garden Pringle begged me to say to you that he wrote about a fortnight ago and hopes you will answer the letter. He says he was very sorry that he could not pay you a visit in the country or even see you in town to say Good bye—I heard from our dear Father

22 Richard Gough Simons (1816–1836) & Pillings were officers returning from the Seminole war when they had a quarrel that resulted in a duel. www.genealogy.com/ftm/g/r/i/Kim-E-Grissom/GENE7–0007.html, accessed 06–03–2015.

this week he was in that detested Orangeburg—I wrote & told Charles all that you said—Have you written to William—I hope you will—it is dreadful that Brother should not correspond—My paper tells me stop though my inclination tells me to go on[.] I must obey the former. So Adieu and accept with this the sincere love of your Sister—

~

ELIZA ALLEN SINKLER TO SEAMAN DEAS SINKLER IN PHILADELPHIA
CHARLESTON JUNE 11–SATURDAY [1836]

I thank you sincerely My dear Brother, for your affectionate letter of the 31st— your letters, be assured, are a great source of delight to me and they always receive a hearty welcome. What pleasure is greater than that of receiving letters from our friends? Father & Charles got here safe last Monday evening—to my infinite delight though as they are staying at Stewarts I do not see them as much as I wish— however Father calls for me generally in the in the [*sic*] evening and we take a pleasant ride—he told me he wrote to you a few days ago—therefore I suppose you know that my fate is not yet decided—he says if I go at all it must be for 1½ years—this is a very long time (and now, My dear Brother, I suppose you you [*sic*] know what it is—though I believe you always did but would not acknowledge it) but if he does carry me you will I hope be with me. If I stay here this summer I will be very uncomfortable with him & you all away—and were it but for the summer I would be very glad to go—I long to see Anna Thomson—do when you see her, give my love to her—and beg her to write—she has owed me a letter a long time but I would not mind that had I any time—do you attend Madame G's soirees? do tell me all about Anna and her mann[ers.] Brother James yesterday looked at a house (Mrs. Keating Simons') but I do not know if he has made up his mind to go to housekeeping. Mrs[.] S and her whole family are going to the north the last week in the month so perhaps you will see your friend K. S. Robert Smith has had a tedious sickness: I do not believe he has been out yet— Some people seem to have a suspicion that Cousin Daniel is highly pleased with a little lady—Aunt Lesesne[23] is expecting Cousin Tom to visit this place some time in the summer— Both she & Cousin Anna look very thin—Dr. H [Nott] & Cousin Deas have not moved to Broad Street—but expect to do so soon—he has fitted out the house very nicely— Where we are living now is a horrid place though our chamber is pleasant enough—the yard is but a slip of land and the parlours hot as fire—the family occupy the upper piazza in the evening—unless when it rains and then we descend to the box—it is the eastern tenement of the house at the N E corner of Tradd & Meeting Streets—

23 Aunt Lesesne would be Mary Deas Broün's older sister, Anna Caroline (1786–1874), who was married to Thomas Lesesne.

Both Father and myself have got letters from William this week and he says he has written to you—he seems shocked at seeing so many go on <u>tick</u>[24]—he is to be down the 1st of July—Charles is studying navigation with Mr. Leland—and I do not see very much of him— Cousin Nancy I suspect will go about the middle of next week—their present plan is by the Florida route, as several persons have come on in that way safe—Friday—Dear Brother you will really think me negligent—but it is a fact that I have not had time to finish my letter. Every day I run in from school study my lessons and then Father calls for me—and you know that I cannot withstand—I believe you will forgive me as this is my first transgression—I hope you do not include me in your reproof in Father's letter— cousin Nancy went off this morning. I cannot say by what route for I hear they were obliged to alter after they got up to the Rail Road—they had intended to go to Greenville—Yesterday we all dined with Father he got a private parlour— I wished that you and William were there—Father is suffering much from his foot—I only wish you were here to doctor it—and yet is not that selfish? Do Brother when you write tell me what you think candidly about my going—I am really in an uncomfortable state—I would much rather go than stay here in the summer but then that 1,000 miles between Fa[ther] & myself in the winter— and then not certain of having you—My heart is pulling me in every different direction—Where Charles will be I cannot say—Father hopes to get him on board the vessel that is now preparing—They have called me to dinner—so I will close my letter—it is not worth going but to you—and I could not think of making you pay the enormous sum of 2 cents—as the planters here are all talking about the rain and I am afraid you do not take exercise enough so Adieu—

Your always affectionate Sister

I believe I must let you off from taking a walk this time but the n[ext] time I will not—

[Postmarked CHARLESTON S.C. JUN 18]

[Addressed to]
Mr. Seaman D. Sinkler
No 14 Sanson [*sic*] Street
Philadelphia
Pa

[Note below address]
Do tell me if I direct merely to Philad[elphia] if you will get it

---

24 Tick refers to leaving bills on credit; WHS was attending South Carolina College in Columbia.

~

WILLIAM SINKLER TO SEAMAN DEAS SINKLER
CHARLESTON 30 JUNE 1836

My Dear Seaman—

I wrote to you, immediately, after my arrival in this place—and enclosed you one hundred dollars—and as the enclosure, would have made an immediate reply necessary—I thought of course, I would by this time have heard from you—I hope no accident has happened to the letter—and that I may soon, have the best testimony and acknowledgement, from you. Tomorrow was the day—I was to have left this for Norfolk, but a variety of circumstances have occurred to prevent—I have been twice, quite sick—but have been detained more particularly to attend the sale of Goshen,[25] which takes place the 6th of July from what I can learn, there is but little chance however of my becoming the purchaser. I have had many things to disturb my tranquility—among the most important of which has been, and now is, to get Charles fixed in some place, what are his ideas, for the future, nay even the present—I am sure I cannot say, how dreadful it is, to see a youth well blessed, with fine intellectual powers, waste his genius on things, frivolous—or spend his time in idleness—. The present rage or fashion in this City, among the well informed and well bred, is to make money—it is quite a fashion—young men, are going into Counting houses—to become, men of business—receiving, while they are obtaining information, salaries, quite sufficient for their support—and of course no longer a tax on their friends or parents—, by the bye your friend Mr. Pringle, has gone to Edisto, to take charge of a school so you see, that he, while he will be preparing himself for the Law will be putting something handsome into his pocket—, it is quite praiseworthy—I wrote you in my last, by Deveaux—I was quite undetermon'd about Eliza—I am equally so, now—if I should bring her on. I would hope Mrs. Greland, will abandon her summer excursions, which I by no means approve—they can have no good tendency. It would have [been] very pleasant could I have left here tomorrow I should have had the advantages of the society [of] Mrs. Simons and her family. I suppose you will of course see Mr. Simons, who will give you the news, of our City—William returned home from Columbia, on Friday last—he looks well, evidently, he has benefitted from the change of Institutions—I hope he will realize my fondest hopes[.] Accounts from home of the cotton crop, are favorable—if I could but pay a visit there, what an advantage it would be to the crop so I have the vanity to believe—. As soon after the 6 of July as possible, I will leave—my health, would induce me to seek first the Virginia Springs, but the welfare of

25 Property located near St. Matthews, in present-day Calhoun County. Neuffer, *Names in South Carolina*, 12:47.

Charles, will not allow me to do so—I must go to Washington, and if possible get him, in some situation, where there will be no more idling[.] I am anxious to see, you, more so my son than words could express—apply your time profitably—, God bless you and grant us a happy meeting—

Your affectionate father

W Sinkler

All friends are well—your sister I saw for a few minutes all tender their love—

~

MARGARET HUGER SINKLER[26] TO SEAMAN DEAS SINKLER [IN PHILADELPHIA] CHARLESTON JULY 7 1836

My Dear Brother,

You are I hope fully aware that my long silence does not proceed from the want of inclination but I have been so much occupied with your brother "as a good wife ought to be" that I have had very little time to call my own, but that I believe is <u>never</u> "a poor womans privilege" he has been very sick since his return from the Country & you know it is a <u>family failing</u> not to be able to make up his mind immediately, what would be his movement for the Summer but now he is off for Virginia.[27] I have more leisure & determined that a letter to you should be the first thing I would do—but dear Seaman I hoped before this to have received one line of remembrance from you your Brother received your letter & it was his determination to have answered it but a few days after he was taken sick, but he has in anticipation the pleasure of seeing you in the course of the Summer—Both of my little children have been sick & I am in fear of the Hooping Cough and Measles which is prevailing very much in our city—I was very glad to hear that you are so well pleased with your situation[.] I hope however you will not like it so well as to induce you to be absent during the winter remember when we are all around the hearth at the Eutaw of our vacant chair which cast a gloomy [*sic*] on us—Our Tailor of course we cannot calculate on—I need not be drawing all these dear home scenes to your mind often I expect you have them "in minds eye" I am sinful enough to be wishing the time between this & October would pass quickly by—Our city is very dull the latest news is the engagement of my friend Julia Ancrum to Mr. Davidson a widower with <u>two</u> children and another her age[.] What do you think of the report says Maria Simons is engaged to Gibbes Elliott but I cannot vouch for the truth of that—I see a good deal of aunt

---

26 Margaret Huger was married to Seaman's oldest brother, James, and they had two young children, ages one and two.

27 White Sulphur Springs, Virginia.

Mary & Eliza since they have moved in our neighborhood—your father has been indisposed but he is never well & looks better than I have seen him for some time he leaves us on the 15th for Norfolk with Charles and William—Adieu my dear Brother I shall be very happy to hear from you when ever you can find a leisure moment—Mother desires her love to you & accept the affectionate love of William & Anna sends a Kiss—   Your Sister

    MHS

[Addressed to]
Mr. Seaman D. Sinkler
No 14 Sansom Street
Philadelphia

MARY DEAS BROÜN TO SEAMAN DEAS SINKLER IN PHILADELPHIA
[CHARLESTON] AUGUST 5TH: 1836

My Dear Nephew—
      Your letter of the 26th I received yesterday you may judge how truly welcome it was by my promptness in replying to it[;] it is impossible for my feeble pen to express how much pleasure your affectionate communications always give me[;] continue to write me and always write me as a <u>true</u> <u>friend</u> who loves you dearly—I am glad to hear you have moved out of the City such excessive heat was enough to have <u>unstrung your</u> nerves & rendered you incapab[le] of any exertion[.] I really think you deserve credit for your selfdenial [*sic*] in not accompanying your fath[er] to New York[.] I trust there is much pleasure & enjoyment in store for <u>you</u> & indeed for <u>you all</u>[.] I long to see you very much[;] when I think of the pleasure I will feel when I meet you I am in a tremor[;] I am sorry to hear your father's spirits are not good they were much deprest when here last—I attributed it to the unkind manner in which he was treated by those he had believed to be his <u>friends</u>[.] Mrs. L has litterally taken possession of the house[;] she appears to think the world made for her & her Children[;] the dea[r] <u>gentleman</u> does not appear at all satisfied I would not be surprised if he removed from the house he said the other day "that Anna was so completely absorbed in her Children but he supposed it was natural[.]" They are uneasy about the dear Dr. he has a bad cough the sighs would fill the sails of a Man of War & Deas is quite delicate they both look very badly[.] the two pair dine here every Wednesday[;] they have not yet quit playing the <u>Lovers</u>[.] I have not heard of our dear James for ten days[;] his last letter was dated Salisbury[.] Margaret & the dear children are well[;] they are engaging little creatures William has a cry almost every morning to come & see Aunt <u>Ma</u> ought I not to love the aff[ec]t[ionate little rogue[.] Anna runs about & can say some few words[.] I know you will laugh at me when you read all this but

excuse a <u>doting</u> old <u>Aunty</u>[.] Margaret has got your letter & says she will try & be a regular correspondent[.] Mrs. M is in great trouble her housekeeper was struck with <u>Palsy</u> & of course will never be of use to her again—I had almost forgot to tell you the news you know T Lesesne is here & there is not the smallest doubt— <u>on my</u> mind that he has renewed his addresses to our fair cousin in [word unclear] Street[.] She drank tea here an evening or two since & the <u>Manouvering</u> Mother soon got him fixed where he wish[e]d to be[.] I would not venture to give an opinion as to his succeeding—you must even now have a long walk to the <u>Alms House</u>. Ah my dear Seaman be prudent take care of yourself with no unnecessary risk[.] the weather here for the last ten days has been excessively warm the thermometer 91—but this is not equal to Philadelphia[;] if I was a good scribe I would be writing continually for next to the pleasure of mercury is the writing to a dear friend—how is [*sic*] Charles's spirits does he appear satisfied with the profession he has chos[en?] Poor fellow I often think of him[.] I wonder if Mrs. L—[torn] recollects he is her godson give my Love to [him] affectionately & beg him to write me[.] I do not know where to direct or I would write <u>him</u>[.] God grant he may succeed in his profession & be all your father wishes[.] Prof[es]s[or] Smith has received the things from you safe[.] I see him very seldom[.] I do not know if he has got a letter from you recently—I am glad you have young friends with you who are agreeable[;] as soon as you have determined let me know if you return here this winter—my dear Eliza desires her [words unclear;] for she is well but her spirits are deprst [*sic*] but I suppose it proceeds from her being separated from you all[;] she is very anxious to reside continually with your father[.] In reading over this scrawl I see so little to interest or amuse you that I am half inclined to destroy it & try & do better but perhaps it would be worse—do use every precaution in visiting Patients at the Alms House[.] I never knew the City duller than it has been this summer I have not heard of a tea fight[28] do take Dr. Huger's advice & cultivate the acquaintances of the Ladies[;] you require some recreation & relaxation from study let it be in associating with them—I wish I could be transported to the Banks of the Schuylkill[29] for a little while[.] I have a thousand things to say to you Heaven Bless you my dear Nephew Your Sincere Friend

MDB

---

28 A tea fight was a public, or large private tea party. Eric Partridge, *Slang: To-Day and Yesterday* (N.p.: n.d.), 203, ebook available at Google Books, https://books.google.com/ books/about/SLANG_TODAY_AND_YESTERDAY.html?id=LeVRnQEACAAJ (accessed October 30, 2015).

29 Seaman had recently moved close to this river, which runs through Philadelphia.

[Postmarked CHARLESTON S.C. AUG 6]
[Addressed to]
Mr. Seaman D. Sinkler
Philadelphia
Pennsylvania
Steamer

WILLIAM SINKLER TO SEAMAN DEAS SINKLER IN PHILADELPHIA
WHITE SULPHUR SPRINGS 15 [AND 16] AUGUST 1836

My Dear Son—

We arrived at this place yesterday evening—all things considered, we had rather a pleasant time—I found your brother here—looking unusually well, and getting on well, in consequence of his being here, we are comfortably accommodated, which I assure you is no easy matter—There are a great number of persons on the mountain & a vast number at these springs—and tho' they have added many cabins—and a general improvement, in everything—there is much difficulty, to procure accommodations as ever—I believe, if fifty cabins were to be put down by magic, they would be filled in a day or two—The young Frenchman has stuck to us—is pleased with every thing—he is deficient in judgment, but has good feelings—and quite agreeable—he did not get as much money, as he expected in Baltimore, this I thought strange, has therefore only returned thirty dollars—but promises to pay the balance of seventy ($70) dollars to you— which I hope he will do, promptly—will that sum be sufficient—to enable you to allow Charles Sixteen dollars for a Cocked hat and as much as four or five dollars more? James speaks of having this for him next week—we have not determined whether he will take the stage or his carriage—I have met with many acquaintances here, among them—The Mess^r Taylors and the Rev. Mr. Hanekell, and his daughter—I could spend my time pleasantly here—but when I think of Charles—and some <u>matters</u> I am made gloomy—. I saw young Mr. Singleton at Charlottesville—they say he is positively to be married—and I do hear, that his father is <u>much</u> <u>opposed</u> to it—if it be true—it will be an awkward situation, for the son—. I wish you could have spared the time, to visit, this place. I am sure the waters, would be of great service to you—you would be astonished to see in what a short time, great changes are produced—James looks like another person—. Let me hear from you immediately—and as often as you can—I think you had better conclude, to return home this Winter—you will have great advantages—I do not think it would be a bad plan, for you to enter Dr. Frost's office—he has a great deal of practice—and while you are attending the Lectures you could be preparing medicines—for the patients he may be attending, and gain a knowledge of his practice—which <u>has</u> become <u>extensive</u>—I think I

South lawn of White Sulphur Springs, VA, where WS frequently visited.
Courtesy of the Library of Congress.

shall remain in these mountains, until the 15th of September—, I will not hurry
myself for fear, I may become too anxious when I get near home—. I got a letter from Eliza—all friends are well—Richard Richardson [JBR's youngest son]
left here, before my arrival, for Philadelphia. I hope you will make it a <u>point</u> to
<u>see</u> him—, James & William desired to be remembered to you, adieu my dear
Seaman

    Your affectionate father

    W Sinkler

Tuesday 16th I have just had a conversation with Mr. Richard—he says in about
ten days, he will be in Philadelphia—and he positively, will, pay you the seventy
($70) dollars—, when he sees you in New York—I hope he will do so—if he
should propose to send it by mail—I would advise you, to say, you would prefer
to wait, until you went to New York—unless you <u>knew of any person</u>, by whom
he could send it—and who you <u>would be willing to place confidence in</u>—. This
young man appears to mean well, he certainly is very goodhearted, to use a common phrase—but is inexperienced, and entirely deficient in judgment, and in the
<u>ways, of the world</u>—he made his debut in the Ball room—and was introduced to
one or two young ladies. <u>At his request</u>—this by Mrs L—guest—was a <u>delicate</u>

Residences on Paradise Row in White Sulphur Springs, VA. Courtesy of
the Library of Congress.

matter—. In consequence of his coming in with me and having had an introduction, to one or two young man [*sic*]—and James kindly taking him into his room,
(until he can do better,) were advantageous circumstances[.] I have felt very awk-
ward, when I have been asked—who he was—I could say no more than he was
introduced to me, by an acquaintance—and I believed him to be respectable—. A
man cannot be too cautious <u>who</u> [he] <u>associa[tes]</u> with, or who <u>he introduces</u>—,
the responsibility in the latter is too great to be assumed—. While on this subject, let me advise you not to encourage too great an intimacy <u>with persons</u> you
do not know—for instance this young man[;] you can be polite, and courteous,
without <u>creating too great an intimacy</u>—he speaks of visiting the South, in the
autumn, therefore be <u>silent</u>, on this <u>subject</u> of <u>your plans</u>—lest a proposal be
made to <u>accompany</u> you—in saying thus much, my object, is not to <u>injure</u>, an
<u>unoffending</u> individual, whose conduct has been all politeness—and who seems
perfectly <u>grateful</u> for the <u>attentions</u> received—but to put you on your guard. I
will write you again in a few weeks. <u>Read</u>, and then <u>burn this letter</u>. I have just got
a letter from, my dear Charles—it is quite satisfactory. I have every reason now
to hope that the cause of my unhappiness, may be removed—he is quite a smart,
fine looking youth, and if he conducts himself properly—he will be <u>worthy</u> of
the <u>finest woman</u>, our country affords—I love him truly and hope, God will

bless him, and make him a comfort to me—an honor to his profession—and to his family—he is anxious to see you—you will not however go, I presume before September—it is the best time to go. [The end of the photocopied letter possibly covered by the envelope].

[Addressed to]
[Postmark WHITE SULXSPRS Vạ AUG 16]
Mr. Seaman Deas Sinkler
Philadelphia

WILLIAM SINKLER TO SEAMAN DEAS SINKLER [IN PHILADELPHIA]
WHITE SULPHUR 19 AUGUST 1836

My Dear Seaman—
    Your kind, and acceptable letter of the 10th Inst[ant] reached me yesterday[.] It gave me much pleasure to hear from you, and to have such good evidence afforded me of your improvement—and determination to prosecute your studies with zeal, which must terminate in success—I have thought frequently of you, and the best plan for you to adopt, for the Winter—I am under the impression, that it would be a good plan to return to Charleston—I refer you my son, to my letter, by the last mail—for my opinion fully on the subject—I have given you my opinion and you are now at liberty to make your selection—so that you, apply your time profitably—and graduate with credit—I will be satisfied—. Your brother James, has, <u>after, a variety of plans, come</u> to the determination, of turning the Carriage over to me, and is to leave here on Sunday for Philadelphia—where you may expect him by Friday next—, this arrangement, would deprive me of the privilege, of visiting you—I must creep on South, after the 15 of September from these mountains, in order to get William to Columbia by the 1st of October—. He by the bye looks much better—he uses the water, sparingly, he does, not bathe, the baths are not numerous—and too much in <u>requisition by the diseased</u>—I have observed your advice, which I am always willing to treat with respect—and thank you—and feel gratified that I have so occupied your attention my dear Seaman[.] I use the waters sparingly, it is the only way to get the system, properly impregnated were it not for the <u>spot, which</u> you have seen I would not use them at all[.] A great number of persons are here, about five hundred—and persons daily arriving and turned off as many as one hundred and fifty made application to get in, day before yesterday—and only fifty succeeded—The evenings amusement are [*sic*] dancing, a great many very pretty ladies are here—I often wish for you—and wish for Charles too, a sight of <u>some of these</u>—would <u>soon obliterate</u> the recollection of __, which were to lift a great load from me[.] The gentlemen, during the day—hunt, play cards (a party on now, in hearing,

only in the Piazza—engaged at that business), and visit the ladies—Richard,[30] is
going on very well—and has made a tolerable good impression he is quite a ladies
man—and is not over burthened with modesty—I think very well of him—although, his conduct, in the circumstances of the loan was rather singular—if
however he pays you, it will remove any unpleasant reflection—, but that of his
being imprudent—I will endeavor—to get James—to make some arrangements,
with you for money you may require—I will write you by him—if only to tell
you, what I wish you to procure for me—I am sensibly obliged to Dr. Chap-
man—whose acquaintance I beg you will cultivate, visit his house as often as you,
can, and your company is acceptable, which no doubt, will always meet, with a
good reception—I heard from my dear Eliza her letter dated the 8th the city is
healthy and all are well—she is indeed a good child and deserves all—I can possibly do for her—my happiness, seems to be, her study to promote—O what a
blessing is such a child—I presume, you will go on with James, to see Charles—it
is his intention to go to see him—I observe by the papers—from an advertisement of Petigru & Lesesne[31]—that, a letter sent by them to Phil[a]delphia on the
8 of June, with three hundred dollars, is missing—this looks bad—and gives less
hope for the recovery of yours—. I beg you will write me, as often as your time,
will admit—it gives me pleasure to hear from you—this is my third letter, since I
have parted with you—. God bless you my son
    Your affectionate father
    W Sinkler

Remember me to Mr. Stoney—if Mrs. Greland has returned, my respects to
her a[nd] love to Anna—

[Addressed to]
[Postmarked WHITE SULXSPRS V<u>A</u> AUG 19]
Mr. Seaman Deas Sinkler
Philadelphia

ELIZABETH ALLEN SINKLER TO SEAMAN DEAS SINKLER IN PHILADELPHIA
CHARLESTON AUGUST 20 1836

What is the reason My dear Brother that I have not heard from you for so long a
time—I have not got a letter from you since Father went—I hope it is only that

---

30 A friend of Seaman's who owed him money; he was also referred to as "the Frenchman."

31 Henry Deas Lesesne, William Sinkler's nephew, was an accountant and a law partner
with his father-in-law, James L. Petigru.

you are busy—As long as he was with you—I did not expect you to write—but now he has left you and it is the vacation time—I hope to hear very soon—Aunt Mary [Mary Deas Broün] got a letter from Father as far as Fredericksburg. I am sorry to say he was in bad spirits—but that was I suppose at having just left you—and Charles—I wish that you and C. were in the same city—however you can get to each other in very little time—I am very anxious to hear from him[.] Sister[32] heard from Brother James the other day he was at the White Sulphur—and a great deal better though he had been quite unwell at the Gray Sulphur—he is quite homesick. I heard from William in New York—I did not think he seemed very much pleased with the travelling—I suppose Anna will soon be returning to Philadelphia—Do beg her to write to me—I long to hear dear Brother your determination with regard to the next winter—we will all miss you dreadfully but if you think it would be more advantage[e]ous to you to remain there, we will have to submit—but the fact is we will not know what to do without you. I do not like to think of it at all—but I will say no more for you will come if you think you can without injury to the getting the title of M.D. and if you cannot—there is no use to say any thing about it—for we both know that your absence will be a great mar to pleasure and your presence will contribute much to it—Though time does go very fast—it seems dear Brother like a year since I have seen you—consequently cannot help being very very anxious for your return—only to think of it makes me feel joyful—I often recur to the day you left us—and all the feeling I had as you turned from the avenue return—and even then I could not realize that you were going so far—I often think of you—in your beautiful abode on the Schuylkil[l]—and wish we could be there together—I try to imagine the scene but I fear I come far short of it. What a contrast this summer is to me to the last—now Father is away and I have not one of you with me—it is a lonely feeling—There is nothing I look forward to with more horror than our separation for a long time, but I hope and trust when Charles comes back—and you are practicing here—we will have no more of that—It is a long time to look forward to—but I hope all my anticipation will be realized. Sister and the children are well—she looks thin and seems very anxious for the return of Brother James—she says she will never let it be so another summer—that she will go under any circumstances with him since she has regretted not going so much this summer—Willie is very engaging—he is so affectionate—he heard us say we had heard from you and asked "Where is Uncle Seaman?["] He told his mother the other day that he wanted pen, ink & paper to write to his Father—Anna is a little fairy—and runs and chatters all day—they have the highest spirits I ever saw—There is a perfect dearth of news in town—indeed it is almost deserted—I must soon say Adieu My dear Brother [torn] that I will see you

32 "Sister" was probably brother James's wife, Margaret.

in the winter—Aunt Mary & Grandmother & the rest of the family desire me
to send the[ir] love—believe always My dear Brother that you have the sincerest
from

    Your Aff[ection]ate Sister

[Postmarked CHARLESTON S. C. AUG 20]
[Addressed to] Mr. Seaman D. Sinkler
Philadelphia
Pennsylvania
Steam boat via New York

WILLIAM SINKLER TO SEAMAN DEAS SINKLER IN PHILADELPHIA
WHITE SULPHUR–VA 22 AUGUST 1836

My Dear Son—

    I wrote you yesterday, by Mr. Richard—and already do I find my pen in
my hand to address you—I mentioned the circumstances of your brothers have
changed his plans—he left here yesterday, in despite [*sic*] of all I was to say, to go
directly home every person here, gave it as their opinion, that he would decid-
edly run a great risk—he heard too that P[ine]v[i]ll[e] was sickly—but all to no
purpose—go he would—I feel uneasy and the more so, in consequence of a letter
this day received, which mentions one or two cases of sickness in Cordesville—
young Simons, the son of Edward Simons is very ill—this shows conclusively—
that the general state of the atmosphere is bad—I wish he might again change his
plans and remain in Greenville until October—I had hoped my <u>presence</u> here,
were to have induced his longer stay—but neither the desire to be with me or my
advice were <u>strong enough</u>, to have weight—what a mortification if however he
escapes Sickness—I can reconcile myself to the other circumstances—. As I have
to go with William as far as Greenville—and as I wish to delay a little while at
the warm springs in No[rth] Carolina—and to visit Buncombe, I think I shall
leave this quite as early as the 10th of September—I have given you my advice respecting, next Winter—I think yet—it would be best you should return—where
you will have equal advantages—and certainly a better chance of understanding
the diseases of our climate—but as I said before you can do as you please my
dear Seaman—only graduate with credit—and I am satisfied—The longer I live,
the the [*sic*] more I see the necessity, of every young man, studying a profession,
and <u>practicing</u> he must practice, to become <u>conspicuous</u>—The advantages are
manifold—it leads to independence and re<u>spect</u> and often <u>esteem</u>, from every
body, it is the <u>best letter</u> of recommendation—and certainly puts a <u>young</u> man,
on a <u>footing</u>, with the most conspicuous, Look at Dr. Nott—, his fortune is
made—and his reputation, worthy of every man[']s admiration—there is Dr.
Frost—he has made his own fortune—Dr. Dickson would not have been known,

but for education, and his <u>profession</u>—Dr. Prioleau and a host of others—. Pope was right when [he] said "Worth makes the man" I have the greatest confidence in you, and believe you will employ, your time profitably, and do ample justice to the <u>opportunities</u> that are now, and <u>may be afforded</u> you—The young man who I wrote you respecting—I think as I said, has an excellent heart—but he is imprudent—has, I soon discovered, no <u>stability</u>, he is easily lead [*sic*] away—and therefore an unfit companion, for any, but the most <u>steady</u> and <u>positive</u>—it is <u>easy</u> to commence the practice of vice, but when <u>once familiar</u>—there is little <u>chance</u>, of <u>abandoning</u> it—I have concluded to get a cloak made, of such Stuff as I told, Dermont the best <u>Camlet</u>, a <u>dark blue</u>—I wish it <u>handsomely made</u>, large cape, and with armholes to button, when <u>not used</u>—the <u>standing cape</u> to be lined <u>with finest velvet</u>—and a <u>little</u> ornament for such a one, I think he asked $20, or $22—unless I could have an uncommon neat Cloak—I <u>would not have it</u>—direct him also to make me a pair of the <u>best</u>, <u>black</u>, <u>Cashmere</u>, <u>(double milled)</u> pantaloons, they are wanted for dress—then articles direct to the care of Mr. G. L. Deas—they had better not be sent, until the middle of October—Say to Dermont, it <u>depends</u> how I am pleased with the Cloak and pants—whether he is to have my custom—I direct Miles to have the boots made, which can be sent at the same time—the soals [*sic*] must be a little thicker, than those <u>of the shoes he made</u>—I want <u>high heels</u>—If you could without trouble, get some one, to procure, a keg of about 60, or 70 lbs. of the best—butter—I wish you would procure one—and a half keg of good tongues (beef)—These articles, ought not to be sent on, until about the 20th of October—You might get the Lady who you are boarding with to select these <u>articles for you</u>—if however, my son you find the <u>least difficulty</u>, do not <u>trouble</u> yourself <u>about</u> them. If you determine to go home in the fall—you will require money—you can draw on your uncle Charles—at the same time, you can ascertain the am[oun]t of the articles I have wrote for, and include that among, with what you will require for your own use—This will be a <u>year of great expense to me</u>—I must go <u>home</u>, and work hard and try, and make up the <u>deficiency</u> that may <u>be created</u>—.

Charles spoke in his letters, of his situation, and intimated, if he wished to get extricated, from the Difficulty "how it was to be done?" The best and safest is <u>an entire</u> and <u>positive silence</u>—never to <u>commit himself to paper</u>—he [torn] forget—and she if she has <u>sense</u> or feeling—will understand all [torn] meant by it—<u>any</u> woman who wants <u>consent</u>, to yield to the wishes [of] any youth of eighteen—<u>without first</u>, knowing, the opinion <u>of his family</u> ought to expect nothing else—and surely it is better <u>for him</u>, to abandon her [than] <u>to be cast off</u> by <u>his family</u>, which <u>will be</u> the <u>result</u>, if he <u>persists</u> beside they adopt only <u>this mode</u>—of treating <u>her</u> with <u>slight</u>, and <u>contempt</u>—what a [torn] will it be to both <u>parties</u>—to <u>him</u> & <u>her</u>—, Say as much as you [torn] the subject and induce him to abandon, what will inevitable [*sic*] lead to ruin—and I will write to him tomorrow—. I understand Tom Lesesne, and Henry, have gone [to] Buncombe, the latter has gone for his health. They are to return in ten days—Tom, no doubt, means to renew the business with his cousin—I hope Charles will visit, Mrs. Wells and the other lady often—advise him, to avoid all frolicsome company—Michaud i[s] certainly that way inclined—William desires to be remembered to you—my paper as well as time, admonishes me—God bless you,

P.S. Better, <u>burn my letters, such as these</u> Your affectionate father
W Sinkler—

[Addressed to]
[Postmarked WHITE SULXSPRS VA̱ AUG 22]
Mr. Seaman Deas Sinkler
Philadelphia

[Note]
The cloak ought to be lined with some thin woolen stuff, <u>blue</u>—and <u>fine</u>—and the cape to have a chord, to make it secure around the neck—he will understand from that description what is meant—

ROBERT PRESS SMITH TO SEAMAN DEAS SINKLER IN PHILADELPHIA
CHARLESTON SEPTEMBER 23RD 1836

My Dear Seaman,

Your last letter dated at NY was doubly gratifying to me in not only hearing of your health and enjoyment, but also a disreguard of the foolish ceremony of letter for letter, I being in arrears to you for one on the receipt of the last: every allowance should be made for me as you know I am kept much harder at it than any of the fellows here. My dear Seaman you will bear with me when I recount to you a most melancholy occurance; the death of my two little Nephiews [*sic*], in the short space of four days (two each), they were snatched from the heighest health and laid in the silent Grave[.] Oh most horrid PineVille it proves a Buryal Ground to all Children the season was so far advanced I had really flattered myself that all would be well with them for this Summer at least; whent [*sic*] to think with what honor and regret I was struck to hear of the death of both the eldest was but indisposed when his brother died, poor little fellow a few hours before his death, as the paroxisoms [*sic*] of pain would come on his screams could be heard all over the neighbourhod; and evry [*sic*] piece of furniture in the room shook his struggles were so tremendous; although not five years old, their poor bereaved Parents are truly to be pittied, however we are taught to believe that the God who directs all things suits the capacity to the affliction. This City has had, and still has many cases of Cholera, many more than you see reported in the daily papers, in consequence of the irregular reporting of your <u>Brother Chip</u>; notwithstanding that foolish blind that appeared in the papers some time since; an Ordinance of Council inflicting a fine of $500 on any Physician neglecting to report a single case coming under his Knowledge: our young friend Benjamin Murden had it pretty severe, but Dr. Frost cured him in a couple of hours, his has been the only case that has made me think of Noi: it has been making great havock on Daniel's Island at Capers' Plantation he has lost near thirty all fullgrown Negroes, in one day they had as many as 27 cases, Nancy Dawson has been attending Them. Before I forget let me tell you the above named Colt is engaged to just such another, (having Gender) Jane Simons daughter of Dr. Thos Y, such rattle brained people should be prohibited from marrying, particularly getting together. you fellows all give accounts of your Travels, I will tell you of a trip some of us had to Wo[o]dstock on a day of humiliation and prayer ordered by our Sallaried Intendant; among our fellow passengers there were two in black, one calling <u>tother Ruff</u> and <u>tother</u> calling <u>one Dolph</u>, the latter was quite a buckish looking fellow with mighty Jimmy sort of whiskers, but Oh Ruff he looked more like an Apostle than any thing I had ever seen, his stiff whiskers, and mustachios, with hair coming down over his face, all made me think I saw one one [*sic*] of the good old guandam [*sic*] Fishers; as you may suppose I kept very quiet and amused myself with looking at this oddity, when all at once there was the most infernal crash and overturn; the Engine had taken a fancy to quit the Road, (fortunately for our Bacon we were not on one of those low places) I very soon left the Wreck and went to the assistance of a Fireman on the ground, soon after came this mysterious stranger, judge of my amazement when he said to Dolph, how I wish Seaman Sinkler was here to see how strange a face he would put on this Catastrophe[;] upon enquiring found they were your friends the Not[t]s: our party took up the line of march for Woodstock not wishing to be any longer dependant on Steam for our Breakfast, the walk was only a matter of 5 miles about 3 Oclock up came the Car, Dolph and the Apostle came, but to smell the Dinner, for no sooner did they get a mouth full in than it was spit out in calling for the Car to stop that was off.

I must now contude [*sic*] my dear Seaman this doleful Epistle—
Your most sincerely
R P Smith

PS Your aunt has your Cloak I hope it will please; it is the ditto of my own, do write me for any thing you want 4½ yds Cloth   @ 3.50 $15.75

2 " Velvet	@ 4.00	8—
1 Tassle		<u>1.50</u>
		$25.25

[Postmarked CHARLESTON S.C. SEP 2]
[Addressed to]
P. Smith
Seaman D. Sinkler Esq
Steamer Philadelphia

MARY DEAS BROÜN TO SEAMAN DEAS SINKLER IN PHILADELPHIA
EUTAW JANUARY 17TH: 1837

My Dear nephew—

It appears an age since I have written you but my silence has been caused by several circumstances[;] there is some difficulty in getting direct opportunities from this place & when they have offered your father or Sister have written and I thought it unnecessary to encumber you with <u>letters</u> when I could give you no news but what no doubt theirs contained[.] I feel you will accept this as a sufficient excuse for my not having replyed to two or three of your kind affectionate letters ere this. Your communications are always read by me with the most heartfelt pleasure[.] I feel interested in all your plans and arrangements continue to write me unreservedly on this subject[.] I have several times been <u>indirectly</u> questioned about your intentions for the future but I have never given the slightest information sufficient will it be when you return to us that period so ardently & anxiously anticipated it—is impossible for you to imagine with how much pleasure I am looking forward to our meeting in March[.] I am sinful enough to wish the time were already here[;] the moment you have graduated I entreat you to relieve my painful anxiety & write me if you only have time to say "I am M.D." the pain of suspense is beyond leaving, but enough of this subject I find it too <u>exciting</u>[.] We have had quite a dull Christmas you and Charles both absent & to add to our gloom but a day or two previous to the holydays [*sic*] your father got a letter from poor Charles mentioning how sick he had been & was still extremely weak poor fellow I feel more for him than I can describe[.] I trust in heaven he has not allowed himself to get entangled in the snares spread for him if left to himself[.] I am concerned he will act as he ought[.] Mr. A Huger has been extremely kind in working and giving your father all the information in his power respecting how Charles have you heard lately and has he gone to Sea I wish the time had arrived for his return[.] I always disliked the Sea & shall do so more than ever—William spent five or six days with us but that was as long a holyday [*sic*] as he could get[.] James & your Sister & the chicks were with us their prattle & tricks serve to amuse us a little dear little creatures you will find them much improved[.] William called William nothing but Uncle Sea so you see he has not forgot you by name[.] James is incorrigible as a correspondent[;]

I cannot imagine why he has such a dislike to his pen[.] Margaret says she will write you very soon[;] the children take so much of her time is the reason she has not done so before this they will go down the last week in February she will not be able to return this spring your brother will have a dreadful uncomfortable time of it—continually going to & fro[.] Mr. H[uger] will think this nothing[;] we came up from St. Stephens about ten days ago—your father speaks of going up to visit your Aunt Richardson in a day or two Eliza & myself will accompany him[;] and as soon as we return we shall be off for Charleston[.] I am sorry to think how lonely he will be left [behind] by himself—Your grandmother says she frequently sits to dinner only two Henry L[esesne] & his Lady have gone to their own house so no doubt your Aunt Ls time is compleat[ly] taken up in writing at the Dr & Henry's—what do you think of a gentleman walking up to Ann Deas & speaking to her as Mrs. Lesesne rather embarassing her[.] Sister Allen quickly explained [matters.] I suppose she will be married in [the] e[arl]y part of the sum-mer & steam away f[or] Alabama what ocean of tears shed on the occasion poor girl it really will be a trial [for] her—you tell me you have again changed your abode surely my dear Seaman you are not difficult to please—I have been quite unwell with influenza for the last week if you had been here I would have got you to Bleed me[.] I however hope that before the [word unclear] if there is anything you want against you come home let me know & I'll attend to it—your Linen must be getting thin[;] if you wish any write <u>immediately</u>[;] the dinner here ap-proaches I wish you were here to partake your father[']s gave cheer—Heaven Bless you my dear Nephew Eliza joins me in aff[ectiona]t[e] love Yours Ever

   MDB

[Note from WS to SDS on 19 January enclosed]
[Postmarked CHARLESTON S.C. JAN 22]
[Addressed to]
Mr. Seaman D. Sinkler
Philadelphia
Pennsylvania

~

[ENCLOSED WITH 17 JANUARY 1837 LETTER FROM MARY DEAS BROÜN]
WILLIAM SINKLER TO SEAMAN DEAS SINKLER IN PHILADELPHIA
[EUTAW] 19 JANUARY 1837

My Dear Seaman—

   Your affectionate letter of the 4th Inst[ant] reached me yesterday—it is indeed gratifying and rendered infinitely so, on account, of the happy tidings of my dear Charles—God grant, he may now be well, attending Strictly to his duties—for which I hope he is perfectly prepared—I hope he will return to us, reaping every advantage from the opportunities afforded him—<u>well</u> and <u>worthy</u>. The idea of your return, gladdens my heart—and fills it with expectations, delightful to dwell on—I often think of you, and am anticipating a <u>rich</u> <u>reward</u> for the <u>pain</u>, that <u>your</u> <u>absence</u> has caused me[.] It is now to my children, I must <u>look for</u> happiness—every thing <u>depends on them</u>—this, they ought to keep in mind and <u>act</u> <u>accord-ingly</u>—. In the course of the next week I expect to go to Charleston—when I will write you fully—and I trust more satisfactorily than I have hereto done. I will then forward you a draft, for the amount you require and probably more, & should I conclude, for you to purchase any thing for me—. I think you were right to make an early application, allways be, <u>before</u> hand with <u>time</u>—I have not the least objection for you to visit Washington when, by all means, call and see The President (Gen Jackson) with even his faults he is a great man[.] I have not had time to write a regular letter and knowing your great dislike to waste—have filled up this <u>little space</u> in your Aunts letter. I know too your <u>hate for postage</u>—Attend closely to your studies—I have great confidence in you my Son—God bless you. Your affectionate father   W Sinkler

Building called "The Lodge," at Eutaw Plantation; family tradition is that it was built for Seamon Deas Sinkler's medical use. 1938 photograph by Frances B. Johnston. Courtesy of Library of Congress.

1901 photograph of Eutaw, by Morton Brailsford Paine.
Courtesy of the Charleston Museum, Charleston, South Carolina.

1901 photograph of Eutaw avenue by Morton Brailsford Paine.
Courtesy of the Charleston Museum, Charleston, South Carolina.

Chapter 7

Reflections

After William Sinkler's wife, Eliza, died in 1824, he never remarried. The only suggestion that he might ever have considered doing so is an oblique reference in a letter James B. Richardson wrote him in June 1826, in which JBR suggested "that a faint heart never woos a fair Lady." No name is mentioned, and the matter is never repeated, so it may have been more JBR's idea than Sinkler's. In any case, William had many matters to claim his attention, not the least of which was the responsibility of raising six young children—his five, plus a niece for whom he was guardian. As mentioned elsewhere, he had abundant assistance from his mother-in-law and other family in Charleston, but letters reflect how serious he was about guiding and educating all of them.

Among the numerous other issues claiming his attention, business matters included running Eutaw Plantation and other properties he owned. He undoubtedly had overseers, but crops and planting details were frequent topics of letters—especially those exchanged with his son, William Henry, who inherited Eutaw Plantation. A letter of August 5, 1828, from Peter Gaillard (1757–1833) gives details of constructing ditches and banks at the Rocks, a nearby plantation he had built shortly before William built Eutaw. While the surviving letter does not include the referenced diagram, it contains minute details, including how the "spades must be heated & hammered quite flat, & ground very sharp." The Rocks was located on a creek feeding into the Santee River, somewhat as Eutaw Creek did, so perhaps WS had been seeking advice on draining his property.

Horse racing remained a primary interest, as did breeding. A January 6, 1837, letter from William Henry—still at South Carolina College in Columbia—makes it quite clear that he was already involved in racing, having a colt of his own. In

The Rocks, Peter Gaillard's plantation near Eutaw Springs.
Courtesy of the Library of Congress.

1839 the Pineville Jockey Club awarded William Sinkler a silver trophy,[1] still owned by the family. On February 3, 1841, WS wrote to Richard Singleton, reminding him that he had paid him in person for stud-service charges for his mare Non Plus, then was dunned by "the gentlemen . . . you had placed in the hands of your book." WS provided details surrounding the agreement, then told Singleton that if he still considered that he owed him anything, to "let me know the amount, and I will at once pay it."

Several letters refer to breeding services he provided or that others were seeking. On May 16, 1853, less than a month before William Sinkler died, John G. Guignard wrote to him requesting that Shark and his groom "visit" Williston, in Upper Orangeburg County, for two to three weeks.

From about 1830, there was an exodus of South Carolina cotton farmers as they left the state for land in Alabama that had not been exhausted.[2] One of these was Thomas Gaillard (1790–1864), the son of the previously mentioned Peter Gaillard of the Rocks. On July 9, 1833, Gaillard wrote a long letter to WS from Claiborne, Alabama; while much of the letter is devoted to politics, he also extolled the

1 The trophy seems to have been awarded for general excellence, rather than for a specific race, although the family had generally associated it with the horse Jeannette Berkeley.
2 Edgar, *South Carolina,* 275–76.

1839 racing trophy awarded to William Sinkler by the Pineville Jockey Club (the irregular spelling of "jockey" on the trophy seems to have been acceptable at the time). Courtesy of William Henry Sinkler.

advantages of what he called the Prairie Lands of Alabama. It is clear that he still owned property in Upper St. John's Parish, as he mentioned having William gin his cotton at Dorshee. He also noted that he had asked his brother, James, to lease out portions of that plantation that could not be sold. The same letter offers to sell WS two hundred acres of Dorchee adjacent to Eutaw for $1,200. There is no inference that he was in debt to WS, but he seems to have been consolidating his holdings.

Another planter who went to Alabama was James S. Deas (1784–1864), the younger brother of William Sinkler's mother-in-law. Letters and other documents make it clear that he was indebted to WS. On May 10, 1837, he transferred from Colonel James Chestnut to WS a $16,992.31 bond mortgaging his "plantation four miles below Camden." This debt was payable on November 1, 1838, and precipitated letters explaining why he could not make payments. A letter of July 1, 1837, acknowledged that WS had sent him an additional $3,100, and makes reference to a previous $3,115, which would appear to have been separate from the bond.

In his April 2, 1842, letter, Deas acknowledged being late making a payment, fearing that "it will be sometime yet before you will be in funds." A year later, on June 18, 1843—and again late—he complained of "the ruinous state of exchange" and begged that WS would allow him to wait to make payment when the rate

Certificate for nineteen shares in the Bank of Charleston, Issued on February 25, 1836, and acknowledging that the first two shares have been paid on this date. On the back is a receipt for the fourth installment of $475 paid the following day. Courtesy of the South Caroliniana Library, University of South Carolina, Columbia, SC.

improved. Again, on August 3, 1849, James Deas was unable to pay his debt, claiming losses and delays due to flooding in Alabama and Louisiana, which he described in detail.

In a long, newsy letter of October 25, 1850, James S. Deas acknowledged William Sinkler's recent letter, and included details of family affairs, politics, and crops—cotton "not very good, but as yet hope a reasonable crop," and corn "a good one." Written the following day, perpendicularly across the lines of the first page, he described losing his home and an outbuilding to fire the previous night: "I was upstairs when the roof fell in & my life saved with some difficulty."

In other business, William Saab Thomson (1785–1841), the older brother of William Sinkler's deceased brother-in-law, John Linton Thomson (1792–1825), wrote to WS on June 25, 1838, reporting having collected bonds owed WS, evidently in the Amelia–Ft. Motte area. In the same letter, he requested that WS arrange for his niece Anna to come visit her grandmother.[3]

Other business matters of this period include William Sinkler's having invested in the newly formed Bank of Charleston. In addition to the nineteen shares represented by an 1836 certificate, there is also a detailed receipt that William Henry Sinkler sent his father after his 1841 marriage to his first cousin Anna. It includes thirty-five shares in the same bank.

In a letter of August 25, 1849, Henry D. Lesesne suggested to William Sinkler that Eliza—WS's daughter and HDL's first cousin—consider moving to Sullivan's Island in an effort to improve her health. He described a house for rent close to his own, apologizing for not being able to invite her to stay with them. Ironically, he referred to his wife's ill health, suggesting that she would probably not improve until cool weather. The same letter notes that "by grandmother's[4] request" he was enclosing a bill of sale of two slaves for $600 and her request that the payment go against her bond; the letter also requests a receipt.

Meanwhile, social life continued, and many letters relate to family activities. On August 22, 1836, Margaret Huger Sinkler, wife of William Sinkler's oldest son, James, wrote to WS at White Sulphur Springs. The letter contains extensive local and family news, especially regarding their two young children, William and Anna. It is clear from her letter that her husband was in Virginia with his father: it mentions her being pleased to hear from him once a week and hoping his health had improved.

William Henry Sinkler wrote his father a puzzling letter on March 26, 1837, stating that he was giving up "all my right to any and every thing" with regard to

---

3 Elizabeth Sabb Thomson, who died on November 8, 1838, was the mother of Anna's father, John Linton Thomson.

4 "Grandmother" would have been Mary Deas Broün, the mother-in-law of William Sinkler, who had apparently loaned her money.

his older brother, Seaman, who was graduating from medical school. It is unclear what he referred to: it seems unlikely that money or property would have been an issue. Likewise, it is hard to believe that he resented the attention paid to educating his brother. William Henry was graduating from South Carolina College, after which he would take over the management of Eutaw. Seaman was making plans to continue medical studies in Paris.

It seems strange that there is no reference in letters—or addresses—to the summer home in Eutaw Village (later Eutawville). The exact date of construction of the Eutaw summer home is not known, but most of these homes were built starting in the mid-1830s. It is a documented fact that families moved away from the creeks and rivers during the summer, and, although no longer inhabited, this house—located about two miles from Eutaw Plantation—still stands.

Business and horses were often the topics of letters exchanged between William Sinkler and his son William Henry. From addresses, it appears that WHS and Anna, who had married in 1841, were living at Eutaw, and although WS maintained his home there, he was frequently in Charleston or traveling. WS wrote a letter to Anna on June 13, 1844, in Charleston, where she had just arrived to stay for the summer and presumably until the birth of their first child in October.

A June 20, 1846, letter Eliza Sinkler Manning wrote to her father thanks him for the "chair" (baby carriage). She described the new baby—her first—and lamented that he would not be present for the baptism the next day, albeit noting that he probably would not like to see her immersed. The Manning and Sinkler families belonged to the Episcopal Church, which did not practice immersion, so it seems highly unlikely that she meant total immersion; however, it is certainly not clear exactly what she meant.

She also referred to her brother, Seaman, having plans to go to Europe for health reasons. Another family letter at the time of his death (January 1847) refers to his having had plans to go to Cuba. But apparently he did neither.

It is also surprising that no letters of this period mention the March 28, 1848, death of William Sinkler's half-sister, Ann Cantey Sinkler Richardson. Considering how close the two families were, and especially William and Ann, it would undoubtedly have been a major loss to both families.

During the latter part of his adult life, William Sinkler seems to have suffered gastrointestinal ailments, most likely what would now be called diverticulitis, or perhaps irritable bowel syndrome. We know from letters that he made frequent visits to White Sulphur Springs, Virginia, as early as 1835. While there was undoubtedly a social attraction, it was probably a serious attempt to find relief. Frequently, his sons accompanied him, and letters suggest that both James and William Henry had health issues.

In 1852 William Henry Sinkler took another step and made a journey to Europe. This is perhaps not surprising, inasmuch as his brother Seaman (1816–1847)

William Henry Sinkler, photograph courtesy of the South Caroliniana Library, University of South Carolina, Columbia, SC.

had studied medicine in Paris, as had numerous others during that period.[5] In any case, he carried with him three letters of introduction, all written on June 23, 1852: Alfred Huger wrote to William C. Rives, U.S. minister to France, and Benjamin Huger and Wade Hampton each wrote to Abbot Lawrence, U.S. minister to Great Britain.

William Henry's passport application describes him as being five feet, nine inches tall with light brown hair, a straight nose, an oval face, and a large mouth. It is dated June 30, but with no year; however, it was likely 1852. While it is definitely his signature on the document, it is difficult to tell whether the rest was his handwriting.[6]

It is known that WHS spent August in Paris, as there exists a translation of Dr. Palmier's lengthy letter, detailing his diagnosis of the medical problems and "Mode of treatment." It is interesting that this letter mentions "a tremendous fall which broke his right wrist, wounded the fore part of the arm & the right shoulder" and "cerebral spinal injury resulting from the fall," but nowhere in any other letters is there any mention of such an event. A few days later, another Palmier letter notes having sent lotion and syrup plus a bag of woolen straps "to rub yourself

5 According to historian David McCullough, from 1830 to 1860 "nearly seven hundred Americans came to Paris to study medicine." McCullough suggested that the advantages were the size of the hospital, which allowed the study of a large number of different sick and wounded, and the supply of cadavers, which were not available in the United States. David McCullough, *The Great Journey: Americans in Paris* (New York: Simon & Schuster, 2011), 111, 115, 132.

6 Passport application at *Fold3.com,* https://www.fold3.com/image/86564875 (accessed June 4, 2015).

with." The letter includes an account "for all my visits & disbursements for you up to this Day" of 1,450 francs or 58 British pounds (equivalent to about $252.00).

There is also an August 23 German customs receipt (see appendix D), probably comparable to a visa, from Kehl, Germany, just across the Rhine River from Strasbourg, France (about 250 miles east of Paris). This suggests that WHS may have combined some pleasure travel, as the "Legitimation Document" indicates that he was "taking the route via the border area Through the neighboring town." By September he appears to have been at the Adelphi Hotel in Liverpool, where he received yet another letter on September 16 with further instructions from Dr. Palmier. This one includes a note from the translator requesting to be remembered kindly to WHS.

Back in Charleston, William Henry wrote his father a long letter on December 31, 1852, noting first that "Anna had another child" but not sharing either gender or name.[7] Most of the letter consists of horse racing matters, one particularly interesting issue being the fact that WHS was going to be away from Eutaw when a Mr. Rives planned to visit, and he expected his father to deal with it. He went on to say that "it will not be pleasant for you . . . if he is not satisfied" with his horse, adding, "I presume he will take him home." It is not clear whether this is the same Mr. Rives, the U.S. minister to France, whom WHS would likely have met in Paris the previous summer.

Despite all William Sinkler's attempts to attain good health, he died on June 8, 1853 at Eutaw Plantation. His obituary appeared in the *Charleston Daily Courier* on June 15.

OBITUARY[8]

DIED, on Wednesday, 8th instant, at his residence, in St. John's, Berkley, WILLIAM SINKLER, Esq. aged 65 years. It is by a hand well used to the warmth and fervor of his greeting, that this mournful record is made; and it is a heart which has been sensibly affected by a character, full of excellence, and rich in virtue, that now carries this feeble expression to his grave! With the attributes of manly strength; with a fixed integrity; with an inherent love of truth, with an instinct of what is honorable, and with an impulse to pursue it, the respect and the confidence of other men were a necessary and

---

7 Family records indicate that this daughter, Elizabeth Allen, the fourth of their six children, was born on December 14, 1852, and died on March 21, 1854.

8 Judging by the writing style and the family connection, it seems likely that this obituary was written by Samuel DuBose, Jr. (1786–1859), whose mother was the daughter of Peter Sinkler, making him the first cousin once removed of William Sinkler. They were contemporaries; both had attended the Rogers School in Newport, Rhode Island (possibly at the same time); and DuBose was an executor of the will of WS's mother, Margaret Cantey Sinkler.

William Sinkler, repro-
duced from a portrait
by Henry Bounetheau.
Courtesy of the South
Caroliniana Library, Uni-
versity of South Caro-
lina, Columbia, SC.

involuntary offering; but in the social relations of a well-spent life, let those speak, who to the departed spirit, were as neighbors, as kindred, as family, as children! There it is, and in a hallowed place, that the blandness and gentleness of his manner, the purity of his motive, the tenderness of his every action are written down on hearts, that make no boast of sorrow, but cherish the opinions which affections will register!

Who that knew him will not join in this tribute? Who that has witnessed his reverence for the old, or felt his protective fondness for the young, or met him, as co[n]temporary or as comrade, will either hesitate or falter? Who that appreciates the delicacy and refinement of a gentleman, or values the constancy and fidelity of a friend—who that has seen his mild and generous hospitality, or been the object of its kind and courteous dispensation, can remember him without emotion. And who that contemplates the softness and sweetness of demeanor, which renders the sternness of rectitude and of principle, the more impressive and the more imposing, will ever marvel that those who knew him best, loved him most. In life, without fear and without reproach, in death without a murmur or a tremor, has a good man passed to the presence of his God!

A tribute is contained in a June 21 letter from Thomas Porcher Ravenel (1824–1898) in Pinopolis to his brother, René Ravenel (1826–1875), who was studying medicine in Paris:

> They [the community] met with great loss on the 8th of June in the death of Mr. W. Sinkler, Sr. He died of inflammation of the bowels. He had been, to my surprise, for some time sick with an affection of the bowels. I did not know he was unwell until I heard of his death. He will be a great loss to the community in which he lived. He was an elderly man of so high a moral character & so finished a gentleman, the example of such a one is much felt in the community of young men, as we are becoming very fast. Our old men are jewels among us, which some few are silly enough not to value or have not sense to appreciate. Our Parish will feel the loss deeply when they are taken.[9]

Another tribute is contained toward the end of Irving's *History of the Turf:*

> Mr. Sinkler was for many years a steady and zealous supporter of the Carolina Turf; his horses were generally trained for the Pineville and Charleston Races. At the former he was frequently a winner, and at the latter he came in for a tolerable share of distinction. Among the horses of his own breeding, Rienzi and Jeannette Berkley [*sic*], both by Bertrand, Jr. out of Carolina, by Buzzard, were the best. He had in his stable, during the campaign of 1839, Santa Anna, and a bay filly by Humphrey Clinker, out of imported Mania by Figaro. Kate Converse, by Non Plus, out of Daisy by Kosciusko, ran honestly, and won several good purses for him. This mare passed into other hands, and formed part of Mr. Singleton's stud. Mr. Sinkler was fortunate to possess one of the most faithful colored grooms in the State. It is due to the integrity and character of this man to notice him favorably in this place. In his attachment to his master, and devotedness to his true interests, he reminds us of . . . a feature in the crowd upon a race field.[10]

9 SCHS 12–213–05, Thomas Porcher Ravenel Papers.
10 Irving, *South Carolina Jockey Club,* 187–88.

~

Peter Gaillard[11] to William Sinkler[,] Esquire
[The Rocks] Aug[us]t 5, 1828

Dear Sir

Enclosed you have the plan[12] of my ditches & Banks at the Rocks, & I will now give you my mode of executing the work. But it is very probable that some more approved plan may have been introduced into the neighborhood by foreigners employed by Dr. Rave[nel] at Ash Hill, & by Mr. Deve[a]ux at Woodlawn.

I first dig my ditch as you will observe 4 ft. deep & 4 wide at the top, throwing up the dirt as near to the edge of the ditch as it will stand, leaving it in this situation to settle as long as possible, & when I return to finish it off, a line is stretched along the Bank so far on the dirt that has been thrown up, as will when sliced down make the ditch 5 feet wide upon the top. The line must be supported every 18 to 20 feet with small stakes to prevent swaging [*sic*], and with a long handle spade take a slice from the line down to the bottom of the ditch, other hands following & throwing up the dirt 2 spades with long handles to slice down will be sufficient to furnish work for a number of hands to throw up, giving them one days start. The spades must be heated & hammered quite flat, & ground very sharp, it will make the work easier, & it will be better done. Other hands must follow to finish off with long handle paddles walking backward on the top of the Bank, placing the dirt & slapping it as it is thrown up to him, perhaps 2 or 3 paddles will be enough. Perhaps it would be better to have your Bank a foot instead of 2 feet wide upon top, but of this you will be a better Judge when you see some of it finished. Any ditch at all on the inner side will increase the labor, & be worse than useless, it will weaken the foundation of your Bank, & heavy rains running along it will Wash away its base—If you were to leave the Slice within the dotted line, for a shoulder it[']s weight would soon carry it down. By taking it away, it gives a more gradual slope to your Bank of course not so apt to cave— Any further explanation you may Wish will be given with pleasure when we meet.

Y[ou]rs very Sincerely
Peter Gaillard
5 Aug[us]t, 1828

11 This is probably the older Peter Gaillard (1757–1833), not his son Peter Gaillard II. In 1865 his great-granddaughter Cleremonde Gaillard married WS's grandson, WHS, Jr.

12 No plan or diagram was with this letter. The Rocks plantation was not far from Eutaw and had been built by PG several years before Eutaw. Samuel Gaillard Stoney, *Plantations of the Carolina Low Country* (1938; rev. ed. 1955, Charleston: Carolina Art Association), 75.

[Addressed to]
W. Sinkler Esquire

THOMAS GAILLARD[13] TO WILLIAM SINKLER IN CHARLESTON
CLAIBORNE, ALAB[AMA], JULY 9TH, 1833

Dear Sir/

Were I now to acknowledge the receipt of your letter written more than twelve Months ago, and to intimate that this would be received by you as a reply to it—I would perhaps but encite your smile. It is certainly out of common place to make a voluntary acknowledgment of an obligation when it had already been barred by limitation. I shall take it however as a running account upon good faith and shall endeavour to make amends for not having liquidated it sooner by making a return with Interest. I did not see Mr. Brown by whom it was intended that the letter should be delivered—nor did I receive it until some considerable time after he left Alabama[.] I had previously however made my arrangements for the transaction of my Business in Mobile—having soon after my arrival in this Country—confided it with Mr. Duke Goodman—My acquaintance here, at the time, was too limited (as you might suppose) to render any interposition in his behalf advantageous to him. I therefore have made no communication to others on the subject. With respect to the employment of an Agent (as Factor) to execute Commissions for me—I at that time put aside all consideration of party differences. Although I had witnessed in Carolina—a feeling the reverse of that of conciliation actuate those to whom I was opposed in all political questions I determined on my removal here—to endeavour to obliterate every impression having such a tendency. But I became fully sensible afterwards of the folly of cherishing so friendly & forgiving a disposition. I perceived that the Nullifiers proceeded with a determined spirit, in every measure they dared to attempt to bear down & oppress their opponents[.] Threats of Confiscation of the suspension of the privilege of Habeas Corpus & the ordinance of the convention—the levying of Troops all united to exhibit on their part an unnatural feeling of unappeasable

---

13 Thomas Gaillard (1790–1864) graduated from South Carolina College in 1809 and was a member of the South Carolina bar, a land surveyor, an accomplished draftsman, an author and historian, and compiler of the Gaillard Chart. After representing St. Johns in the legislature for eight years, he moved in 1832 to Monroe County, Alabama, where, according to Louis Towles, "he failed as a planter." He was the son of Peter Gaillard, Sr., builder of the Rocks plantation and author of the previous letter. Dorothy Kelly Mac-Dowell, *Gaillard Genealogy* (Columbia, S.C.: R. L. Bryan, 1974), 20; Louis P. Towles, *A World Turned Upside Down: The Palmers of South Santee, 1818–1881* (Columbia: University of South Carolina Press, 1996), 968.

Hostility—To these manifestations of their diabolical purposes—those of the—same same [*sic*] fraternity in this section of the Country, although powerless—by the weakness of their Numbers—most heartily responded—I discovered the delusion under which I laboured 'It was a natural but an honest delusion'—From the Date of the proceedings of the convention in So:Ca [South Carolina] I proved myself as relentless as those who, I perceived, designed & wished the prostration of every Individual of the Union Party—I determined at once to withdraw my Business as soon as practicable from one—who although a Minister of the Gospel, had indulged in expressions which would well have characterized a Danton or a Robespierre[14]—& will give you <u>one</u> instance of his Christian temper—you may rely upon its [veracity.] He affirmed in a conversation—that in the event of a conflict by arms between the Nullifiers & Unionists—he would shoulder his Musket; & at every halt would cry out 'God help their Souls'! Having determined to withdraw my Business with a view of transferring it to one who would entertain no such feelings of hostility either towards my person or property—I enquired what were the political opinions of Mr. Brown—but could not learn. Had I been assured of his being of the same side with me (of which I am yet ignorant) I would have transferred it to him without hesitation. I go against the Nullifiers with all my heart, with all my Soul & with all my strength—with a Temper at once of unappeasable—against them—as Disorganizers, as Banditti in feeling & principle, & as the most Dangerous Enemies of our common Country—I am against them in whole & in part—and I say too 'God turn their Hearts from the wickedness of their ways.'

I have partly expected you in this Section of Country—I have understood that J[oh]n Davis & S Gourdin were making arrangements to pay us a visit & supposed you might accompany them—I think the most favourable Season of the year, for travelling as well as for a satisfactory examination of the Lands—is the early part of the Winter. I shall expect you to give us a call. This Country unquestionably presents to the Farmer many advantages—not to be procured in Carolina. Opinions, as to what description of lands should have a preference are yet divided—Were I to empress mine—I would say—select a prairie soil—not distant from a navigable Water Course—Many insist upon the 'river Lands as the best in the State.' When I state that they are liable to Inundations—you can draw deductions for yourself—Prairie Lands—at a distance from the river—have the disadvantage of difficulties of the transportation of Produce—of which, those who have rivers witnessed them can have no correct conception—Imagine a good ferry of ten Miles, through the low swamps of the Santee—in a wet Season it

14 Georges Danton and Maximilien de Robespierre were lawyers and fiery orators who attempted to overthrow the monarchy during the French Revolution. Both died at the guillotine.

would not be more impassable—than a road through the Prairies. Under similar circumstances—But the prairie soil is not stable—I would declare—that my
opinion inclines in their favour. What is called however [torn] open (or bald)
Prairie—I would reject— Your former Overseer Mr. McNeal has the management of a Plantation about 30M[torn] [long] wine—He owns, I have been told
ten Workers & a Track of [torn] Land—and is doing well in the advancement
of his interest—Our Crops generally may be said to be good—although—somewhat backwards. The swamp corn—has been injured by a Worm—which made
their appearance in the Fields soon after the Freshet in April—and are still destroying the late Corn—I have a very fine Crop of Cotton (Green-Seed) and if no
untoward accident befall it I expect that I shall make as much as I shall be able to
harvest—I wrote to my Overseer some time last Winter to make an engagement
with you for saw ginning my Cotton at Dorchee[15]—I wish, if practicable, to remove my Negroes to this State before the 1st of January; & directed him to make
arrangements accordingly—will you be good enough to procure for me the ped-
igree of your Horse <u>Nicholas</u>—I have a beautiful Colt—from him—I think he
will not disgrace his Sire—In what relationship does your Horse stand—to Mr.
Richardson's Julia or little Venus for I would be glad to have his <u>Pedigree</u> <u>fully</u>—
can you procure one—of Buzzard—the Sire of my Psyche? I have requested my
Brother James to lease out such part of Dorchee as he can—in the event of my
not effecting a sale—L Porcher had rejected the first offer—as he has Hands
already settled there—You can have the Field bounded by the two public Roads
& your Eutaw Tract containing—I believe <u>about</u> 200 Acres—in fee simple—
for the Sum of Twelve Hundred Dollars—payable on the 1st of January next—
possession to be taken as soon as the Crop now growing upon it shall be harvested. I suppose you may have heard that the Cholera has paid us a kindly
visit. It has been very fatal on some of the Plantations on the River[.] I had
many cases of premonitory Symptoms—as the Physicians terms Th[em]—but
was successful in effecting a cure in every instance—the disease has entirely disap-
peared—and the country is again restored to its accustomed Health—Since my
removal here—I have paid but about $5 for medical attendance—on my Negroes
& Family—You may judge from this of the Health of the Country—I remain
very respectfully yours
    Thomas Gaillard

[Addressed to]
Mr. William Sinkler

15 Dorshee was a plantation near Eutaw Springs and may have been owned by WS at
that time. There are several different spellings, probably because it was usually pronounced
"Dawshee."

Charleston
South Carolina
Care of—Messrs. Deas & Brown—Factors Charleston

WILLIAM HENRY SINKLER[16] TO WILLIAM SINKLER, ESQUIRE[,] AT EUTAW
COLUMBIA, JANUARY 6, 1837

Dear Father

I received your letter by Snow just before entering [the] recitation room[.] I
got leave of absence and attended immediately to the business which you wrote
about[.] I saw Mr. Tradewell and told what you said and delivered the letter. He
mentioned that Col. Elmore[17] had left nothing for you, and that he was ignorant
w[h]ether he got permission from the court or not, but that he would read the
letter and if he had anything to say would write. I also delivered the letters to Mr.
Thomson and Col. Flud, the latter said that he thought all hopes of recovering
the money was lost, as even those from the same place with the man could not
tell any thing more about him, than that he had left for the West. When I saw
Charley I really thought that you had arrived, but was soon informed to the
contrary by Snow. I was truly disappointed as this is a part of the week, in which
we don't do much and I could have seen you often, but I am sensible that it was
almost impossible for you to leave home[.] I have put the letters in the P Office
as you directed. I suppose you will be disappointed when you hear that the colt
was unable to [race] from being lame (but I am glad to say that it is not serious)[.]
A great many think that he would have done well, on either day, Col. Flud has
taken no purse as yet. I suppose that by this time you have heard of the result of
each day's race, therefore it will be unnecessary to make mention about them. I
see the C[ol.] D. Broün is here. I have not had a chance to speak to him however
to him [*sic*]. It is now about 4 oclock P.M. I must retire, if I [have] time in the
morning I will extend this letter if not I hope you will excuse it. The night is past
and I resume my pen. Col[.] Flud intends sending the horse today and I would
have written by him had you not sent Snow. I will start him off early so that he
can get home tomorrow evening. I suppose if you come at all you will come before the Charleston races. I hope so at any rate. I have left my measure with Paris,
so that if it is convenient to you, you can get a cloack [*sic*] for me. Do remember
me to Sister Ann and Marg[18] and all of them. Tell Sister I will write shortly to

16 WHS would have been seventeen.
17 This suggests that Colonel Elmore may have owed WS money.
18 "Sister" would have been Eliza Allen, who was two years younger than William
Henry. "Ann" was probably Anna Thomson (1823–1873), and "Marg" was Margaret Thomson (1818–1891), his first cousins.

her. It is drawing near to near to [*sic*] the breakfast. I must therefore stop[.] After getting the letter from Mr. Tradewell, I will immediately send off Snow.

I remain your fond son

W H Sinkler

P.S. I have seen Mr. Tradewell, he say's that Col. Elmore left no message for you, and that he knows nothing at all about it, or he would have written to you. Mr. Thomson says he will write, as well as Col. Flud. I will write you shortly more fully. Hoping that I will soon see you. I must again bid you adieu.

[Addressed to]
William Sinkler Esquire
Eutaw
St. John's
By Snow on horse

WILLIAM HENRY SINKLER TO WILLIAM SINKLER
EUTAW [PLANTATION] MARCH 26TH, 1837

My Dear Father

I am sorry truly that you have been so much bothered of late. I have endeavoured to do every thing I could to assist you but to no purpose. I think that you and you <u>alone</u> should arrange every thing connected with brother Seaman's affairs.[19] I therefore give up to you all my right to any and every thing, to do as you please with it. I hope you will allow me to do this as it relieves me of much disagreeable feeling.

I take this opportunity to say also that, the valuation which was made, (and <u>I</u> consented should be shown to you,) was altogether erroneous, and I beg that, as far as I am concerned, you will not be governed by it.

Your affectionate son

W H Sinkler

I will consider this as binding on <u>me</u> as a <u>legal</u> instrument.

[Addressed to]
William Sinkler Esquire
[NOTE: Penciled on envelope "WHS/SDS"]

19 Seaman would have been graduating from the University of Pennsylvania Medical School and planning to pursue further studies in Paris. It seems unlikely that this concerns money or a disproportionate share of attention paid to educating his older brother.

⁓

JAMES S. DEAS[20] TO WILLIAM SINKLER
[CLAIBORNE, ALABAMA] MAY 10, 1837

Col. James Chesnut's Bond to James S. Deas secured by a Mortgage of his plantation four miles below Camden in the Wateree River on which there is a balance due of . . . $16,992.31

Drawing Interest from 17 Dec 1836 & pay[a]ble 1 Nov 1838. I hereby assign and transfer unto Mr. William Sinkler the above described bond & Mortgage and hereto annexed with authority to him to transfer the same to any one else or to retain & receive the proceeds of the same and apply it to the payment of any debt due by me.

 10. May 1837
 James S. Deas (Seal)
 Witness S. D. Sinkler

⁓

JAMES S. DEAS TO WILLIAM SINKLER, ESQUIRE[,] IN CHARLESTON
MOBILE [ALABAMA] 1 JULY 1837

My dear friend

 I received last Evening your Letters of the 20: & 26: ult[im]o, the last covering a draft [u]pon The Planters & Mechanick Bank on the Branch of the Bank of the State of Alabama at this place for three thousand one hundred dollars which has been duly paid—I feel very much indebted to you indeed for this fund and also the very interested part you have taken on my behalf and I assure it shall not be very early forgotten—I shall send you by Savage Deas who leaves here to day to join Tho[ma]s Lesesne[21] at Montgomery a Bond for the amount say including the previous $3115. I am doubtful whom to make it payable to and on reflecti[o]n think it may be best to put at foot an obligation for the money which will be replaced by a proper bond when I know to whom you wish it payable which please inform me. I shall close this as it is the mail hour and will more fully by another conveyance is Col. Chesnuts bond deposit where you please subject to your or my order for it & if I have occasion for it I can send an order—[torn] here all a [torn] & [th]ings more quiet tho' otherwise Much as they have been—the crops of Cotton are promising & the corn very fine. What a dry year so far but within a few days we have had a superabundance of rain.

---

20 James Sutherland Deas (1784–1864) was the younger brother of Mary Deas Broün, WS's mother-in-law.

21 Thomas Lesesne was married to Anna Broün, the younger sister of WS's wife, Eliza.

As ever
Most truly Yours
James S. Deas

[On a separate page, possibly the back of the envelope page, but struck through, and having no signature]

One year after date I promise to pay to William Sinkler Esq[uir]e on his order Three Thousand dollars

[Addressed to]
William Sinkler Esq[ui]r[e]
Care of C. D. Deas, Esqu.
Charleston
So[uth] Ca[rolina]

[Note on envelope]
Col Deas—for money loaned—WS

～

RECEIPT FROM C. D. DEAS[22] TO WM SINKLER E[S]Q[UIRE]
CHARLESTON, JUNE 12, 1838

Rec'd Charleston 12 June 1838 of Wm Sinkler E[s]q[uire] Eight hundred & twenty Seven on acc[oun]t Ja[me]s Sinkler, being amo[un]t of order & paid to Cap[tain] Gaillard[.][23]
$827 C. D. Deas

～

WILLIAM S. THOMSON[24] TO WILLIAM SINKLER, ESQUIRE[,] IN CHARLESTON
OAKLAND, 25TH JUNE 1838

Dear Sir[,]
    have just arrived from Totness and find your boy at my house; the bonds I received from you I have collected but one, & that is Cates' bond the amount I do not recollect, but I have the bond & statement, not knowing how to get the

22 Charles Dundas Deas (1778–1854) was a brother of WS's mother-in-law, Mary Deas Broün, and James Sutherland Deas.

23 Captain Peter Charles Gaillard (1812–1889), after leaving the army, became a cotton factor from 1838 to 1861 and 1865 to 1875. He was a grandson of Peter Gaillard of the Rocks. Towles, *A World Turned Upside Down,* 967.

24 William S. Thomson (1785–1841) was a brother of William Sinkler's brother-in-law, John Linton Thomson. Totness (near Ft. Motte) was the location of a Thomson family

money to you or when I would see you. I offered the money to my Brother, he has not yet taken it, but will in a few days. I hope it will be satisfactory to you. I shall be glad to see you on your way to Virginia, & hope you will bring Anna home this fall as Mother is very desirous to see her, I hope she she [*sic*] may live to do so. I have heard various reports of myself & only hope some were true, but assure you that if I am to be marri'd I know nothing of it myself.

We had heard of the loss of the Pulaski[25] a dreadful accident indeed, we understood from the Papers there were ten persons saved names not known, which leaves some hope with the relations of Mr. Bull that himself & family may be of that number, should I not see you I wish you a pleasant summer.

Yours truly
W. S. Thomson

[Addressed to]
William Sinkler Esquire
Charleston
By Henry with horse.

◠

[SCL: SINGLETON FAMILY PAPERS]
W[ILLIAM] SINKLER TO RICHARD SINGLETON, ESQUIRE
EUTAW 3 FEBRUARY 1841

Dear Sir

When in Camden, on my way to the Course, I was called to, by the gentleman, who it appears, you had placed in the hands of your book, relative to Non Plus—stating that my name, was among those, who had not settled. This surprised me not a little; [I] dislike to be <u>dunned</u>. I have always been prompt in paying my debts, particularly those of that Character. I told the gentleman, that I had paid you in person, in the street in Charleston, the am[moun]t of the season of my mare to Non Plus. This I certainly did. The first year, that the mare was sent to Non Plus—she returned immediately home—at the period for her return to the horse. The water was up and I was told, the horse would not get back to True Blue in time for the ninth day. Therefore I did not send my mare. She proved not in foal. This I related to your son John, who invited me to send the mare back. The succeeding spring, free of any charge for the season—which I

---

summer home. Anna was raised by WS after the early deaths of both her parents. "Mother" would have been Anna's grandmother, who died in November 1838.

25 The American steam packet *Pulaski* was lost thirty miles off the coast of North Carolina when its starboard boiler exploded on June 14, 1838. About 128 persons died; about 59 survived.

did. If not withstanding what I have stated, you consider that I owe anything, let me know the amount, and, and [*sic*] I will at once pay it. I should have written to you earlier, but expected I might have the pleasure of seeing you. I beg you will tender my respects to Mrs. Singleton—and believe me,

>Yours truly
>W Sinkler
>Richard Singleton, Esquire

>Attention of
>Col. James B. Richardson [JBR's nephew]

∽

WILLIAM HENRY SINKLER TO WILLIAM SINKLER [RECEIPT]
CHARLESTON, JUNE 10, 1841[26]

Charleston June 10th 1841 Received from William Sinkler Esq. Guardian of my wife, Anna L. Sinkler, late Anna L. Thomson, transfer of the following Bank Stocks: viz.

>35 Shares in The Bank of The United States.
>49 Do. in The Planters & Mechanics Bank of S. Carolina.
>44 Do. in The Bank of South Carolina.
>39 Do. in The Bank of Charleston, S. Carolina: and
>31 Do. of the increased Stock of The Bank of Charleston, S.C.

Also received Col. James S. Deas Bond to the said William Sinkler Guardian aforesaid, conditioned for the payment of ($3115.50) Three thousand and one hundred and fifteen 50/100 Dollars, and W. L. Lewis' note to the same for Seven hundred Dollars: Also received the said William Sinkler's order on the Commissioner in Equity for Orangeburg District, in my favor, for the balance due on my wife's shares of the proceeds of sale of Pond Bluff Plantation, and his order on W. S. Thomson Esq. for the balance of a Bond of Christian Gates to the said Guardian given for the purchase of part of my wife's negroes, which balance has been collected by the said William S. Thomson, and I hereby acknowledge myself to be indebted to the said William Sinkler on his account as Guardian, in the sum of One thousand and sixty two 95/100 Dollars.

>Note WH Sinkler

26 WHS and his first cousin Anna Linton Thomson, seventeen, had married on March 4, 1841.

[Attached page: note later date]
77 ½ Acres of wooded Land
<u>110 ¼</u> Do of cleared Land
187 ¾

Surveyed by Thos I Mellard, D. S.
May 9th 1843

JAMES S. DEAS TO WILLIAM SINKLER AT VANCE'S FERRY P.O.
   [SOUTH CAROLINA]
SPRING HILL [ALABAMA], APRIL 2ND, 1842

Dear Sir,

The time has been so long since I informed you that I would make you a payment that I write now to say to you I have not forgotten it & that the payment Shall be made to you. The delay has been occasioned by the raft, but now that obstruction is removed & I am looking for my cotton daily. I fear it will be sometime yet before you will be in funds but I shall most assuredly send it, without some unforeseen or improbable accident. I have been for a long time under so severe an attack of rheumatism that I have been unable to place myself in any position to be able to write without very great pain. I leave for the Hot Springs in Arkansas in a few days, for a stay of three weeks or a month & I hope to be here again by the first of June.

As this is a letter on business, I shall add no more than the assurance that I am as ever
   Most truly Yours—
   James S. Deas
If I do not succeed in finding health at Arkansas, I shall go to the Virginia Springs this summer will you be likely to be there.

[Addressed to]
William Sinkler Esq[uire]
~~Care of C. D. Deas Esq[uire]~~
Vances Ferry P.O.
~~Charleston So[uth] Car[olina]~~

[Note above address] Col[.] Deas received on the 14 inst[ant] (April) Postmarked Mobile, Ala. APR 8 and Charleston, S.C. APR 9.
[NOTE: Other than the signature, this does not appear to be the handwriting of JSD.]

～

JAMES S. DEAS TO WILLIAM SINKLER, ESQUIRE[,] AT FULTON P.O. [SOUTH
    CAROLINA]
NEAR MOBILE [ALABAMA], 18 JUN 1843

My dear Sir,

I have but just returned home and lose no time in placing upon you the
causes of the delay in the payment promised you—as I wrote to you I directed
my Cotton in N. Orleans shipped & the bills sent to Mr. C. [Amze] who now
has in hand three thousand four hundred dollars which have not been sent in
consequence of the ruinous state of exchange & the hope that arrangements were
making by the Bank to make it much less. That exchange is now 32 per cent—I
hope that the situation of things with you may authorize you to let it stand a
while till things get some better and I pledge myself that the fund shall remain in
bank or be converted into a certificate of deposit in your favor as preferred—So
soon as the loss on exchange shall not exceed 6 or 800 dollars the amount shall be
transmitted to you thru Mr. D. Lesesne—I am not insensible of the obligation
conferred on me in the loan or of the obligation of paying it in Charleston, but
the price of cotton is very low, and the exchange at a price that is unusual & cannot last long, and the present times with me pretty hard.

I shall be pleased to hear from you and I beg you to receive the assurance that
I am as ever Sincerely &

    Truly Yours
    James S. Deas

[Addressed to]
William Sinkler Esq[uir]e
Fulton P. O. ~~Charleston~~
Sumter Dist. S[outh] Carolina
[NOTE 1: Postmarked Mobile, ALA Jun 21]
[NOTE 2: In different hand in upper left: Col Deas 1 July—1842]

ARTEMAS T. DARBY TO WILLIAM SINKLER [RECEIPT]
[CHARLESTON]FEBRUARY 24, 1844

Charleston[,] February 24, 1844 Received from William Sinkler Esquire One thousand and forty five Dollars 95 cents in full of my wife Margaret C. Darby's[27] share or half part of the net sales of the following tracts of land Viz. Beckford and Effingham, Flower Cane, Lequeux and the tract of four or five hundred acres of swamp belonging thereto. Received the same in Settlement of my share of the purchase of said lands.

$1045.95 Artemas T. Darby

[Note on back]
February 24, 1844
Dr. Darby's Receipt for share of proceeds of sale of Lands.

WILLIAM HENRY SINKLER TO WILLIAM SINKLER [RECEIPT]
[EUTAW] FEBRUARY 24, 1844

Eutaw[,] February 24, 1844 Received from my father William Sinkler One thousand and forty five Dollars 95 cents in full of my wife Anna L. Sinkler['s] share or half part of the net [*sic*] sales of the following tracts of land Viz. Beckford and Effingham. Flower Cane. Lequeux and the tract of four or five hundred acres of swamp belonging thereto. Received the same in Settlement of my share of the purchase of said lands.

$1045.95 WHSinkler

Received 24 February 1844 of my father W. Sinkler One hundred & Sixty six dollars 93/100, the same being the balance paid him for me by Messrs Martin Walter & Co. on acc[oun]t of M. Singleton[']s note.

$166.93/100   WHSinkler

27 Margaret Cantey Thomson Darby (1818–1891) was the oldest daughter of Margaret Anna Sinkler and John Linton Thomson, and the older sister of WHS's wife and first cousin, Anna Linton Thomson.

WILLIAM SINKLER TO MRS. W. H. SINKLER IN CHARLESTON
[VANCES FERRY] EUTAW, 13 JUNE 1844

My Dear Anna—[28]

The return of Sampson, last evening, was a great relief to me—I had suffered much from anxiety—I hope you are now safe in the City, with our kind friends, that you may suffer no inconvenience from your journey—that you may have a pleasant summer, and may return safe in Autumn, to Eutaw, <u>happier</u>, than when you left it—with <u>cause</u>, for gratitude to God, it is only necessary to trust implicitly in Him—to serve Him faithfully—and we will always be as happy as we deserve. The day you left, was one of intense anxiety to me. I felt more than I would be willing to express. I roved about, like a disturbed spirit—but when night came—and I retired, I became tranquilised [*sic*], was blessed with sweet sleep— and thank Heaven I am now enabled to go throughout my business, with ease and comfort. Thus you see my Daughter—how I love you, how I have missed you & William, you deserve much at my hands, for your attention & kindness— has been always as it ought to be—and has made impressions, that will be as lasting, as life— I hope William, will return with his brother, for the sooner he gets the waggons [*sic*] off the better, I shall expect them to today—I suppose you saw Eliza on your arrival—and if Charles & Emily [Charles's wife] are to come, hope you will soon see them. At this dull season, you could not expect news. Give my warmest love to Deas, and my best respects to the Doctor,[29] their kindness, lays me under great obligation—These humble lines will show you—how your absence has been felt—adieu my dear daughter—and ever believe me

Your fond father

P.S.
My love [to] the children—W Sinkler

[Addressed to]
Vances Ferry
14 June
Mrs William H. Sinkler
Charleston

28 Anna Linton Thomson (1823–1873) was WS's niece, whom he raised after the deaths of her parents. She married her first cousin, William Henry Sinkler, in 1841. Their son, WHS, Jr., was born on October 5, 1844.

29 This was probably WHS's first cousin Mary Deas Lesesne (daughter of Anna Carolyn Broün) and her husband, Dr. Henry R. Frost.

～

ELIZABETH SINKLER MANNING TO WILLIAM SINKLER AT EUTAW
SAND HILLS, 20 JUNE 1846

How cordially do I wish My beloved Father that you were here to night that you might hear from my own lips how fully and heartily I enter into your feelings, grieving at all your griefs—and further that I might tell you in person how delightful are your continual attentions & kindnesses. The news of my dear Brothers[30] [*sic*] departure for Europe created feelings you can better imagine than I describe but I am glad he has gone trusting he will derive all the benefit we can fondly hope and return to us well & happy. I do long to see you dearest Father to tell you what however I hope you never will doubt, that my love for you increases instead of losing any of its vigour and that unceasingly my heart craves for you the richest blessings as Mortal can enjoy—rest assured your daughters [*sic*] heart always turns towards you with love and reverence. The chair is delightful and has already been enjoyed and I am sure the baby[31] will be delighted with her beautiful little carriage[;] the other good things Hercules brought were also very acceptable. Our darling little one is to be christened tomorrow and I know your prayers will be added to ours that she will be indeed a Lamb of the blessed flock and fulfill the solemn engagement of this holy & beautiful sacrament. I feel deeply and I know you would too and we would have liked you to be present but I know as she is to be immersed you would not like to see it. I have felt so much anxiety that it should be done as soon as possible that I do not think it right to put it off[;] the earlier the better she is sleeping sweetly in her crib now[.] I wish you could see the sweet picture of happy innocence—but I will lay aside my pen now & tell you all about it tomorrow night—she is not quite as meek & submissive as she was when you saw her for she is very timid & afraid of any one she is not accustomed to—but she is still very good. And now my beloved Father Goodnight—my heart is too full of wishes for you, to say what they are.

Sunday evening—I am now seated in your chair out in the Piazza and where my dearest Father are you. The baby has been lying on my lap looking up at the sky and [scratched out] we poor mortals will no [doubt] have been looking into a future which may be very different from that I have been picturing but this is one of the days I must always look to with comfort & pleasure—our little one to day thru the waters of Baptism was admitted into the visible Church of our

30 "Brother" was probably Seaman, who had health problems; he died on January 19, 1847.

31 Family records show that EASM's oldest child was born in 1852. The Baskin/Cathcart family chart shows that Elizabeth Peyre Manning was born on December 21, 1845, and died on September 10, 1852. "W" and "A" referred to her brother William Henry and his wife, Anna.

Saviour which beautiful type and the gracious promise accompanying the faithful observance of this Sacrament fills my heart to overflowing so excuse my saying so much about it. Ann Richardson was at church. I h[ave] not been able to see her for we have not the horses here yet. You do not say when William is coming up. We will look for you on Thursday when I trust we will happily meet my beloved Father[;] till then Adieu with warmest love to W & A and a hug to Harry. Mr. Manning desires to be very affectionately remembered—he says the rains have injured the crops very seriously—I cannot see but to say that I am

> Your ever Aff[ection]ate
> Daughter EAM

Mr. Manning says he hopes you will come up as soon as possible and that you keep in mind your contract to tarry long.

[Addressed to]
William Sinkler
"Eutaw"
By Hercules

~

JAMES S. DEAS TO WILLIAM SINKLER AT FULTON P.O.
NEAR MOBILE, 3 AUGUST 1849

Dear Sir,

This letter is a most painful one to me to write as I have no apology suitable to make for not complying with my promise to make you a payment the past spring save that I have really been unable to do so—I must ask your indulgence for yet another crop and I hope I am safe in saying that with it I will assuredly make you a payment and to all the extent I can. I think I am engaged in a good business and an increasing one but it has so far not yielded what I expected from it. I am absent from home two thirds of my time and only got home yesterday or would earlier have replied to your Letter.

We are all well Mrs. D. is on a [page torn] visit to Mrs. Huger—We have had an unreasonable quantity of rain for the last month and the crops are miserable—the river is high & the river plantations are generally under water here. The Rio river is out of its banks and nearly as high as at any time the past winter but my levee has kept me safe. They are calculating in N[ew] Orleans that the crop will be 400,000 bales cotton under average. The rains have been general thro'out all the Cotton Country and the summer so far cool & favorable for all the tribes of insect that prey on Cotton—all this region of country has been healthy & N. Orleans was never more so notwithstanding their alarms from the overflow. As ever my good friend

Most truly yours
James S. Deas

[Addressed to]
William Sinkler Esq[uir]e
Fulton Post Office
Sumter Dist.
South Carolina

[NOTE: Postmarked Mobile, ALA Aug 3]

HENRY D. LESESNE[32] TO WILLIAM SINKLER, ESQ[UIRE]
CHARLESTON, AUGUST 25, 1849

My dear Uncle,

I suffered a severe disappointment the other day in not being able to make you a visit after finishing my business at Sumterville. I was afraid however that William would not get my note in time. I had written one two days before and given it to young Dyson who kindly undertook to get it to the Sand Hills but it seems he was not able to find an opportunity. It would have afforded me peculiar pleasure to find myself among such kind friends after a week of hard labor at the wretched Court House, which is much worse even than old Orangeburg. Since my return I have been quite indisposed—so much so that for two days I did not leave the house.

I am greatly concerned to hear that Eliza's[33] health is so far from good. Do you not think that the climate of Sullivan's Island, which would be such a change from that to which she has been accustomed, might be of service to her? There is a comfortable house with good standing furniture, quite near to us, for rent, and I would be most happy to have her for a neighbor. I only wish that the accommodations of my house were such that I could offer the hospitality of it. Do make me affectionately remembered to her, and tell her I was very much gratified and flattered by her letter in reply to the hurried lines I wrote her from Sumterville during my visit there in May.

My poor wife, I am sorry to say, is in very feeble health. She had a severe attack of illness in June which quite prostrated her strength. She recruits slowly, and I'm afraid a decided change cannot be expected till cool weather comes.

32 Henry Lesesne (1810–1886) was the son of Anna Caroline Broün, the younger sister of WS's wife, Eliza, who had died in 1824. His wife was Harriette Louise Petigru (1812–1877).

33 The Eliza referred to here was undoubtedly WS's daughter (1821–1908), who was married to Richard Irving Manning, Jr. She was HDL's first cousin.

By grandmother's[34] request I send you a Bill of Sale of the two negroes Flora and Betty, at the price agreed on, six hundred Dollars. She begs that you will write off that sum on her Bond, and send a loose receipt also for the same.

With affectionate remembrances to William and Anna, and Charles and his wife when you see them. I remain, dear Uncle,

Very sincerely yours,

Henry D. Lese*sne.*

William Sinkler Esq.

COL. JAMES SIMONS[35] TO WILLIAM H. SINKLER AT EUTAW
CHARLESTON, MARCH 13, 1850

Dear William,

I received your letter of the 12 on the same day, and hasten to reply in time for the Mail of Thursday.

I had a very satisfactory interview with Colonel Moore,[36] whilst he was here. He mentioned that Mr. James B. Richardson did settle Wm H B Richardson in his lifetime—That he[,] Col. Moore settled the Lot in question in 1831, not 1832. Some 4 or 5 years before the death of JBR—& has been in possession ever since—which would be near 20 years.

I conceive his Title to the Lot, in right of his wife, pretty clear for the other Children of Testator having accepted of their several Lots of 100 Acres, of the Sand Hills, would be banned to their Election[.]

If Wm H B Richardson or even Richard Richardson under the particular devise of Testator, had any claims to the particular Lot, then Mr. Moore's possession would give him a good Statutory Title as against either of them.

Perhaps as against all the Children of the Testator, Mr. Moore['s] possession might give him a good Statutory Title in his own individual right, but I am willing to regard his title as in right of his wife.

Then as I have said before he would be entitled to ⅓ & his 2 sons to remaining ⅔ as Distributors of the late Mrs. Moore.

34 "Grandmother" would have been Mary Deas Broün, WS's mother-in-law. The last paragraph refers to William Sinkler's sons William Henry and Charles.

35 James Simons (1813–1879) was a Charleston attorney and contemporary of WHS. He handled legal work for the Sinklers, including, eventually, William Sinkler's estate.

36 Colonel John Isham Moore (1794–1852) was the widower of James B. Richardson's daughter Hermione, who died after her father but before the date of this letter. It is unclear why WHS was involved in this dispute, as he does not appear to have been an executor of JBR's will.

He proposes to give a guaranty Title, to covenant that his sons will release their rights & interest on Coming of age, & as he is a man of fortune & likely to continue to be so, I think such a Deed may be Satisfactory.

If therefore you will Send me an accurate description of the Lot stating the number of Acres, if you can, & the boundaries accurately, I will immediately prepare a Title which you can send up to Col. Moore & have Executed. I will expect to hear from you [by return] Mail on Tuesday

Pray present my regards to Mrs. Sinkler & your father, &

Believe me

Very truly &

Sincerely

Yours

James Simons

[Addressed] To:

Wm H Sinkler Esqu[ire] Eutaw—[word unclear]

[outside]

From Col[.] James Simons

About title for Col[.] Moore

~

WILLIAM SINKLER TO WILLIAM HENRY SINKLER AT FULTON POST OFFICE,
SUMTER DISTRICT
WHITE SULPHUR, SEPT[EMBER] 17, 1850

My Dear William

It gave me much pleasure, to receive last evening, your very kind letters of the 6th & 8th inst[ant]. it always affords me satisfaction to hear from you, particularly, at this season when so many things, are occurring to make it interesting. I am very glad to hear things are all well at home—the crop, as you and Mr. Thurston describe it, bids fair, to exceed my expectations. I hope you may both be correct, a good crop, would be acceptable and much desired, the chances of good prices I think good. I am glad you have got the Stoney Colt with you—it was the only way to get him in condition to be trained. Hercules, is the first person, that the idea <u>originated</u> with, of injury to horses feet from the Limestone water. Nothing of the kind ever occurred until he came to the Eutaw. I cannot <u>abide his prejudices;</u> how glad I am to hear that the little horse Zar or Kit—is well—I will require his services—Janette's[37] Colt I hope continues promising, I have named

37 Janette refers to WS's racehorse Jeannette Berkeley, considered one of the two best that he bred. Irving, South Carolina Jockey Club, 187.

it after Jenny Lind. That is her name. The arrangement about the horses you must make as you see best. I think my chances in Pine Ville <u>first rate</u>, if <u>Hercules</u> will only attend <u>to his business</u>, do <u>his duty</u>, and <u>make less excuses</u>. I think it is highly probable Mr. Singleton will be on the turf again—he is here, looking well but leaves in the course of this week.[38] You have not said a word about the crop of rice—I have my fears about it. It is of more consequence than the swamp corn—by the by, corn will be high—extravagantly high. Every days accounts are worse and worse. I feel alarmed about it. I hope you gave directions that George and Mingo should cut grass in abundance for the horses. Buff ought to cut for the mules—or he will not <u>have employment</u>. I am sorry to hear that Lawyer is no more—I hope he was not allowed to be in want of any thing, that tended to his comfort—or such as he desired. With regard to Cin'den—I think now her fate is <u>sealed</u>—I never knew a case to recover that was tapped, I have never seen a case of Dropsy to be benefitted by a physician—it would have been better, much better that Cin'den, should have been sent to the Sand Hills—common remedies, with change, might have saved her—it is a folly for a man to give way to the foolish prejudices of negroes. I hope you urged Thurston to make everything <u>go as the cotton</u>, and let every good day be used to advantage, his letter was satisfactory on the [w]hole. What can Elsy do with two girls, at this season. The stock of poultry is much more limited than I expected[.] You say, you are using, the rice from home—and that you have ordered an amount kept—I have no objection—and do <u>not</u> <u>know</u>, if I <u>may</u> require a return. much depends on this present crop and Charles's[39] crop. I never felt more anxiety to be at home and yet I do not know if all that I am constantly hoping for, is <u>to be realized</u>. [crossed out] The Source, of my comforts seem to be diminishing. The fashion of the age, is "self" and when, that prevails to full extent—adieu to the happiness—of him, who is dependent on others for <u>his</u> happiness. I am truly sorry to hear of Mr. Deveaux's death. What torture, must be endured, by those, who were on bad terms with him, persons should be ever be [*sic*] on their guard, in indu<u>lging</u> in pre<u>judices</u> again<u>st those</u>, that God intended we should always be in harmony and live in peace with— when ever the <u>affections are allieniated</u> [*sic*] and diverted from<u> their proper source</u>—it is hard for us even to think favorable of much less to love than that we are bound, by all the ties of nature—to live in the closest terms of intimacy ~~with~~ always <u>favorable to</u> our self we always make excuses, <u>we are not to blame</u>, when family difficulties occur; that will not avail—When the time comes—and come

---

38 "Richard Singleton first came to the springs in 1818, and by his death in 1852, he had become the outstanding resort figure of his time . . . by a gracious and unobtrusive personality, and by his amiable willingness to lend money [to the owners of White Sulphur Springs]." Conte, *History of the Greenbrier,* 13.

39 Charles would have been WHS's older brother, who planted Belvidere Plantation.

it <u>will</u> when we will meet our punishment; how <u>monstrous</u>—is it to see Children of the same parents nursed from the same source—living regardless of each others [*sic*] comfort. It is a crime of great magnitude—unhappiness the result, perhaps to both parties.

Hot Springs 19 Sept—We came here last night, on our way to the Warm—are now delayed for want of conveyance—we will go, when we can, remain at the Warm, until Monday when we will go on to Richmond. It is highly probable, that Richard & party will go from there to Mr. Clarks. I think I will go on to Philadelphia to stay, but two or three days. I will come back to Richmond, and from there leave immediately to Charleston—if so fortunate as to get there safe, I will proceed directly for the Cars [train], for the Sand Hills. I will write you, when to send for me—if there be any failure in the mail. When I get to the Middleton Station I can proceed on to Camden. That I trust will not be the case. The night before I left the White Sulphur I got my dear Anna's letter, which was satisfactory and highly pleasing. She has been fortunate in every way and I do trust you will all continue so. Are you sure that the little strangers[40] name is not Peter! Tell Henry that I fear his nose is disjointed. I think Peter, will cut him out. The difficulty of getting him is always an obstacle to travelling in public Conveyance. There is less certainty. [words struck through] No situations are however exempt. I never felt more desirous to be at home—I want retirement. I rather expect my anxiety must exceed yours. My love to Anna, I will certainly reply to her, very affectionate ~~children~~ letter. The first moment I have a chance—I am glad my plan, has been, more than supplied[.] It gave me much satisfaction to find that Margaret[41] has been so long with her, and that she has had so many visits from other friends—which furnished a variety that must have caused time, to pass pleasantly. I will write you as soon as I can make any just calculation of the time—when I trust I may be permitted to return to you—a period the heart, is anxious for. May God grant that my humble exhortations may be realized. Kiss Anna & your children fondly for me—and ever believe me my dear Son, in the language of undisguised truth. Your affectionate father

    W Sinkler

I think the corn ought not to be harvested until they get a <u>head of</u> the cotton and then I beg, you will Direct, that they should take <u>good weather</u> for it. Say to Mr. Thurston <u>provisions are</u> <u>too valuable to run the least risk</u> with them. I wish him to select <u>good, fair, weather</u> to break corn. I hope you have directed G<u>rass cut in abundance for the ant creatures.</u> George, Mingo and Buff with whoever Carts

<hr>

40 John Linton (named for Anna's father) was born on August 31, 1850. Henry (WHS, Jr.), his brother, was born on October 5, 1844.

41 Margaret was probably Anna's older sister, Margaret Thomson Darby (1819–1881).

ought to cut enough for all. While the cattle do well on high land, they can remain—and pens for manure making. If I could get home without risk—I would
not go to Philadelphia—should I miss this chance to go there I might never have
another. Gabriel ought to be intrusted.

[Addressed to]
Mr. William H. Sinkler
Fulton Post Office
Sumter District
So Carolina

∾

JAMES S. DEAS TO WILLIAM SINKLER ESQ[UIR]E[,] AT
    FULTON POST OFFICE, SUMTER DIST[RICT]
NEAR MOBILE, 25 OCTO[BE]R 1850

My dear Sir,
    Your very acceptable Letter of the 10 ult[imo] was received a few days and I
thank you for your good opinion of me and mine—My children have all been
brought up to regard you as a near relation and their father's friend and I assure
you there is no home where your reception would be more cordial—Sally is again
among us quite well and with her fine health is in high spirits—We are all well
save and except one convalescing from the dengue.[42] We have had a summer of
uncommon health and of uncommon drought and no frost in this place nor
have I heard of it any where except so slight as produce little or no effect on the
Cotton Crop—My own accounts are not very good but I yet hope a reasonable
crop we are backward in opening and advantage has been taken of it When the
entire crop of corn which was finished on the 20 Ult[imo] and is a good one. We
have corn much earlier and in much worse weather than your nicer husbandry
would justify. John leaves in a few days for the plantation, but the water [courses]
are so low as to make very uncertain his getting there. The Crop of this state will
be larger than earlier expectations about it. The planting interest is generally in
a state of unprecedented prosperity. The uncertainty of our political [prospects]
prevents their purchasing negroes and their caution keeps the funds in hand. I've
confidence and a negro would readily command a thousand Dollars cash—I view
with much anxiety and alarm the progress toward emancipation which has been
steadily advancing since "93[*sic*]—and embraces any west indies Island except
Cuba—the advance in our own Country makes it probable that in ten years
there will be an accession of States sufficient to alter the Constitution or it may
be done earlier by the "higher law"—the better among the abolitionists regard

---

42 One of the mosquito-borne fevers. McCandless, *Slavery, Disease, and Suffering,* 43.

the institution as a crime & that it is their duty as Christians to get rid of it. We have nothing to expect by saying or doing nothing to offend them, nor is there any certain measure that gives us security. The Stake is worth fighting for and the odds in this are much against us. The enquiry of every reflecting man is what is best to be done and he is a smart fellow who can give the proper reply to this. The least unobjectionable to me is to seek by political organisation what is the point on which the South will agree and take no step that will not be acceptable to a very large majority in the State, and that to be such as the other Southern States will accord with. Your State may have unanimity enough to justify Secession but I think no other State is yet prepared to go this length and that step taken alone will retrograde the cause for I feel very certain that no other state will march [troops.] When protection, if the means of coertion [*sic*] is Embargo & no landing & marching of troops—It would be safest to wait till the leaven of discontent has worked our masses into the proper spirit. I feel very sure that Emancipation is the end and not of distant approach and that the abolition in the "District" and at our forts and naval stations will be the next sessions work. The only issue that I think at this time that the South would be united in is the "Right of Secession" and such a declaration united in in [*sic*] a few states with a good military defensive organization I regard the least objectionable. This union is a government of consent & not office and the caution of three states Virginia[,] New York & Rhode Island in reserved this right in their act of acceptance and ratification—Secession is a question of expediency and [blurred] right and not one that would be probably resorted to or for light reasons. I see no stronger reason for the North objecting than that we are convenient to them and give them advantages that might be lost by our withdrawal and this could hardly be a good reason. The present government of the U.S. was by secession from that Government that carried us thru' the war of the revolution, and one of the premises on which it was to go into effect was the concurrance in it of something less than ¾! of the states accepting it. It got that majority leaving one or two states still in the Old Government. So far as [to the] right now as [to the] expediency I would not secede without more than one State till yet greater aggression. Our safety lays in State unanimity and much sacrifice of individual opinion must be made for this great object. I think that there will be no call made of by the Governor of our Legislature or Convention & am doubtful that the Nashville convention[43] will yield to another Southern Convention if called. My paper bids me stop about politics and every thing so I should not have said so much on the subject but that you have asked my opinion. I am much out of the way of hearing the opinions of others as my time is much taken up by my Mills at which I am doing well after

43 After a prior convention on June 3–12, there was a second scheduled for November 11–18 to promote a southern secession. Rogers and Taylor, *South Carolina Chronology*, 90.

however a world of trouble. I hope you are making a fine crop and that to long cotton there will be a long price. I shall not probably get mine into market before March but when I do you shall hear from me. I fear prices won[']t hold when they hear the quantity already gathered. It will all be out by Christmas. All under this roof send their best wishes to you and yours.

Your friend

James S. Deas

[Written perpendicularly across p. 1]

Saturday 26. After writing this I had the missfortune of having my fine Home and a large outhouse destroyed by fire & with it, much valuable furniture—It occurred from a spark on the upper shed while it was blowing very hard & it is a matter of surprise that so much has been saved. I was upstairs when the roof fell in & my life saved with some difficulty. I cannot say what I have lost but I fear five Hundred Dollars will not more than cover the loss. I had an insurance only of fifteen hundred Dollars—It is not agreeable to be turned out of house & home just on the approach of winter—P and [words unclear] has been opened on me a long time.

Your friend

James S. Deas

[Addressed to]

William Sinkler Esq[uir]e

Fulton Post Office

Sumter Dist.

South Carolina

[NOTE: Postmarked Mobile, ALA Oct 26]

∿

ALFRED HUGER[44] TO HIS EXCELLENCY, WILLIAM C. RIVES[45] IN PARIS
CHARLESTON, S. C., JUNE 23D, 1852

My Dear Sir

I venture to a friend, that I continue to have a place in your remembrance. And I ask leave to present to your kind consideration, My Valued Relative and friend, Mr. William Sinkler of South Carolina. The Claims of this Gentleman,

44 Alfred Huger (1788–1872) was a brother to John H., Margaret Sinkler's father; he was also a first cousin to William Sinkler's wife, Eliza. A lawyer and Charleston postmaster, he had helped get WS's son, Charles, into the navy.

45 William C. Rives (1793–1868) was U.S. minister to France from 1849 to 1853. He also appears to have had WHS train a horse for him: see December 31, 1852, letter (WHS to WS).

with myself, are far beyond those which were consanguinity would Establish and it gratifies me to hope that he may be appreciated abroad, as he undoubtedly is at home. With the Influence of an Ancestry, always devoted to the Integrity and Honour of our whole Country, and with the qualities which belong to him as an Individual, I can have no hesitation in Commending him to your Notice.

[I am Dear Sir]
With the highest Respect
& Regard
faithfully Yours
Alfred Huger

[Addressed to]
His Excellency
William C. Rives
Paris

BENJAMIN HUGER[46] TO EXCELLENCY ABBOTT LAWRENCE [IN LONDON]
CHARLESTON, S.C., JUNE 23., 1852

My Dear Sir
I take the liberty of introducing to your acquaintance & notice my relative & friend Mr. William Sinkler who visits England in pursuit of health. I need not say that Mr. Sinkler is advantageously known in our community for otherwise I could not ask for him the kindness of Mrs. Lawrence & yourself. I am aware that your time is valuable but I am equally aware & not unmindful of the kindness which has been uniformly extended to my friends when introduced to Mr. Lawrence.

I will only trespass upon you further to say that Kindness & attention shown to Mr. Sinkler will add to the obligation I am already under to you & yours.

With most respectful compliments to Mrs. Laurence [*sic*] & assurances [of profound] respect for yourself.

I remain dear Sir
Your obliged & obedient
Benj[amin] Huger
To his
Excellency Abbott Lawrence

---

46 Benjamin Huger was a brother to John and Alfred Huger, and a first cousin to WHS's mother, Eliza. Abbott Lawrence (1792–1855) was U.S. minister to Great Britain from 1849 to 1852.

~

W[ADE] HAMPTON[47] TO HON[ORABLE] ABBOT LAWRENCE IN LONDON
CHARLESTON, JUNE 23, 1852

My Dear Sir

Allow me to make known to you my young friend William Sinkler Esq[uire]. Besides being my friend, and one in whom I take much interest, he is a gentleman of the first respectability, & of high character, & I shall be exceedingly obliged, if you will extend to him every attention in your power[.]

Very truly yours
W. Hampton

[Addressed to]
Hon[ora]ble Abbott Lawrence
London
Introducing
Mr. Sinkler
W. Hampton

~

PALMIER MEDICAL DOCTOR TO [WILLIAM SINKLER IN PARIS]
PARIS, AUGUST 12TH, 1852

[Translation from the French]

A thing must not be lost sight of, viz: that nervous affections are not <u>primitive</u> in their nature, but what they are <u>consecutive</u>, that an effect at first they become the cause by the importance which the nervous system has in all the vital action, and that it thus throws all its influence upon the whole of the organization, according as how it has been troubled, led away or injured in its vital action upon the organization generally and upon each system in particular; it is by it that simple diseases in their origin become complex or composed.

What is of great importance in order to cure, is to search for the primitive cause, so as to drive away the complications which impeding the natural progress of events, fetter nature in its means of expelling Disease and to cure the patient; but the disease is rendered chronically by incomplete or unrational [*sic*] treatments which have only searched for the Symptoms without [torn] the causes.

Mr xxx has a Disease call[torn] shooting burning pains, which extend sometimes to the sto[torn] to the chest, although its origin is on the right side of the stomach, the right shoulder [and] the right leg are sometimes affected by this pain. Melancholy, Sadness, weariness and disgust of life. There is also a "Tic

47 WS and WHS would have known Wade Hampton well through horse racing circles.

douloureux" in the face (face ague) more or less intense, drawing towards the eyes, to the cheekbones, round the neck and to the lips, with fits more or less regular. Finally some <u>cerebral spinal</u> phenomenon (affections of the spine) without its having arrived at <u>spinal</u> <u>consumption</u>, although when I began to prescribe for the patient he was growing very thin but luckily this thinness is now daily decreasing.

If the patient will recollect that he had [a] tremendous fall which broke his right wrist, wounded the fore part of the arm & the right shoulder, he will understand the nature of the commotion which was propagated to the Spine & to the head and has thus developped [*sic*] a rheumatic shape.

On the other side his constitution, which is of a Nervous Lymphatic sort, has acquired a Lymphatic predominance, either by a bad mode of living, bad diet, or by a treatment the activity of which has acted too much upon the liver and complicated by the excitement of this organ the constitutional state of the patient, and injured the normal nutrition by the impediments placed in the abdominal organs (the stomach).

Laying aside what are only effects, we find a defect in the nutrition on account of the lymphatic predominance, an injury of the great abdominal sympathetic, caused either by the constitution or by the <u>cerebral</u> <u>spinal</u> <u>injury</u> resulting from the fall and as an effect of the excessive ex[c]itement of the whole ner[v]ous system, glandular by the great sympathetic being hurt by the defect in the nutrition, Cerebral Spinal by the fall, and this state being developped [*sic*] by the <u>lymphatic</u> <u>nervous</u> <u>constitution</u> of the patient and kept up by the [torn] and the treatment of the Symptoms instead of the [torn.]

1° We have to regulate [torn] [an]d restore nutrition in order that a salutary Diet m[torn]ck strength which only want to be helped and this Do a[torn] with the <u>lymphatic</u> <u>predominance</u>.

2° We have to fortify the muscular System, and by it moderate the nervous influence, which Depends of the diet aiding the assimilation of a more rational nutrition.

3° The System of the blood becoming more powerful by a more appropriate nutrition, the nervous state will cease to have a predominance. Then after the equilibrium in the functions, health will result, and it is important to regulate it by a constant exercise of all the faculties (occupation is the most powerful means of doing away with weariness and Melancholy).

Mode of treatment

Mr xxx will rub his body with Dry wool in the morning on rising and in the evening at the time of going to bed.

Every other day or twice a week at least he will take Baths and shower baths with aromatics as he has Done in Paris with a measure full of the liquor, which he is taking with him to America, in each bath that is five pails of warm water which the pump will throw violently upon him along the spine upon the chest on the belly & upon the limbs after which he will be frictionned [*sic*] & shampooed in this water and frictionned [*sic*] with a bag of Dry wool. Coming out of the bath or after the shower bath after being wiped dry he will have to lie Down in wool for an hour.

Every morning fasting he will have to take a wine glass of quinkina wine and continue this for three months. In the day time he will make use of flowery Pecko tea, orange water with a tea spoonful of good brandy, or Champaign wine mixed with ¾th of water.

In order to have his body free every day, he will make use of a glass of water in an injecti[torn] (lavement) morning & evening should the stools not be su[torn] ill take a lozenge of the purgative chocolate; but a [torn] accustom itself to every thing, every morning after [torn] or his bath; Mr xxx will put himself upon his j[torn] remain sometime until he can make a stool; the body can be regulated by habit better still than by medicine.

Every day Mr xxx will take exercise in the open air, riding is the most salutary exercise I know of. Mr xxx must not forget that that [*sic*] whenever he gets home and is tired, he must change his linnen and rub himself well before Doing so; the substances which he is taking with him are most important and capital things for him, they alone can restore strength and do away with enervation, activate circulation and cure the Rhumatic state.

Mr xxx will make at least three meals per Day, the diet consisting of full grown animal meat roasted and rare done without any fat neither spiced nor kept till it is high. Game, fried or boiled fish, fresh vegetables, good fruit, Chester or Roquefort cheeses. Drink Bordeaux, Champaign and Madera wines during the meals but always with the addition of one half or three quarter of water. Take Flowery Pecko tea.

Abstain from, Salt meat or fish, and pork meat as a habit usually oil, acids, spiced dishes, ragouts, fat grease and skin of animals, flatulent vegetables such as cabbages or haricots (beans), Pastry coffee & liquors, and all exicting [*sic*] things. Avoid numerous assembly of people and close places. Try and find daily and varied occupations.

Signed Palmier Medical Doctor

Paris August 12th 1852

~

[Dr. Palmier to William Sinkler in Paris]
[Paris, August 16, 1852]

[Translation from the French]
Dear Sir

I have the honor of sending you yesterday a bottle of the lotion to be employed as you would "eau de cologne" for the toilet by putting in the water either for the face or other parts.

You have also received a bottle of syrup for yourself. I now send you six woollen bags of six woollen straps to rub yourself with and for friction.

According to your wishes I give you my account for all my visits and disbursements for you up to this Day 16th August, amounting to F1450 or £58 [$252.00].

I have also sent you by your friend from America [torn] flagon of concentrated additioned "Paregorique" [torn]ed in frictions upon the loins of the liver a [torn] ntity of one tea spoonful each time the cost [torn]ich is F50. or £2.

I remain my dear Sir your's very truly
Signed Palmier
August 16th 1852

~

Dr. Palmier to William [H.] Sinkler at Adelphi Hotel
in Liverpool
Rue de la Paix [Paris], September 15, 1852
[15 Sep 1852]

[Translation]

My dear Sir. I immediately beg to answer your letter which has been <u>Delayed two Days</u>. Your state of health & the Diversions which you take have pleased me, but the ~~constipation~~ costiveness you complain of must be attributed to your mode of living. You must eat fresh vegetable, cooked fruits Drinks made of fruits, such as orange, raspberries, cherries. Those syrups being Drunk in water (one table spoonful to a glass of water) will cool the blood, facilitate the letting of water & the stools. Now & then take your lavements (Injections) with olive oil and usually with water only and the lozenges or pills only as you have been directed. When once you are arrived at home, the Shower baths, baths, frictions and mode of living will Satisfy all the conditions and cause to continue and [r]eturn permanently the state I was happy enough to produce in Paris.

Your's very truly
Signed Palmier M. D.
W Sinkler, Liverpo[ool]

The translator [torn] remember himself kindly to W [torn]
[torn]ry Dumelate
Rue de la Paix

[Addressed to]
Angleterre
William B. [*sic*] Sinkler Esq[ui]re
Adelphi Hotel
Liverpool

WILLIAM HENRY SINKLER TO WILLIAM SINKLER [PROBABLY AT EUTAW]
[CHARLESTON], DECEMBER 31ST, 1852

My Dear Father

Anna had another child last night,[48] and 'tho not as violent as the last, the fever which followed has prostrated her very much[.] She is quite sick, and I dread
a further recurrence of the terrible afflictions[.] I hope however that this may be
prevented she is now taking Quinine. I will leave my letter open until morning
and let you know at that time if any change either for the better or worse has
taken place[.] It is impossible to fix upon any time for coming home now and
I must beg you to have my business attended to, as in your judgement seems
best. Charles will go down to Belmont when necessary, and save you that much
trouble. Of course, if I can will be in time for the Pineville, Races, you will give
such directions as are necessary. Do have my new horses used regularly. They are
not yet broke and use is the only thing to them. Fisher must stay until then, ride
down on errands etc. under your directions. Do make him attend particularly to
Henry's poney Doctor. I want to bring him to town looking well[.] My brown
horse "Rock" you have the refusal of. I wish Charles could be persuaded that
he will not suit him. I am ready to turn him over as soon as his leg gets well. If
Charles wants my new horses and I can [find] others to suit me I may be induced
to let him have them but horses are so scarce, that I could not venture to sell before I saw another pair that [I] can buy. The cotton market (for long cotton) has
been perfectly quiet for some days—but today there was a sale made at 38 c[en]ts
which is regarded as a decline of 7 c[en]ts. I suspect plan would be to sell at once
or keep untill very late in the spring[.] I am sorry it so happens that Mr. Rives
will visit Eutaw when I am away. It will not be pleasant for you. I wish if he has
any thing to say about his horse, it would be to you, and not through any other

48 According to family records, Elizabeth Allen Sinkler, the fourth of their six children,
was born on December 14, 1852, and died March 21, 1854. It appears that the family was
staying with the Broün cousins in Charleston; WS was at Eutaw.

person. If he is not satisfied with his trial of course he wo[uld w]ish him thrown out—in that case I presume he will take him home. I will expect to hear soon of this. I did not think that Lot exhibited as much foot as he has done heretofor[e.] This ought to be attended to, no excuses will be received on a public race course and I am satisfied that in condition for two mile heats, he is equal to any and superior to a large majority. I dread to hear of any injury he may receive, for I am certain almost, he is my only [one] dependable for a saddle horse. My love to all with you. I wish we were there. Our friends here are more than kind. The obligations I am under can never be canceled [*sic*]—in fact. The Doctor and Cousin Deas[49] have been unremitting in their Kindness [to] all of us, your whole family, some may not acknowledge, but this does make it otherwise. I must arrange so as not to leave home again for a very long time and make up somewhat for lost time—

If I could think that Anna contracted her fever in the Sand Hills, I would unhesitantly give them up—and go further. Her constitution must seriously be impaired by these [torn.]

I suppose you may [have] heard something of cholera, the accounts carried into the country are generally exageration [*sic*] but I think that there have been some cases.

I will leave my letter open until morning[.]

Your affectionate son

WH Sinkler

[In pencil] Saturday Morning Anna is better now, but feels very weak.

[Dr.] John G. Guignard to William Sinkler
Charleston, 16th May 1853

Dear Sir

I take the liberty of inquiring whether it would suit you to send your Horse Shark & his Groom to my house to stay some two or three weeks say as soon as he can be spared from this present location—as it would be much more convenient for myself & one or two more to have him there to serve a few mares, should you comply with our desire every attention will be paid that he & Groom require as well as Compensation for his services—

Respectfully Yours

John G. Guignard

---

49 This refers to Dr. Josiah Nott and his wife, Sarah Deas, who was WHS's first cousin, once removed.

[Please] address
   Dr. JG Guignard
   Williston
   SC

P.S. I live just thirty miles above Orangeburgh C[ourt] H[ouse] on the South Edisto river & your servant can have no difficulty in finding the way by enquiring at Orangeburgh & crossing the North Edisto at the Orangeburgh Bridge—JGG

[NOTE: WS died June 8, 1853.]

Collage of images from Shark journal. Courtesy of the South Caroliniana Library, University of South Carolina, Columbia, SC.

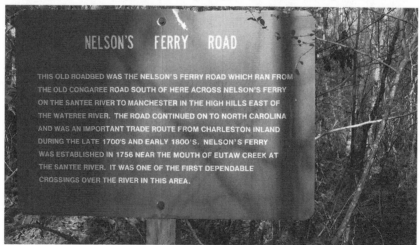

NELSON'S FERRY ROAD

THIS OLD ROADBED WAS THE NELSON'S FERRY ROAD WHICH RAN FROM
THE OLD CONGAREE ROAD SOUTH OF HERE ACROSS NELSON'S FERRY
ON THE SANTEE RIVER TO MANCHESTER IN THE HIGH HILLS EAST OF
THE WATEREE RIVER. THE ROAD CONTINUED ON TO NORTH CAROLINA
AND WAS AN IMPORTANT TRADE ROUTE FROM CHARLESTON INLAND
DURING THE LATE 1700'S AND EARLY 1800'S. NELSON'S FERRY
WAS ESTABLISHED IN 1756 NEAR THE MOUTH OF EUTAW CREEK AT
THE SANTEE RIVER. IT WAS ONE OF THE FIRST DEPENDABLE
CROSSINGS OVER THE RIVER IN THIS AREA.

Photos of a portion of the original Nelson's Ferry Road.

Epilogue

Two of William Sinkler's surviving sons died shortly after he did. The oldest, James, died of typhoid fever in 1854 at age forty-three, and William Henry died in 1856 at age thirty-six. The remaining son, Charles, lived to the age of seventy-six, and William's daughter, Eliza Manning, lived to be eighty-six. By the time of Eutaw Plantation's demise, there had been six generations of Sinklers to inhabit the plantation.

James B. Richardson's two sons, William H. B. and Charles, lived to be seventy-four and sixty-one. The oldest daughter, Dorothy, lived to be fifty-four, but the other five died younger. Neither son followed their father into politics, although several nephews did, keeping the Richardson name politically prominent for many years.

All the family homes are gone. Most of the Richardson homes succumbed to fire, and the Sinkler homes to the creation of Lake Marion. Likewise, the racecourses—Charleston, Pineville, Manchester, and Belvidere—are long gone. The latter had a brief resurgence in the late 1930s before being subsumed by Lake Marion.

And the iconic Nelson's Ferry died the same way. When the water rose in the early 1940s, it engulfed wide swaths of land on both sides of the Santee, becoming the largest lake in the state, at more than 170 square miles. The bridge to cross the new lake near that location was nearly a mile long, as is the interstate highway that later replaced it. While this provided a recreational paradise for fishermen and boaters, it marked the end of a way of life for many families, including the Richardsons and the Sinklers.

Appendix A People and Places of Interest

NOTE: Most of the people and places named below are self-evident, or explained within each chapter or family chart; however, it may be helpful to have more information listed alphabetically.

People

Alston, Colonel William (1756–1839)—A founding member of the South Carolina Jockey Club in the 1780s and one of about twenty planters who established the Washington Race Course in Charleston, which opened in 1792. When he retired, many of his horses were sold to Richardsons.

Broün, Captain Archibald (1752–1797)—Son of Dr. Robert Broün and Elizabeth Thomas, husband of Mary Deas, and father of William Sinkler's wife, Eliza. He was commissioned a captain in the Revolutionary War. The name was pronounced somewhat as a cross between "brown" and "broon."

Broün, Elizabeth Allen (1784–1824)—Daughter of Archibald and Mary Broün; wife of William Sinkler.

Broün, Mary Deas (1762–1857)—Daughter of John and Elizabeth Allen Deas, wife of Captain Archibald Broün, and mother of William Sinkler's wife, Eliza.

Broün, Mary Deas (1789–1847)—Daughter of Archibald and Mary Deas Broün and sister of Eliza B. Sinkler, she was influential in helping William Sinkler raise his five children after the death of her sister.

Peter Burchell (d. 1728)—First husband of Jane Girard, who later married James Sinkler. He was probably the father of Peter (Burchell) Sinkler and Jane (Burchell) Sinkler Cooper.

Cantey, Charles (1718–1780)—Berkeley County planter whose Santee River plantation, Mattasee, was close to James Sinkler's Old Santee.

Cantey, Margaret (1763–1821)—Daughter of Charles Cantey and Ann Drake, she married James Sinkler as his third wife, after the death of her half-sister, Sarah. She was also the stepmother of Ann Cantey Sinkler, who married James B. Richardson.

Cantey, Sarah (d. pre-1780)—Daughter of Charles Cantey and Harriet Drake, she was the second wife of James Sinkler and the mother of Ann, who married James B. Richardson.

Cooper, Thomas (b. pre-1769)—Nephew of James Sinkler and son of Thomas Cooper, Sr., (d. 1772) and Jane Sinkler (pre-1725–1769).

Deas, Charles Dundas (1778–1854)—Son of John Deas and Eliza Allen, he was a younger brother to Mary Deas Broün and uncle to William Sinker's wife, Eliza.

Deas, James Sutherland (1784–1864)—Son of John Deas and Eliza Allen, he was a younger brother to Mary Deas Broün and uncle to William Sinkler's wife, Eliza.

Deas, Mary (1762–1857)—Daughter of John Deas and Eliza Allen, she married Archibald Broün in 1780 and was the mother of William Sinkler's wife, Eliza.

Dow, Robert—Master at Woodville Academy in Sumter County.

Frost, Dr. Henry Rutledge (1795–1866)—Husband of Mary Deas Lesesne, niece of William Sinkler's wife, Eliza.

Furman, Mr. Wood—Master at Furman Academy.

Gaillard, Captain Peter (1757–1833)—Son of Theodore Gaillard and Lydia Peyre, he built the Rocks Plantation in Upper St. Johns, Berkeley.

Gaillard, Thomas (1790–1864)—Son of Peter Gaillard and Elizabeth Porcher of the Rocks.

Girard, Jane (about 1703–1770)—Daughter of Peter Girard, she married James Sinkler after the death of her first husband, Peter Burchell. Mother of Peter and Jane Burchell, as well as Dorothy and James Sinkler.

Hampton, Colonel Wade, II (1791–1858)—Son of Revolutionary War colonel Wade Hampton. A planter (of Woodlands Plantation in Columbia), banker, and legislator, he was one of the wealthiest men in South Carolina.

Hercules—Famous trainer of racehorses at Eutaw Plantation.

Huger, Alfred (1788–1872)—A lawyer and Charleston Postmaster, he was a first cousin of Eliza Broün, wife of William Sinkler. He helped get WS's son Charles into the U.S. Navy.

Huger, Benjamin (1793–1874)—First cousin of Eliza Broün, wife of William Sinkler.

Huger, John, Jr. (1785–1853)—A Berkeley County planter, he was a first cousin of Eliza Broün, wife of William Sinkler. His daughter Margaret married William Sinkler's oldest son, James.

King, Benjamin—Friend of James B. Richardson; builder of William Sinkler's Eutaw Plantation, starting in 1808.

Lesesne, Henry Deas (1810–1886)—The son of Thomas Lesesne and Anna Caroline Broün, he was the nephew of William Sinkler's wife, Eliza.

Lesesne, Thomas (b. 1775)—Husband of Eliza Broün Sinkler's younger sister, Anna, and father of Henry.

Malbone, Edward G. (1777–1807)—Miniaturist from Newport, Rhode Island, who spent five months working in Charleston in 1801–02.

Moore, John Isham (1794–1852)—Husband of JBR's daughter Hermione, who predeceased him.

Nott, Dr.—Probably Josia C. (1804–1873), a surgeon who studied at the University of Pennsylvania and in Paris. One source says that in 1832, he married Sarah Deas, daughter of Colonel James S. Deas.

Peyre, Elizabeth (1787–1832)—Daughter of Francis Peyre and Catherine Sinkler (daughter of Peter Sinkler, half-brother of James Sinkler). She married Charles Sinkler (1780–1817) in 1817.

Peyre, Floride Bonneau (1772–1844)—Daughter of René Peyre, Jr., and Elizabeth Cantey (daughter of Charles Cantey and Harriet Drake, and half-sister of Margaret Cantey Sinkler). She was married to John Peter Richardson. Their daughter was Elizabeth "Betsey" Richardson.

Richardson—Ann Cantey Sinkler Richardson often referred to her husband, JBR, as simply "Richardson" or "my Richardson." The name may also have been used to refer to his nephew JBR, son of John Peter.

Richardson, Charles (1774–1829)—Younger brother to James B. Richardson. He married Elizabeth Eveliegh and lived at Elmswood Plantation.

Richardson, Dorothy (1791–1845)—Oldest daughter of James B. Richardson and Ann Cantey Sinkler; married William B. Mitchell.

Richardson, Dorothy Ann (1808–1894)—The daughter of Charles Richardson and Elizabeth Eveliegh, she married James B. Richardson's son William Henry Burchell Richardson.

Richardson, Elizabeth "Betsey" (1794–1873)—The daughter of John P. Richardson and Floride Bonneau Peyre, she married Richard Irving Manning.

Richardson, James Burchell (1770–1836)—Oldest son of Richard Richardson and his second wife, Dolly Sinkler. He was a prosperous Clarendon County planter and politician, as well as a successful racehorse breeder. He served as South Carolina governor from 1802 to 1804.

Richardson, John Peter (1772–1811)—The next younger brother to JBR, he was married to Floride Bonneau Peyre.

Richardson, Margaret (1794–1845)—The second daughter of James B. Richardson, she married Colonel John Spann.

Richardson, General Richard (1704–1780)—A land surveyor, originally from Virginia, he became a large property owner in Sumter and Clarendon Counties. He married Mary Cantey and, after her death, Dorothy Sinkler. He distinguished himself during the Cherokee War and the Snow Campaign.

Richardson, William H. B. (1804–1879)—Older of two surviving sons of James B. Richardson. After graduating from South Carolina College, he was a Clarendon County planter and married his first cousin Dorothy Ann Richardson.

Robin—A slave boy and self-taught musician on the plantation of James B. Richardson, who promoted his musical prowess.

Rogers, Robert—"Mr. Rogers" in letters, he was proprietor of a Rhode Island boarding school popular with South Carolinians.

Singleton, Colonel Richard (1776–1852)—Wealthy Sumter County planter and racehorse breeder.

Simons, Colonel James (1813–1879)—Charleston attorney and distant relative of the Sinkler family, for whom he handled legal work.

Sinkler, Ann Cantey (1772–1848)—Daughter of James Sinkler and second wife Sarah Cantey. She married her first cousin James B. Richardson, with whom she had twelve children.

Sinkler, Charles (1780–1817)—Son of James Sinkler and older brother of William Sinkler. He was president of the St. Stephen's Jockey Club at the time of his death. He had been a militia captain and represented St. Stephen in the state legislature. Shortly before his death, he married Elizabeth Peyre.

Sinkler, Charles (1818–1894)—Son of William Sinkler and Elizabeth Allen Broün, he lived at Belvidere. He married Emily Wharton.

Sinkler, Colonel—Probably refers to Charles Sinkler (1780–1817) but sometimes appears to mean his younger brother, William, although there is no evidence that the latter served in any militia.

Sinkler, Dorothea/Dorothy (about 1737–1793)—Frequently called "Dolly," she was the daughter of James Sinkler and Jane Girard Burchell and sister of James Sinkler (1740–1800). She was the second wife of Richard Richardson and mother of James B., Charles, and John Peter Richardson.

Sinkler, Elizabeth Allen (1821–1908)—The only daughter of William Sinkler and Elizabeth Allen Broün, she was married to Richard Irving Manning, Jr.

Sinkler, James (d. 1752)—A Berkeley County planter, he is thought to be the first of this Sinkler/Sinclair family to have come from northern Scotland. Some records indicate that he may have died in 1742. He married Jane Girard Burchell, with whom he raised her two children by Peter Burchell. He and Jane had two children, the older believed to be named Jane and the younger, James.

Sinkler, James (1740–1800)—Son of James (d. 1752), he was a successful planter in Berkeley County and an officer during the Revolutionary War; he served in the First Provincial Congress. He was married to Ann Cahusac, Sarah Cantey, and Margaret Cantey and was a brother-in-law to Richard Richardson, the father-in-law to James B. Richardson, and the father of William Sinkler.

Sinkler, James (1810–1856)—The oldest son of William Sinkler, he married Margaret Huger.

Sinkler, Margaret Anna (1793–1829)—The sister of William Sinkler, she married John Linton Thomson.

Sinkler, Peter (1725–1782)—Probably the son of Peter Burchell (d. 1728) and Jane Girard. He was raised by his mother, Jane, and her second husband, James Sinkler.

Sinkler, Dr. Seaman Deas (1816–1847)—Second of four of William and Eliza Sinkler's sons who survived to adulthood. Educated at the University of Pennsylvania Medical School and in Paris, he practiced medicine in Charleston.

Sinkler, William (1787–1853)—Second son of James Sinkler and Margaret Cantey of Old Santee. Educated in the North, in 1808 he started building Eutaw Plantation, where he took his bride, Elizabeth Allen Broün, in 1810. A successful planter and horse breeder, he was well known in racing circles.

Sinkler, William Henry (1819–1856)—The youngest of three surviving sons of William Sinkler and Elizabeth Allen Broün, he married his first cousin, Anna Linton Thomson, and lived at Eutaw Plantation. Like his father, he bred racehorses.

Smith, Robert Press (1814–1887)—Friend of Seaman Deas Sinkler. (One source lists his date of birth as 1802.)

Tarleton, Lieutenant Colonel Banastre (1754–1833)—British officer considered especially cruel to the family of Richard Richardson and many others.

Thomson, Anna Linton (1823–1873)—Daughter of William Sinkler's younger sister, Margaret Anna, whom he raised after her parents died. She married her first cousin, William Henry Sinkler (1819–1856).

Thomson, John Linton (1792–1825)—The son of William Russell Thomson and Elizabeth Sabb, he was the husband of William Sinkler's younger sister, Margaret Anna Sinkler. He was the grandson of Revolutionary War colonel William Thomson.

Walker, Benjamin (1786–1845)—St. Stephen planter, a neighbor and friend of James and William Sinkler. His father, Benjamin Walker, Sr., (d. 1800) was married to Charlotte Cantey, half-sister of Margaret and Sarah, which made him the first cousin of William Sinkler and Ann Cantey Sinkler Richardson. He was also a friend of James B. Richardson, for whom he appears to have managed some local property.

Places

Asylum—The name that James B. Richardson's family used for their Sand Hills summer home.

Beard's Ferry—An earlier name for Nelson's Ferry, established in 1756 near where Eutaw Creek met the Santee River.

Belleville—Site of Thomson family home in the Amelia area, near Ft. Motte, in Calhoun County.

Belvidere Plantation—Sinkler family home, built about 1800, but farmed earlier, near Eutaw Springs; dismantled in 1941 in the wake of Lake Marion. The ruins are on an island, not always accessible.

Big Home—Richard Richardson home near Halfway Swamp in Clarendon County, on property granted in 1744 near the present Rimini.

Bloom Hill Plantation—William Richardson (not related to Richard Richardson) family home in Clarendon County.

Buncombe—Popular health resort near Asheville, North Carolina.

Chateau de la Fontaine—Richardson family Sand Hills summer home, named for a fountain on the property.

Claremont Academy—Boarding school in Stateburg that operated briefly in the late 1780s.

Craven County—Early county later absorbed into Berkeley and Georgetown Counties.

Elmswood—Plantation home built by Charles Richardson, younger brother of James B. Richardson.

Eutaw Creek—A tributary of the Santee River, it flowed northwest from Eutaw Springs.

Eutaw Plantation—Sinkler home built by William Sinkler, starting in 1808. It was dismantled in 1941 in the wake of Lake Marion. The site is rarely accessible when Lake Marion is very low.

Eutaw Village—A summer village established in the 1830s about two miles west of Eutaw Springs. In 1888 it was incorporated as Eutawville.

Fredericksburg Township—Established about 1730, it was later renamed Camden.

Fulton—A town about three miles west of present-day Pinewood, it had an early post office. It no longer exists.

Greenland Swamp—Location of ferry on the Santee River between Eutaw Springs and St. Stephen.

Hagan, The—Huger home at the fork of the Cooper River in Berkeley County.

High Hills of Santee—An area on the north side of the Santee River in the western part of what is now Sumter County, it includes bluffs about 430 feet above sea level. It was believed to be more healthful than the low-lying land nearer the rivers, and it attracted summer residents. It was considered to be an extension of the Sand Hills.

Home Pence—Unclear to which Richardson home this referred.

Jamesville/James Ville—Another name for the Rimini area, it had a post office from 1800 to 1840.

Manchester—An early town in Sumter County about nine miles south of Stateburg. It was also the name of a racetrack established by James B. Richardson near the present town of Pinewood.

Manor Plantation—Richardson home in Clarendon County.

Mattasee—Charles Cantey's plantation on the south side of the Santee River, southeast of St. Stephen.

Momus Hall—Richard Richardson home in Clarendon County inherited by his son James B. Richardson.

Nelson's Ferry—Originally called Beard's Ferry (1756), it crossed the Santee River near the confluence of Eutaw Creek. It was also the location of an early post office.

New Belvidere—Probably refers to Belvidere Plantation during the brief period when it was owned by the Richardson family. James B. Richardson appears to have been the only one to have used that name.

Old Santee—Sinkler family home, about four miles southeast of St. Stephen, abandoned because of periodic flooding. James Sinkler's family left it to build Belvidere, on Eutaw Creek.

Pineville—The earliest of what came to be called the "summer villages," it is located in western Berkeley County.

Porcher's Bluff/White Oak Landing—Location on Santee River, east of Nelson's Ferry near Greenland Swamp.

Rimini—Small community in Clarendon County and location of Richard Richardson's Big Home, St. Mark's Episcopal Church, and Richardson family cemetery.

St. John's (Parish)—One of ten parishes in Berkeley County created by the Church Act of 1706, it extended south from the Santee River, between St. James Goose Creek and St. Stephen's parishes, to what is now Orangeburg County and to Goose Creek.

St. John's Santee—Used as an address for William Sinkler, it probably referred to Upper St. John's Parish.

St. Mark's Episcopal Church—Built about 1764 on 150 acres donated by Richard Richardson, it was destroyed and rebuilt multiple times.

St. Stephen's Episcopal Church—Located in St. Stephen, the parish was established in 1754, and the present church was constructed in 1767–69.

Sand Hills/Sandhills—Generally, the wide sandy swath running northeast to southwest across the state through Clarendon and southern Sumter Counties, also known as the fall line. Left behind from the ocean during the Miocene epoch, it is distinctly different from the coastal and upland areas of the state.

Santee—Mail was occasionally addressed there to William Sinkler, so it probably referred to the Eutaw Springs area.

Santee Canal—In 1786 a company was chartered to build a canal connecting the Santee and Cooper Rivers in order to provide direct travel between Columbia and Charleston. It opened in 1800.

Santee River—A major South Carolina river, it is formed by the Congaree and Wateree Rivers, and empties into the Atlantic near Georgetown.

South Carolina College—Established in 1801, it was reestablished as the University of South Carolina in 1866.

Springfield/Spring Field—Probably an early name for Eutaw Plantation, as mail was directed to William Sinkler there. It obviously does not refer to the later plantation of that name.

Summer villages—Communities built on higher ground—initially pineland—not far from plantation homes, to provide respite from what was believed to be "swamp miasma" causing the illnesses experienced during the warm months.

Sumter Ville/Sumterville—Early name for what became the city of Sumter.

Totness—Summer village near Ft. Motte in Calhoun County, where the Thomson family had a home.

Tuckers—Home of the first James Sinkler in what was then Craven County.

Upper St. John's Parish—The northwest part of St. John's Parish, primarily in northwest Berkeley County and a small portion of what is now southeastern Orangeburg County.

Washington Race Course—A successor to the new Market Race Track (1760–1792) in Charleston, it flourished from 1792 to 1882 and later became Hampton Park.

White Sulphur Springs, Virginia—A huge health resort on the border of Virginia and what became West Virginia, it was very popular with wealthy southerners. It later became the Greenbrier.

Woodville/Woodville Academy—School operated from about 1816 to 1821 or perhaps later, about seven miles northeast of Stateburg in Sumter County.

Appendix B   Contract for the Construction
of Eutaw Plantation

[Sinkler family papers, 1705–1984. Courtesy of the South Caroliniana Library, University of South Carolina, Columbia.]

State of So. Carolina
Charleston Dist[rict]

This Indenture made the 28th day of March in the year one thousand eight hundred and eight, between William Sinkler, of the State and District aforesaid of the one part, and Benjamin King of the State and District aforesaid of the other part. Witnesseth, that for and in consideration of the Sum of Four hundred and fifty Dollars, well and truly to be paid by the said William Sinkler, unto the said Benjamin King in the manner and form following viz. one fourth part thereof at the time the House herein after mentioned, shall be commenced; one fourth part thereof at the time the same shall be completely inclosed, and the remaining two fourths when the said House shall be finished, and every thing thereunto belonging or in any wise incident or appertaining, and shall be received and approved by the said William Sinkler. The said Benjamin King doth covenant and contract, and by these presents hath covenanted and contracted with the said William Sinkler, to Build and complete a house of the following dimensions, and in manner herein described. Viz. Forty feet in length, and thirty nine feet in breadth, one and a half story high, the first [page torn] 12 feet in the clear, the second to be [space] feet in the clear, the first f[loor] is to contain four Rooms, agreeable to a plan drawn, & a passage between the [page torn] back Rooms, wherein the Stair case is to go & the two front rooms are to be finished with flat panneling chairbord high bead'd within, with copings & mouldings above, and wash board below, with double architraves to the doors [and] windows, and a Chimney piece & breast work suitable thereto. The back h[all] on the first floor, & the two rooms & passage above stairs & below; [page torn] [da]doed chair boards high, with a cap and moulding above, & wash[board?] below, and the windows & doors to have single architraves. The floor [page torn] house to be tongued & grooved, and to be neatly & smoothly laid, and that of the largest room below to be secret nailed, and the back rooms to have chimney pieces & breast work, and the rooms above, to have mantle pieces to the chimneys. There will be three large Doors, two in front, & one in back [of] the house, Eleven inside Doors, one of which, will communicate from the hall to the Parlour, the others will be Chamber & Closet doors, all of which, are to be made of the usual length & width, and to be flush panel headed; and one large Door in the centre of the division between the back & front of the House, with a circular sash above. There will be twelve windows below stairs with sashes containing Eighteen lights each, and shutters made in the manner of the Doors. Above Stairs, there will be four end windows, and three Dormants [*sic*], the latter, in the front part of the Roof, and each to have like sashes & shutters, and to be apportioned in size to suit the pitch of the story. A stair case with a[s] many flights as may be thought necessary, is to be run up, and to communicate the lower with the upper story, and to have it compleated with handsome ballisters. The Piazza to be the length of the house & ten feet wide in the clear, to have a neat floor tongued & grooved, five columns & two half D[itt] o against the house, to be neatly Railed & ballistered, and to have a flight of steps at each end descending to the ground, with newels, rails & Ballisters; planed & beaded, and to be shingled on the boarding. The Portico is to be on the back of the house, to have one flight of steps descending to the ground & to be finished in the same manner as the Piazza. The under offices on the ground, are to have Doors, & window frames, and barrs of wood in the windows, & the Doors are to be batten, and underneath the Piazza to be inclosed with railing & barrs in the usual manner. All the Featheredge and flooring to be neatly planed, and the shingling to be well and securely done, and all the work appertaining to the house, to be completed in a neat and workmanlike manner, to be approved of by the said William Sinkler, who is to furnish all necessary materials for the said house, and to find the said Benjamin King in Boarding, washing & lodging such as is necessary & convenient, and five hands until the house is inclosed, and two hands until the same shall be completed.

In witness whereof the parties have hereunto set their hands and seals this day and year first above written

Sign'd & Seal'd Benj[ami]n King

In presence of W[illia]m Sinkler

[Ja]mes Walker

[Editor's Note: There were obvious changes to the original dimensions; for example, the steps to the front porch were not at each end but in the center of the porch. Also, there were not five columns but probably originally six, with the last two likely added when the wings were added, in 1820 and 1838. The alternate possibility is that the house had originally had eight columns with the porch extending beyond the end walls.]

Appendix C Exhibition of Charleston College, 1829 Program

Exhibition of Charleston College, an 1829 program that included recitations by both William Henry Sinkler (No. 15) and Seaman Deas Sinkler (No. 29). William Henry would have been ten years old, and Seaman thirteen. Courtesy of the South Caroliniana Library, University of South Carolina, Columbia, SC.

Receipt for paid customs fee
Number 1600 of Corporate Handbook
Kehl, August 23, 1852
Mr. Sinkler in London
Declared on today's date the following packaged goods and
Declared after required revision—paid the customs fee as follows
[unclear]
Number 38 [Stamp] [Signature]

Legitimation Document

Owner is taking the route via the border area
Through the neighboring town

Present certification is only valid until . . . .
Grand Duke's Office
[Kehl, Germany, across the Rhine from Strasbourg, France, is 250 miles east of
Paris.]

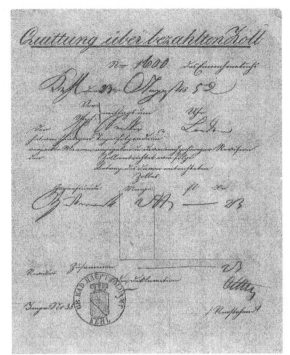

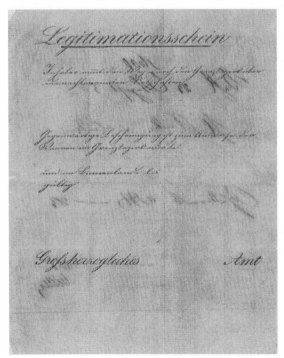

William Henry Sinkler's application for travel from Strasbourg, France, about 250 miles east of Paris, across the Rhine into Kehl, Germany, front (top) and back (bottom). Courtesy of the South Caroliniana Library, University of South Carolina, Columbia, SC.

Translation of William Henry Sinkler's customs document (front)

Receipt for paid customs fee
Number 1600 of Corporate Handbook
Kehl, August 23, 1852
Mr. Sinkler in London
Declared on today's date the following packaged goods and
—after required revision—paid the customs fee as follows
[unclear]
Number 38 [Stamp] [Signature]

Translation of William Henry Sinkler's customs document (back)

Certificate of Authority
Owner is taking the route via the border area
Through the neighboring town

Present certification is only valid until . . . .
Grand Duke's Office

Selected Bibliography

Archival and Manuscript Sources

Duke University, Durham, N.C.

David M. Rubenstein Rare Book and Manuscript Library
James Burchell Richardson papers.

South Carolina Historical Society, Charleston
Henry Ravenel family papers 1731–1867.

University of South Carolina, Columbia

South Caroliniana Library
Richard Irving Manning and Elizabeth Peyre Richardson Manning family papers.
Singleton family papers.
Sinkler family papers, 1705–1984.
Sinkler family papers, 73-VI-19, 1742–1962.
Sinkler, Coxe, Fishburne, Roosevelt, and Wharton family papers, 1801–2010.

Books, Articles, and Other Sources

Bailey, N. Louise. *Biographical Directory of the South Carolina House of Representatives.* Vol. 4, *1791–1815.* Columbia: University of South Carolina Press, 1984.

Bailey, N. Louise, and Elizabeth Ivey Cooper. *Biographical Directory of the South Carolina House of Representatives.* Vol. 3, *1775–1790.* Columbia: University of South Carolina Press, 1981.

Baxter, Angus, "In Search of Your British and Irish Roots," https://www.genealogy.com/articles/research/35_donna.html. (accessed July 10, 2018).

Broün, Robert J. Research notes on Broün and related families, ca. 1971. Sinkler private papers.

Burgess, James. *Chronicles of St. Mark's Parish, Santee Circuit and Williamsburg Township.* Columbia, S.C.: Charles A. Calvo, Jr., Printer, 1888.

Clinton, Catherine. *The Plantation Mistress: Woman's World in the Old South.* New York: Pantheon Books, 1982.

Conte, Robert S. *The History of the Greenbrier: America's Resort.* Charleston, W.V.: Pictorial Histories Publishing, 1989.

Desaussure, Henry William. *Reports of Cases Argued and Determined in the Court of Chancery of the State of South Carolina.* Columbia: Daniel & J. J. Faust, 1817.

Dubose, Samuel. "Reminiscences of St. Stephen's Parish, Craven County." In *History of the Huguenots of South Carolina.* New York: Knickerbocker Press, 1887.

Edgar, Walter. *South Carolina: A History.* Columbia: University of South Carolina Press, 1998.

Faust, Drew Gilpin. *Mothers of Invention: Women of the Slaveholding South in the Civil War.* Chapel Hill: University of North Carolina Press, 1996.

Fishburne, Anne S. *Belvidere: A Plantation Memory.* Columbia: University of South Carolina Press, 1949.

Ford, Lacey K. *Deliver Us From Evil: The Slavery Question in the Old South.* New York: Oxford University Press, 2011.

Fraser, Charles. *Reminiscences of Charleston.* Charleston: John Russell, 1854.

Glover, Lorri. *All Our Relations: Blood Ties and Emotional Bonds among the Early South Carolina Gentry.* Baltimore: Johns Hopkins University Press, 2000.

Graham, S. A. "Inscriptions on Tomb-stones, Private Burial Grounds, on the Santee River in Old St. Stephen's Parish S.C." *South Carolina Historical Magazine,* no. 26 (1925), 113–19.

Gregory, Anne King. *History of Sumter County.* Sumter, S.C.: Library Board of Sumter County, 1954.

Irving, John Beaufain. *The South Carolina Jockey Club.* Charleston, S.C.: Russell & Jones, 1857.

Holcomb, Brent H. *Marriage and Death Notices From the Charleston Observer 1827–1845.* Greenville, S.C.: A Press, 1980.

————. *Petitions for Land From South Carolina Council Journals.* Columbia: SCMAR, 1996.

Kapsch, Robert J. *Historic Canals and Waterways of South Carolina.* Columbia: University of South Carolina Press, 2010.

Kierner, Cynthia A. *Southern Women in Revolution, 1776–1800.* Columbia: University of South Carolina Press, 1998.

Kirk, F. M. "Eutaw Plantation." *Charleston News & Courier,* October 7, 1935.

Long, Grahame. *Dueling in Charleston.* Charleston: History Press, 2012.

Long, Kate. "The Chemical Era," 1–2. https://sites.google.com/site/kateannelong/the chemicalera. 1–8.

Lossing, Benson. *The Pictorial Field Book of the Revolution.* New York: Harper & Brothers, 1860.

MacDowell, Dorothy Kelly. *Gaillard Genealogy.* Columbia: R. L. Bryan Company, 1974.

Mason, George Champlin. *Annals of Trinity Church, Newport, Rhode Island.* Newport, R.I., 1890.

McCandless, Peter. *Slavery, Disease, and Suffering in the Southern Lowcountry.* Cambridge: Cambridge University Press, 2011.

McCord, David J., ed. *The Statutes at Large of South Carolina*. Columbia: A. S. Johnston, 1844.

McCrady, Edward, LLD. *The History of South Carolina in the Revolution 1780–1783*. 1902; repr., New York: Russell & Russell, 1969.

McCullough, David. *The Great Journey: Americans in Paris*. New York: Simon & Schuster, 2011.

Medical Society of South Carolina Minutes: February 7th 1847. Lowcountry Digital Library, http://digital.library.musc.edu/cdm/compoundobject/collection/min/id/10868/rec/1 (accessed July 10, 2018).

Meriwether, Robert L. *The Expansion of South Carolina 1729–1765*. Kingsport, Tenn.: Southern Publishers, 1940.

Mooney, Katherine C. *Race Horse Men: How Slavery and Freedom Were Made at the Racetrack*. Cambridge, Mass.: Harvard University Press, 2014

Neuffer, Claude Henry. *Names in South Carolina*. 12: 47, and 28:24. Spartanburg, S.C.: Reprint Company, 1983.

Orvin, Maxell Clayton. *Historic Berkeley County, South Carolina, 1671–1900*. Charleston: Comprint, 1973.

Partridge, Eric. *Slang: To-Day and Yesterday*. N.p.: nd. Ebook available at Google Books.

Porcher, F. A. "South Carolinians at the Partridge Military Academy, 1826." *South Carolina Historical Magazine* 44, no. 3 (1943), 11.

Richardson, Louise Simons. "History of Pinewood." Unpublished memoir, 1938. Sumter Genealogical Society.

Rogers, George C. *The History of Georgetown County, South Carolina*. Columbia: University of South Carolina Press, 1970.

Rogers, George C., and C. James Taylor. *A South Carolina Chronology, 1497–1992*. Columbia. University of South Carolina Press, 1973.

Shields, Carol. *Jane Austen*. New York: Penguin Putnam, 2001.

Sinkler, Anna L. "A History of the Sinkler Family." Unpublished memoir, ca. 1945. SCL, Sinkler Family Papers, 1705–1984.

Steeler, Kathleen, and Jessica Brislen. "Women in 19th Century America." http://womeninhistory.tripod.com/.

Stauffer, Michael E. *South Carolina Antebellum Militia*. SCDAH, 1991.

Stoney, Samuel Gaillard *Plantations of the Carolina Low Country*. 1938; rev. edition, Carolina Art Association, Charleston, South Carolina 1955.

Stowe, Steven M. *Intimacy and Power in the Old South*. Baltimore: John Hopkins Press, 1987.

Teal, Harvey S., and Robert J. Stets. *South Carolina Postal History, 1760–1860*. Lake Oswego, Ore.: Raven Press, 1989.

Terry, George D. "Champaign Country: A Social History of an Eighteenth Century Lowcountry Parish in South Carolina, St. Johns Berkeley County." Ph.D. dissertation, University of South Carolina, 1981.

Towles, Louis P., Ed. *A World Turned Upside Down, The Palmers of South Santee, 1818–1881*. Columbia: University of South Carolina Press, 1996.

USGenWeb Project. "Naming Patterns in England, 1700–1875." http://usgenweb.org/research/names/shtml.

Wallace, David D. *The History of South Carolina.* 4 vol. New York: American Historical Society, 1934.

Index